THE NATIONAL CURRICULUM ...
... AND BEYOND ...

Sureshot

A Sureshot Guide

to

The National
Curriculum
and GCSE
EXTRA

Tier 3 – 6
Topics 8 – 13

by

Barbara Young

Tarporley High School
Cheshire

Bob Percival

Whitby High School
Ellesmere Port

Illustrators

Matthew Staff, Jennifer Smith, Chris Bujac, Luke Young and Joanne Young

Acknowledgements
to the students and teachers who trialled this new approach,
who worked with enthusiasm
and made suggestions for improving
both content and presentation.

Thanks to the students and teachers of:

France Hill School, Camberley

Whitby High School, Ellesmere Port

St. John's School, Episkopi, Cyprus

and, above all, to Phil Navin

of St. John's School

for all his help and encouragement

This edition was first published in Great Britain 1997
British Library Cataloguing–in–Publication Data

ISBN   1 – 874428 – 44 – 1

Printed and bound by PRINTCENTRE WALES, Mold, Flintshire

THE NATIONAL CURRICULUM ...
... AND BEYOND ...
EXTRA

The EXTRA course :
- has been specially written for low attainers
- is a version of the mainstream course
- has lots of EXTRA practice on all techniques
- can be run alongside the mainstream course
- can stand on its own

Each student:
- takes responsibility for his/her own learning
- can decide how much practice (s)he needs to do for each technique
- can try Star Challenges when (s)he feels ready for them

The authors firmly believe that all students can tackle Levels 3 – 6 in the National Curriculum for Mathematics.

However, some students need :
- more time to get to grips with the ideas and techniques involved
- lots of EXTRA practice
- one idea at a time introduced step–by–step
- to meet ideas and techniques over and over again

Most students in lower sets are underachieving.
This course aims to raise the level of achievement of these students.
Students can transfer to or from the mainstream course (Tier 5–8)

Sureshot

CONTENTS

The topic titles correspond to the topics in the original mainstream course. When redone for the EXTRA course, two of the Y11 topics were split, as they were too long.

"Developing Efficient Calculator Techniques" is repeated at the start of the Y11 text, so it can be tackled either at the end of Y10, or the beginning of Y11, or bridge Y10 and Y11.

Understanding Geometry *Part 2* makes an excellent start to a GCSE revision course.

Teachers may change the order of the topics.

These topics are independent and so can be done in any order.

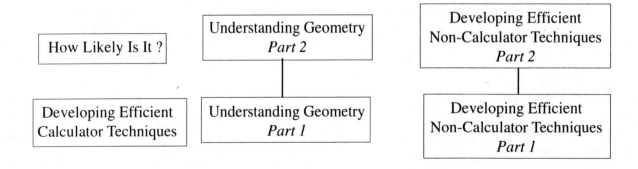

THE NATIONAL CURRICULUM ...
... AND BEYOND ...

Sureshot

Developing Efficient
Calculator Techniques
EXTRA

Developing Efficient
Calculator Techniques EXTRA
Section 1: Divisibility

In this section you will:
- understand what is meant by "divisible by";
- find and work with divisibility rules;
- understand the connection between "divisible by" and "multiple of";
- find multiples of numbers.

DEVELOPMENT

D1: Which answers are whole numbers ?

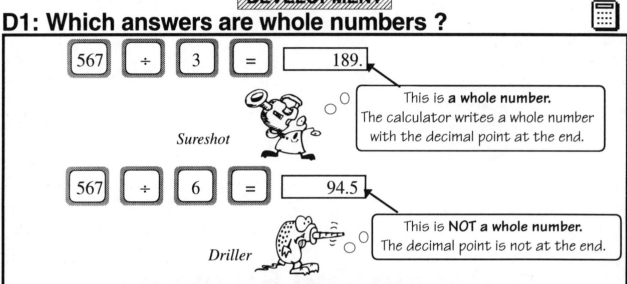

| 567 | ÷ | 3 | = | 189. |

Sureshot

This is **a whole number.**
The calculator writes a whole number with the decimal point at the end.

| 567 | ÷ | 6 | = | 94.5 |

Driller

This is **NOT a whole number.**
The decimal point is not at the end.

Which of these give answers which are whole numbers ?

A: 96 ÷ 4   B: 98 ÷ 4   C: 24 ÷ 3   D: 42 ÷ 3   E: 65 ÷ 7

F: 431 ÷ 5   G: 469 ÷ 7   H: 1350 ÷ 13   I: 768 ÷ 16   J: 1037 ÷ 29

• *Check answers.*

D2: What does "divisible by" mean ?

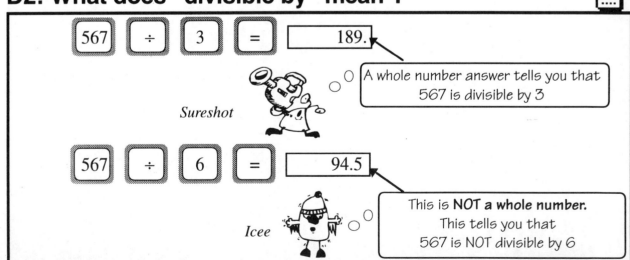

| 567 | ÷ | 3 | = | 189. |

Sureshot

A whole number answer tells you that
567 is divisible by 3

| 567 | ÷ | 6 | = | 94.5 |

Icee

This is **NOT a whole number.**
This tells you that
567 is NOT divisible by 6

1. Is 789 divisible by 6 ?   5. Is 24 divisible by 8 ?   9. Is 26 divisible by 2 ?
2. Is 435 divisible by 5 ?   6. Is 27 divisible by 3 ?   10. Is 14 divisible by 5 ?
3. Is 435 divisible by 7 ?   7. Is 18 divisible by 9 ?   11. Is 44 divisible by 13 ?
4. Is 32 divisible by 3 ?   8. Is 20 divisible by 6 ?   12. Is 48 divisible by 16 ?

13	35	72	55	63	46	49	81
64	56	93	21	26	84	41	

13. Six of these numbers are divisible by 7. Find them.

40	65	29	16	30	24	14	92
95	12	47	49	108	52	26	

14. Seven of these numbers are divisible by 4. Find them.

• *Check your answers.*

D3: Numbers that are divisible by 2, 5 or 10

60	75	30	36	70	45	69	100
95	40	300	125	240	450	35	

1. Eight of these numbers are divisible by 10. Find them.

Possible rules

A number that is divisible by 10 ends in 0 or 5   A number that is divisible by 10 ends in 0

A number that is divisible by 10 ends in 0, 2, 4, 6 or 8

2. Which of these possible rules is the correct one ?

52	55	70	19	80	23	69	20
85	44	900	225	314	128	15	

3. Eight of these numbers are divisible by 5. Find them.

Possible rules

A number that is divisible by 5 ends in 0 or 5   A number that is divisible by 5 ends in 0

A number that is divisible by 5 ends in 0, 2, 4, 6 or 8

4. Which of these possible rules is the correct one ?

24	15	40	16	71	35	68	201
17	28	567	678	120	561	2472	

5. Eight of these numbers are divisible by 2. Find them.

Possible rules

A number that is divisible by 2 ends in 0 or 5   A number that is divisible by 2 ends in 0

A number that is divisible by 2 ends in 0, 2, 4, 6 or 8

6. Which of these possible rules is the correct one ?   • *Check your answers.*

D4: Using divisibility rules

Divisibility rules	A number that is divisible by 10 ends in O
	A number that is divisible by 5 ends in O or 5
	A number that is divisible by 2 ends in O, 2, 4, 6 or 8

Task 1:
Write down all the numbers here that are divisible by 10.

```
24      37      59      65
    90      34      43
75      12      412     501
    105     666     333
2345    5432    231     123
    102     120     250
205     255     946     629
    430     861     579
3570    1437    2369    432
```

Task 3:
Write down all the numbers here that are divisible by 2.

Task 2:
Write down all the numbers here that are divisible by 5.

• *Check your answers.*

Star Challenge 1

All correct = 1 star

2310 is divisible by … ?

Numbers to try   2   3   4   5   6   7
                  8   9   10   11   12   13

2310 is divisible by	2310 is not divisible by

Try each number and put it into the correct set.

• *Your teacher has the answers to these.*

Star Challenge 2

17-18 correct = 1 star

Copy and complete this table:

number	is divisible by 2	is divisible by 10	is divisible by 5
45	No	No	Yes
70	…	…	…
24	…	…	…
47	…	…	…
235	…	…	…
470	…	…	…
2344	…	…	…

• *Your teacher has the answers to these.*

D5: "Divisible by" and "multiples of"

> A number is a multiple of 3 if it is divisible by 3
> 3, 6, 9, 12, ... are divisible by 3
> 3, 6, 9, 12, ... are **multiples of 3**

1. Write down all the multiples of 10 between 14 and 52.

2. Write down all the multiples of 3 between 10 and 20.

3. Write down all the multiples of 5 between 17 and 57

4. Write down all the multiples of 7 between 20 and 30.

> 45   27   30
>
> 99   75   14   60
>
> 5. Four of these numbers are multiples of 3 _and_ multiples of 5. Find them.

• *Check your answers.*

EXTENSION

E1: Divisibility puzzles

1. Put all these pieces together to make a number that is divisible by 5

2   5   6

2. Put all these pieces together to make a number that is divisible by 6

4   2   3

3. These pieces can be put together to make a number that is divisible by 4.
   It can be done in two ways.
   Find both of these numbers.

6   7   8

• *Check your answers.*

Star Challenge 3

All correct = 1 star

4. These pieces can be put together to make a number that is divisible by 4.
   It can be done in four ways.
   Find the largest of these four numbers.

4   6   8

5. Put these pieces together to make a number that is divisible by 15.

5   2   8   9

6. Put these pieces together to make the largest possible number that is divisible by 6.

2   8   4   1

• *Your teacher has the answers to these.*

Section 2: Quotients and Remainders

In this section you will:
- understand what is meant by "quotient" and "remainder";
- find quotients and remainders without and with a calculator;
- solve practical problems using quotients and remainders.

DEVELOPMENT

D1: Introducing quotients and remainders

counters

Share 7 sweets between 2

 =

This shows that
$$7 \div 2 = 3$$
with 1 left over

Sureshot

Copy and complete:

1. Share 9 sweets between 2

$9 \div 2 = \ldots\ldots$

with $\ldots\ldots$ left over

2. Share 8 sweets between 3

$8 \div 3 = \ldots\ldots$

with $\ldots\ldots$ left over

3. Share 3 sweets between 2

$3 \div 2 = \ldots\ldots$

with $\ldots\ldots$ left over

4. Share 7 sweets between 4

$7 \div 4 = \ldots\ldots$

with $\ldots\ldots$ left over

Use counters to work these out.
Copy and complete each statement.

5. $5 \div 2 = \ldots\ldots$ with $\ldots\ldots$ left over   8. $7 \div 3 = \ldots\ldots$ with $\ldots\ldots$ left over

6. $5 \div 3 = \ldots\ldots$ with $\ldots\ldots$ left over   9. $11 \div 2 = \ldots\ldots$ with $\ldots\ldots$ left over

7. $9 \div 4 = \ldots\ldots$ with $\ldots\ldots$ left over   10. $12 \div 5 = \ldots\ldots$ with $\ldots\ldots$ left over

$$7 \div 2 = 3 \text{ with } 1 \text{ left over}$$

quotient   remainder

11. *Copy and complete this table of quotients and remainders:*

	$13 \div 2$	$10 \div 3$	$5 \div 4$	$7 \div 5$	$10 \div 4$	$11 \div 5$	$11 \div 3$
quotient							
remainder							

• Check your answers.

D2: Using a calculator to find quotients and remainders

To find the quotient:

7 ÷ 3 has quotient 2 and remainder 1

| 7 | ÷ | 3 | = | 2.33333333 |

Blurbl

The whole number part of the answer is the quotient

Use your calculator to work out the quotient:

1. 17 ÷ 4　　2. 53 ÷ 5　　3. 47 ÷ 3　　4. 71 ÷ 8　　5. 39 ÷ 6
6. 31 ÷ 3　　7. 86 ÷ 9　　8. 32 ÷ 5　　9. 111 ÷ 6　　10. 458 ÷ 9

• *Check answers*

To find the remainder:

7 ÷ 3 has quotient 2 and remainder 1

Step 1 | 7 | ÷ | 3 | = | 2.33333333 |　　Divide 7 by 3

Step 2 2.33333333 – quotient = 0.33333333　　Take the quotient from the answer

Step 3 0.33333333 x 3 = 1 = remainder

This is the number you divided by.

Taz

Multiply the result by the number you divided by. The answer is the remainder

Use your calculator to work out the remainder:

11. 13 ÷ 2　　12. 10 ÷ 3　　13. 5 ÷ 4　　14. 7 ÷ 5　　15. 10 ÷ 4

• *Check your answers using the answers you worked out in D1, question 11.*

Use your calculator to work out the quotient and remainder for each of these:

16. 17 ÷ 7　　17. 97 ÷ 8　　18. 235 ÷ 13　　19. 492 ÷ 5　　20. 85 ÷ 13

• *Check your answers.*

D3: Division problems

1. There are 9 players in a netball team. 47 students want to play netball. How many complete teams will there be. How many students will be left over ?

2. 162 seats in the hall. 24 in a row. How many rows ? How many seats left over ?

3. 350 cans of cola. 6 cans in a pack. How many packs ? How many cans left over ?

Star Challenge 4　　• *Check your answers.*　　All correct = 1 star

4. 500 eggs. 6 eggs in a box. (a) How many boxes ? (b) How many eggs left over ?

5. 640 newspapers. 50 newspapers in a bundle.
　　(a) How many bundles ? (b) How many newpapers left over ?

6. 243 pupils are going to Alton Towers. A coach will take 53 pupils.
　(a) How many full coaches will there be ? (b) How many pupils will be left over?
　(c) How many coaches will need to be ordered ?

Section 3: Factors and prime numbers

In this section you will:
- use divisibility to find factors;
- meet and understand factor pairs;
- find prime prime numbers.

DEVELOPMENT

D1: What are factors ?

16 ÷ 2 = 8.

Sureshot

A whole number answer tells you that 16 is divisible by 2

We say that 2 is a factor of 16

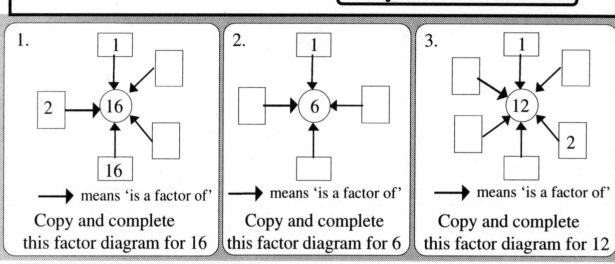

1.

2 → 16

1, 16

→ means 'is a factor of'

Copy and complete this factor diagram for 16

2.

6

1

→ means 'is a factor of'

Copy and complete this factor diagram for 6

3.

12

1, 2

→ means 'is a factor of'

Copy and complete this factor diagram for 12

4. | 1 is a factor of every number. | Is this true ?

5. | Any number is a factor of itself. | Is this true ?

6. 8 has four factors. Find all the factors of 8.

7. 10 has four factors. Find all the factors of 10.

8. 9 has three factors. Find all the factors of 9.

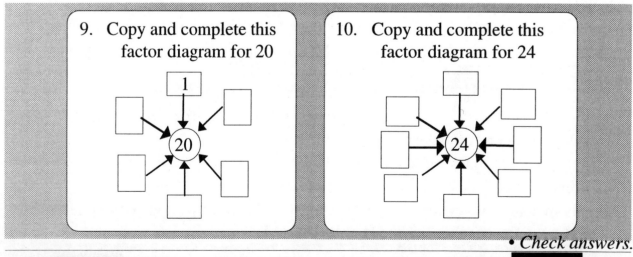

9. Copy and complete this factor diagram for 20

1

20

10. Copy and complete this factor diagram for 24

24

• *Check answers.*

D2: Factor pairs

1. *Copy and complete:*

$6 \div 2 = \ldots$ 6 is divisible by 2   … is a factor of 6

$6 \div 3 = \ldots$ 6 is divisible by …   … is a factor of 6

2. *Copy and complete:*

$6 \div 1 = \ldots$ 6 is divisible by …   … is a factor of 6

$6 \div 6 = \ldots$ 6 is divisible by …   … is a factor of 6

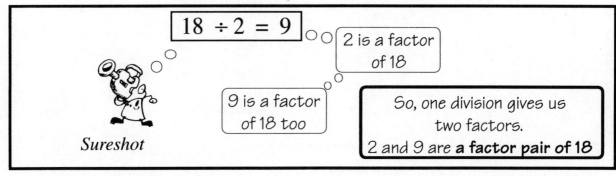

$18 \div 2 = 9$

2 is a factor of 18

9 is a factor of 18 too

So, one division gives us two factors.
2 and 9 are **a factor pair of 18**

Sureshot

3. Find two factor pairs of 10.
4. Find three factor pairs of 18.
5. Find three factor pairs of 20.   • *Check your answers.*

D3: A systematic way of getting <u>all</u> the factors of a number

$18 \div 2 = 9$ & $18 \div 9 = 2$

because $\mathbf{18 = 2 \times 9}$

EXAMPLE: Use factor pairs to find all the factors of 28

Calculator working	What you write down
$28 \div 1 = 28$	$28 = 1 \times 28$
$28 \div 2 = 14$	$28 = 2 \times 14$
$28 \div 3$ not possible	
$28 \div 4 = 7$	$28 = 4 \times 7$
$28 \div 5$ not possible	
$28 \div 6$ not possible	So, factors of 28 are 1, 28, 2, 14, 4, 7
$28 \div 7 = 4$	
(already have 4x7)	

Use factor pairs to find all the factors of each number.
Set your working out as in the example.

1. 15   2. 24   3. 30   4. 25

5. 36   6. 40   7. 49   8. 48

• *Check your answers.*

$9 = 1 \times 9$
$9 = 3 \times 3$
Factors of 9 are 1, 9, 3

We only write
the 3 down once.

Yerwat

D4: From factors to prime numbers

1. *Copy and complete this table of factors:*

Number	Factors	Number of factors	Number	Factors	Number of factors
1	1	1	11		
2	1, 2	2	12		6
3			13		
4			14		
5			15		
6			16		
7			17		
8			18		
9			19		
10			20		

2. **A prime number** has exactly two factors.

   Write down the prime numbers between 1 and 20 .

   • *Check your answers.*

Star Challenge 5

All correct = 1 star

1. Find all the factors of 21 22 23 24 25 26 27 28 29 30   [4 marks each]

2. List the prime numbers between 21 and 30.   [4 marks]

   • *Your teacher has the answers to these.*

D5: Prime factors

1. | The first eight prime numbers are : 2 … … … … … … 19 |

   Copy and complete this box of information. Use your answers from D4.

EXAMPLE: Find the prime factors of 12

The factors of 12 are   1   2   3   4   6   12

The prime factors of 12 are   2   3 ← These numbers are factors of 12 <u>and</u> prime numbers.

Spoton

Copy and complete. Use the box of prime numbers from Q1 to help you.

2. The factors of 15 are ……………   The prime factors of 15 are …………

3. The factors of 20 are ……………   The prime factors of 20 are …………

   Find the prime factors of each of these numbers:

        4. 6   5. 21   6. 18   7. 8   8. 10   9. 14   10. 24

   • *Check your answers.*

E1: Prime factors of large numbers – using factor trees 🖩

EXAMPLE   Find the prime factors of 60

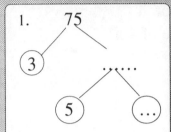

Step 1: Find any number that is a factor of 60
The second line is that number and its factor pair.
If either of these factors is prime, put a circle round it.
The circle shows that this branch of the factor tree
stops here.

Step 2: Repeat Step 1 with any two factors of 30.
......

> The prime factors of 60 are 2, 3 and 5

Copy and complete these factor trees:

1.   75

(3)   .·....

(5)   (...)

The prime factors of
75 are ....

2.   180

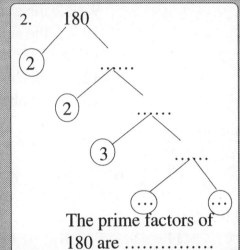

The prime factors of
180 are ....

3.   200

10   ..·..

(...) (...) (2)   (..)

(..) (...)

The prime factors of
200 are ....

Draw your own factor trees for each number below.
Find the prime factors of each number.

4. 30   5. 45   6. 72   7. 120

8. 105   9. 225   10. 495   11. 91

• *Check your answers.*

Star Challenge 🟆6 🟆6

> 8 correct = 2 stars
> 6-7 correct = 1 star

Find <u>all</u> the factors of each number :

   1. 60   2. 90   3. 51   4. 84

Find the prime factors of each number :

   5. 57   6. 36   7. 156   8. 500

• *Your teacher has the answers to these.*

Section 4: Squares, cubes and roots

In this section you will:
- work with squares, cubes, square roots and cube roots;
- use 'trial and improvement' techniques.

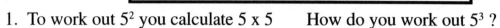

D1: Squares and cubes

square of 5	= 5 squared	= 5^2	= 25
cube of 5	= 5 cubed	= 5^3	= 125

1. To work out 5^2 you calculate 5 x 5   How do you work out 5^3 ?

Calculate …

2. … the square of 13
3. … 6 cubed
4. … 15^2
5. … 21 squared
6. … 3.5^2
7. …the cube of 1

8. …11^3
9. … the cube of 4
10. … the square of 4.5
11. … 123^2
12. … 321^3
13. … 7 cubed

14. *Copy and complete this table:*

Number (N)	2	10	7		5				
Square (N²)	4			9	25	64	36	144	441

15. *Copy and complete this table:*

Number (N)	6	4	11		8	15			
Cube (N³)			1331	1000			8	343	2744

- *Check your answers.*

D2: How good are you ?

You may only use these keys

$\boxed{x}$ $\boxed{=}$ $\boxed{1}$ $\boxed{2}$ $\boxed{3}$ $\boxed{4}$
$\boxed{5}$ $\boxed{6}$ $\boxed{7}$ $\boxed{8}$ $\boxed{9}$ $\boxed{0}$

Find the value of each letter:

$A^2 = 289$	$B^2 = 625$	$C^2 = 121$

$D^3 = 512$	$E^3 = 125$

- *Check your answers.*

Star Challenge 7 7

10 correct = 2 stars
9 correct = 1 star

Find the value of each letter:

$F^2 = 169$	$G^2 = 1156$	$H^2 = 1681$	$I^2 = 4489$	$J^2 = 2809$

$K^3 = 1728$	$L^3 = 3375$	$M^3 = 9261$	$N^3 = 729$	$P^3 = 12167$

- *Your teacher has the answers to these.*

D3: Square roots and cube roots

5 squared	= 25
5^2	= 25

square root of 25	= 5
$\sqrt{25}$	= 5

Task 1: *Complete these two tables.*

In the first table, join each number to its square, using an arrow.

In the second table, join each number to its square root, using an arrow.

Number (N)	Square (N^2)	Number (N)	Square root ($\sqrt{N}$)
7	1	64	7
1	49	9	3
5 ⟶	25	49	8
6	9	25 ⟶	5
3	36	4	10
0	121	100	2
15	225	169	9
11	0	81	13

5 cubed	= 125
5^3	= 125

cube root of 25	= 5
$\sqrt[3]{25}$	= 5

Task 2: *Complete these two tables.*

In the first table, join each number to its cube, using an arrow.

In the second table, join each number to its cube root, using an arrow.

Number (N)	Cube(N^3)	Number (N)	Cube root ($\sqrt[3]{N}$)
2	216	125 ⟶	5
3	1	64	2
6	27	1331	10
1	8	8	4
10	729	1000	11
9	3375	512	8
15	1000	2744	7
5 ⟶	125	343	14

• *Check your answers.*

Task 3: *Complete each statement:*

1. The square of 4 is ......
2. The square root of 4 is ......
3. 6^2 is ......
4. One squared is ......
5. $\sqrt{9}$ is ......

6. 7 squared is ......
7. $\sqrt{36}$ = ...
8. 10 squared is ...
9. the square root of 16 is ......
10. $\sqrt{0}$ is ......

• *Check your answers.*

Write down…

1. … the square of 2
2. … the cube of 2
3. … the cube root of 27
4. … the square of 8
5. … the cube of 4

6. … the cube root of 8
7. … $\sqrt[3]{125}$
8. … the cube of 10
9. … 1 cubed
10. … the cube root of 1

• *Your teacher has the answers to these.*

Star Challenge 9 9 9

48 squares correct = 3 stars
43-47 correct = 2 stars
38-42 correct = 1 star

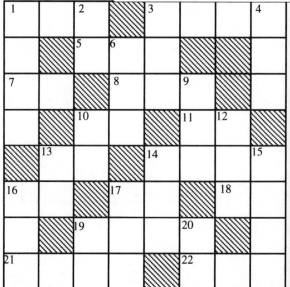

Across

1. 13 squared
3. 17^3
5. a dozen dozen
7. the cube of 3
8. 22^2 — the square of 5
10. square root of 529
11. $\sqrt{8464}$
13. square of 8 + 1
14. $16^3 + 10^2$
16. six squared + 2 cubed
17. cube root of 5832
18. square of 9
19. (number of Heinz varieties)^2
21. $15^3 + 10^3$
22. $28^2 + 4^2 - 3^3$

Down

1. 12 cubed
2. $\sqrt{8281}$
3. $21^2 + 2^2$
4. $15^2 + (3 \times 5^2)$
6. 7 cubed + 10 squared
9. 10 cubed – 3 squared
10. $\sqrt{625}$
12. $17^2 + 3^2$
13. a number that is both a square and a cube
14. square of 22
15. square root of 37491129
16. $23^2 - (5 \times 3^2)$
17. cube of 5
19. $\sqrt[3]{50653}$
20. $\sqrt{9409}$

• *Your teacher has the answers to this.*

Section 5: Decimals

In this section you will:
- name points on a decimal number line;
- mark points accurately on a decimal number line;
- estimate sums and differences of decimal numbers.

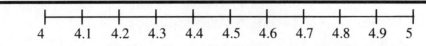
DEVELOPMENT

D1: Simple decimal number lines

| | | | | | | | | | | |
4   4.1   4.2   4.3   4.4   4.5   4.6   4.7   4.8   4.9   5

This decimal number line is labelled in 0.1 divisions between 4 and 5

1.
2   3

Draw a line 10 cm long. Label the line in 0.1 divisions between 2 and 3

2. *Give the number that is shown by each letter. Give answers in the form b = ...*

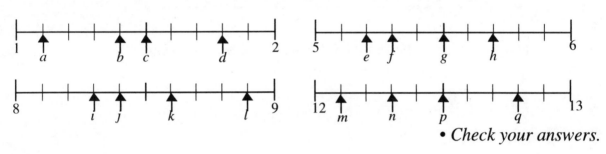

• *Check your answers.*

D2: Zooming in

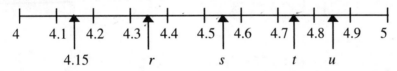
4   4.1   4.2   4.3   4.4   4.5   4.6   4.7   4.8   4.9   5

4.15   r   s   t   u

1. *Give the number that is shown by each letter.*

2.
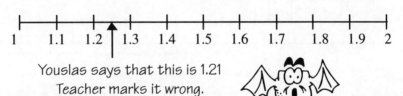
Youslas was asked to
show where 1.21 is on
the number line.

1   1.1   1.2   1.3   1.4   1.5   1.6   1.7   1.8   1.9   2

Youslas says that this is 1.21
Teacher marks it wrong.
Explain why Youslas is wrong.

Youslas

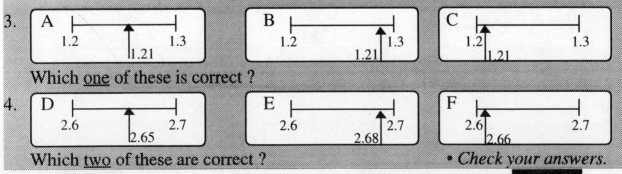

3. A
    1.2   1.3
           1.21

    B
    1.2   1.3
         1.21

    C
    1.2   1.3
      1.21

Which <u>one</u> of these is correct ?

4. D
    2.6   2.7
         2.65

    E
    2.6   2.7
         2.68

    F
    2.6   2.7
      2.66

Which <u>two</u> of these are correct ?

• *Check your answers.*

Developing Efficient **EXTRA**
                                                        Calculator Techniques

D3: Taking a closer look

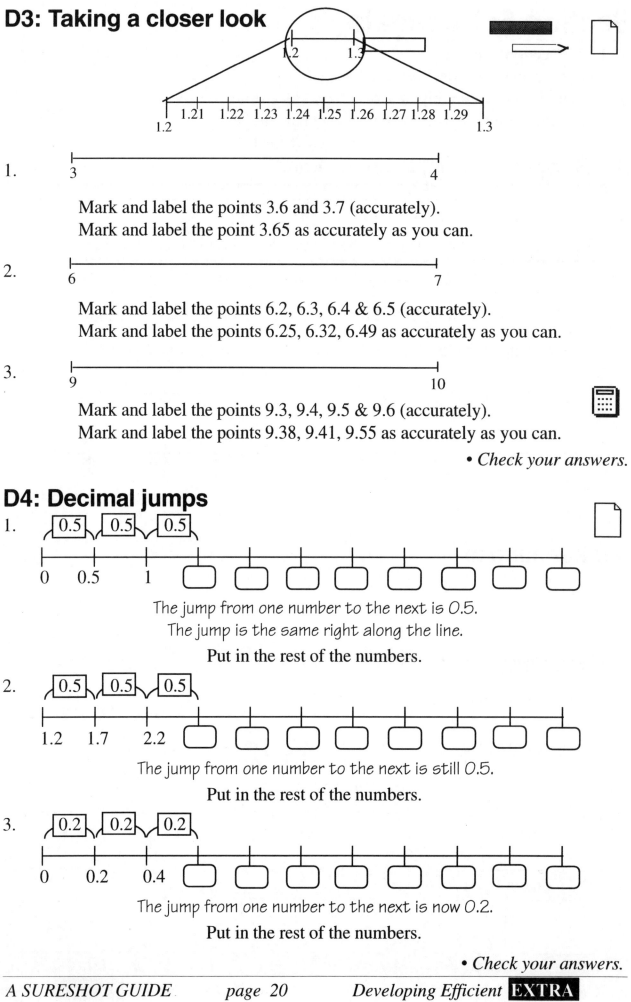

1.21 1.22 1.23 1.24 1.25 1.26 1.27 1.28 1.29
1.2   1.3

1. 3   4

Mark and label the points 3.6 and 3.7 (accurately).
Mark and label the point 3.65 as accurately as you can.

2. 6   7

Mark and label the points 6.2, 6.3, 6.4 & 6.5 (accurately).
Mark and label the points 6.25, 6.32, 6.49 as accurately as you can.

3. 9   10

Mark and label the points 9.3, 9.4, 9.5 & 9.6 (accurately).
Mark and label the points 9.38, 9.41, 9.55 as accurately as you can.

• *Check your answers.*

D4: Decimal jumps

1. 0.5   0.5   0.5

0   0.5   1

The jump from one number to the next is 0.5.
The jump is the same right along the line.

Put in the rest of the numbers.

2. 0.5   0.5   0.5

1.2   1.7   2.2

The jump from one number to the next is still 0.5.

Put in the rest of the numbers.

3. 0.2   0.2   0.2

0   0.2   0.4

The jump from one number to the next is now 0.2.

Put in the rest of the numbers.

• *Check your answers.*

P1: Decimal jump practice

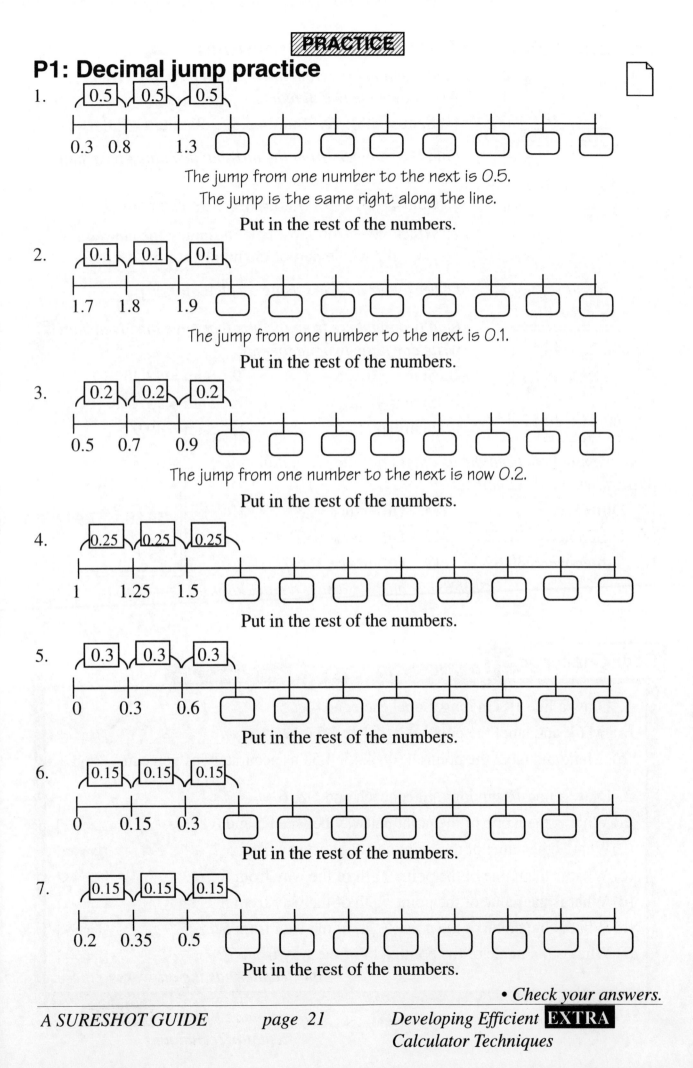

1. | 0.5 | 0.5 | 0.5 |

0.3 0.8 1.3

The jump from one number to the next is 0.5.
The jump is the same right along the line.

Put in the rest of the numbers.

2. | 0.1 | 0.1 | 0.1 |

1.7 1.8 1.9

The jump from one number to the next is 0.1.

Put in the rest of the numbers.

3. | 0.2 | 0.2 | 0.2 |

0.5 0.7 0.9

The jump from one number to the next is now 0.2.

Put in the rest of the numbers.

4. | 0.25 | 0.25 | 0.25 |

1 1.25 1.5

Put in the rest of the numbers.

5. | 0.3 | 0.3 | 0.3 |

0 0.3 0.6

Put in the rest of the numbers.

6. | 0.15 | 0.15 | 0.15 |

0 0.15 0.3

Put in the rest of the numbers.

7. | 0.15 | 0.15 | 0.15 |

0.2 0.35 0.5

Put in the rest of the numbers.

• *Check your answers.*

D5: Estimating additions and subtractions

1.4	2.4
4.4	5.4

Find two numbers from the box that have the given sum. Write down the two numbers.

1. Sum = 3.8   2. Sum = 5.8   3. Sum = 7.8

3.1	4.2
2.5	1.6

Find two numbers from the box that have the given sum. Write down the two numbers.

4. Sum = 7.3   5. Sum = 6.7   6. Sum = 4.7

7. Which gives you most help in finding the answers
   – the whole part of the number or the decimal ?

Hint:
add the whole number
parts in your head !

• *Check your answers using a calculator.*

1.95	8.81
47.97	99.08
60.83	39.57

Find two numbers from the box that have the given sum. 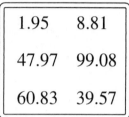 *Write down the two numbers.*

8. Sum = 101.03   9. Sum = 48.38
10. Sum = 41.52   11. Sum = 159.91
12. Sum = 69.64   13. Sum = 49.92

Find two numbers from the box that have the given difference. Write down the two numbers.

7.85	2.1
59.80	37.94
35.1	38.67

14. Difference = 35.84   15. Difference = 33
16. Difference = 51.95   17. Difference = 21.13
18. Difference = 30.82   19. Difference = 5.75

• *Check your answers using a calculator.*

Star Challenge 10

11-12 correct = 1 star

1. Draw a line 10 cm long. Label each end 4 & 5.
   (a) Mark and label the points 4.3, 4.4 & 4.5 (accurately).   [3 marks]
   (b) Mark and label the points 4.39, 4.45, 4.53 as accurately as you can.   [3 marks]

2. Draw a line 10 cm long. Label each end 5 & 6.
   (a) What is the name of the point halfway between 5 and 6 ?   [1 mark]
   (b) What is the name of the point one quarter way from 5 ?   [1 mark]
   (c) What is the name of the point $\frac{1}{10}$ th of the way from 5 ?   [1 mark]
   (d) What is the name of the point $\frac{3}{10}$ th of the way from 5 ?   [1 mark]
   (e) What is the name of the point $\frac{7}{10}$ th of the way from 5 ?   [1 mark]
   (f) What is the name of the point $\frac{1}{5}$ th of the way from 5 ?   [1 mark]

• *Your teacher has the answers to these.*

Section 6: Rounding Techniques

In this section you will:
- review rounding techniques;
- round to the nearest 10, 100, 1000;
- round to nearest whole number.

DEVELOPMENT

D1: Basic rounding

1.

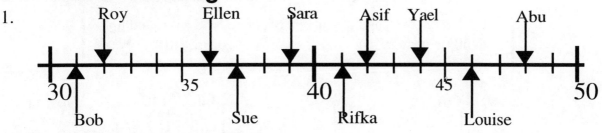

Roy   Ellen   Sara   Asif Yael   Abu

30   35   40   45   50

Bob   Sue   Rifka   Louise

> Roy is 30 years old, to the nearest 10 years.

For each person on this diagram:
- *write down their name;*
- *write down their age to the nearest 10 years.*

2. In 1991, the AA gazette listed the population of the village of Zeals, Wiltshire, as 689.

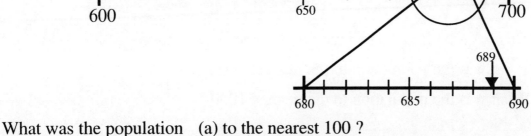

689

600   650   700

689

680   685   690

What was the population   (a) to the nearest 100 ?
(b) to the nearest 10 ?

3. The attendance at the first football match of the season was 5,316.

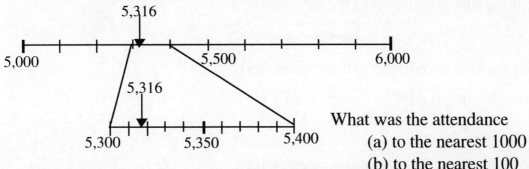

5,316

5,000   5,500   6,000

5,316

5,300   5,350   5,400

What was the attendance
(a) to the nearest 1000
(b) to the nearest 100
(c) to the nearest 10

• *Check your answers.*

D2: Rounding rules

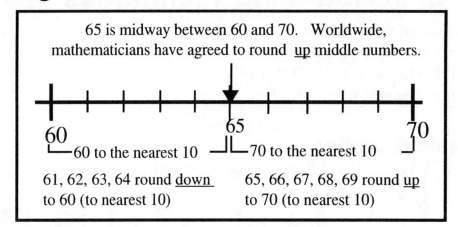

65 is midway between 60 and 70.   Worldwide, mathematicians have agreed to round <u>up</u> middle numbers.

60

65

70

60 to the nearest 10 — 70 to the nearest 10

61, 62, 63, 64 round <u>down</u> to 60 (to nearest 10)

65, 66, 67, 68, 69 round <u>up</u> to 70 (to nearest 10)

1.

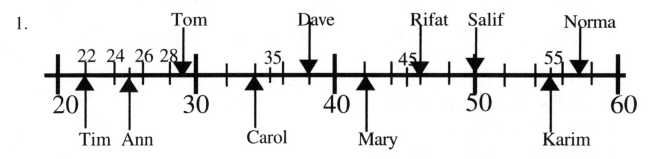

Copy and complete this table:

Name	Tom	Dave	Rifat	Salif	Norma	Tim	Ann	Carol	Mary	Karim
Age										
Age to nearest 10 years										

2. In the 1991 AA gazette, the population of Tarporley, Cheshire was listed as 2 050.

   (a)   What was the population to the nearest 100 ?

   (b)   What was the population to the nearest 1000 ?

3. The population of Otley, W. Yorks, was listed as 14 250.

   (a)   What was the population to the nearest 100 ?

   (b)   What was the population to the nearest 1000 ?

4. The population of Ruabon, Clwyd, was listed as 3 195.

   (a)   What was the population to the nearest 100?

   (b)   What was the population to the nearest 10 ?

5. The population of Trotton, W. Sussex, was listed as 345

   (a)   What was the population to the nearest 100?

   (b)   What was the population to the nearest 10 ?   • *Check your answers.*

PRACTICE
P1: Town and country populations

Population figures for any community can never be exact. They vary from day to day as people move into or out of the area – or as babies are born and people die. Figures given in various gazetteers are only best–estimates on the day that the count was made. The most accurate population count is the National Census, which takes place every ten years, (1971, 1981, 1991, …). However, it does not matter that the figures are never exact. Most of the time when these figures are used, they are rounded to the nearest 10, 100 or 1000.

Complete these population tables for 1992.
CHECK YOUR ANSWERS AT THE END OF EACH TABLE.

> Always round the original figure – not the previous approximation.

Small is beautiful...

Place	Population	Population to nearest 10	Population to nearest 100	Population to nearest 1 000
Scole, Norfolk	1 138			
Taplow, Bucks.	1 710			
Altham, Lancs.	680			
Beetham, Cumbria	1 554			
Beer, Devon	1 328			
Chiseldon, Wilts	2 444			
Chale, Isle of Wight	658			
Stogursey, Somerset	1 246			
Stotfold, Beds.	7 106			
Cromarty, Highlands	878			
Kirkmichael, Tayside	193			
Tywyn, Gwynedd	2 501			
Corwen, Clwyd	2 375			

... but bigger is sometimes better

Place	Population	Population to nearest 100	Population to nearest 1000	Population to nearest 10 000
Birkenhead, Merseyside	99 529			
Huddersfield, Yorks.	123 168			
Maidenhead, Berks.	60 461			
Stretford, Gt Manchester	45 870			
Abergavenny, Gwent	14 871			
Buckley, Clwyd	11 019			
Kilmarnock, Strathclyde	47 158			
Wishaw, Strathclyde	37 187			
Winchester, Hants	35 578			
Mildenhall, Suffolk	12 830			
Douglas, Isle of Man	20 360			

D3: Rounding calculator values

> The instructions on the exam paper said
> *" Give all your answers to the nearest whole number."*

1. ÷ | 5.615386 |

 Spottee says that the answer is 5 to the nearest whole number.

Spottee

Stripee says that the answer is 6 to the nearest whole number.

 Stripee

Who is right ?   Which figure do you look at to decide whether the answer stays as 5 or is rounded up to 6 ?

2. ÷ = | 9.230769 |

Blurbl

Up ? or Down ?

What is 120 ÷ 13 to the nearest whole number ?

3. ÷ | 12.5 |

Icee

Up ? or Down ?

What is the answer to 75 ÷ 6 to the nearest whole number ?

4. *Work out the answer to each of these sums on your calculator.*
   Write each answer down to the nearest whole number.
   (a) 43 ÷ 3   (b) √14   (c) √57 + 5   (d) 347 ÷ 13

   (e) 9.6 x 4.7   (f) √79   (g) √18 x 3   (h) 2321 ÷ 17

   • *Check your answers before doing question 5.*

5. *Work out the answer to each of these sums on your calculator.*
   Write each answer down to the nearest whole number.
   (a) 37.1 x 4.37   (b) √347   (c) 773 ÷ 17   (d) 131.4 x 2.39

   (e) 14.1 ÷ 2.6   (f) √596   (g) √43 x 2.9   (h) 41.6 x 13 ÷ 5.7

   • *Check your answers.*

PRACTICE

P2: Practice in rounding to whole numbers

> *Work out the answer to each sum on a calculator.*
> *Write down each answer to the nearest whole number.*

At the end of each batch of questions, CHECK YOUR ANSWERS.
DO as many of these batches as you need
STOP when you think you are good at the technique.
Do the Star Challenge.

Batch A:	Batch B:	Batch C:	Batch D:
1. 147 ÷ 34	1. 634 ÷ 24	1. 37.87 + 4.3	1. √59.876
2. 35.1 x 2.7	2. √33	2. 67.85 − 5.4	2. 53.8 ÷ 17.3
3. 58 ÷ 39	3. 41.24 + 3.95	3. 38 ÷ 14	3. 46.96 x 2.92
4. 367 ÷ 12	4. 678 ÷ 13	4. 462 x 0.48	4. 57.93 x 4.7
5. 0.34 x 2.7	5. 876 x 0.07	5. √7823	5. 14.56 + 2.96
6. 1.68 x 2.96	6. 437 ÷ 36	6. 34.21 x 2.9	6. 35.77 x 2.22
7. 506 ÷ 3.9	7. √368	7. 53.76 ÷ 6.2	7. 55.44 ÷ 13.2
8. √ 45.78	8. 196 ÷ 27	8. 67.9 ÷ 12.4	8. 14.84 x 45.6

Star Challenge 11

All correct = 1 star

Work out the answer using a calculator.
Write down each answer to the nearest whole number.

1. 56.43 x 0.65   3. 36.89 ÷ 6.7   5. 673 ÷ 57   7. 32.005 ÷ 1.97

2. √142   4. 43.8 x 3.9   6. 14.37 x 7.88   8. 1.47 x 34

• *Your teacher has the answers to these.*

Star Challenge 12

Correct last answer = 1 star

Work out 35.6 x 1.2

Write down the answer to nearest whole number

Multiply the number you wrote down by 2.3

Write down the answer to nearest whole number

Multiply the number you wrote down by 3.4

Write down the answer to nearest whole number

Multiply the number you wrote down by 4.5

Write down the answer

• *Your teacher has the answer to this.*

A SURESHOT GUIDE   page 27   *Developing Efficient* **EXTRA**
Calculator Techniques

Section 7: Decimal places

In this section you will round numbers to a given number of decimal places.

DEVELOPMENT

D1: Rounding to 1 decimal place

√20 to 1 decimal place ?

$\boxed{20}\ \boxed{\sqrt{}}\ =\ \ 4.472135955\ldots$

4.47... lies between 4.4 and 4.5

$\boxed{4.4}7\ldots\ldots$

↑
7 is more than 5 so we round <u>up</u>

Big Edd

$\sqrt{20}\ =\ \ 4.5$ to 1 decimal place

Write down each of these square roots to 1 d.p. :

| 1 d.p. = 1 decimal place |

1. $\sqrt{37}$ 2. $\sqrt{116}$ 3. $\sqrt{69}$ 4. $\sqrt{781}$ 5. $\sqrt{83}$

6. $\sqrt{250}$ 7. $\sqrt{234}$ 8. $\sqrt{5780}$ 9. $\sqrt{13}$ 10. $\sqrt{500}$

• *Check your answers.*

PRACTICE

P1: Rounding square roots to 1 d.p.

Write down each square root to 1 d.p.

Batch A
1. $\sqrt{23}$ 2. $\sqrt{448}$
3. $\sqrt{39}$ 4. $\sqrt{965}$
5. $\sqrt{247}$ 6. $\sqrt{328}$

Batch B
1. $\sqrt{68}$ 2. $\sqrt{457}$
3. $\sqrt{382}$ 4. $\sqrt{35}$
5. $\sqrt{3174}$ 6. $\sqrt{47.3}$

Batch C
1. $\sqrt{491}$ 2. $\sqrt{73}$
3. $\sqrt{242}$ 4. $\sqrt{582}$
5. $\sqrt{37}$ 6. $\sqrt{14}$

• *Check your answers.*

P2: Rounding answers to 1 d.p.

Work out each of these on your calculator. Write down the answer to 1 d.p.

1. $24.2 \div 4.6$ 2. 7.1×13.9 3. $13 \div 8$ 4. 3.7^2

5. $23.45 \div 13$ 6. $4.1 \times 2.3 \times 3.7$ 7. $29 \div 7$ 8. $2.9 \times 3.8 \div 7$

• *Check your answers*

Star Challenge ⭐12

| 7-8 correct = 1 star |

Work out each of these on your calculator. Write down the answer to 1 d.p.

1. $\sqrt{55}$ 2. 5.6×2.7 3. $39 \div 7$ 4. $\sqrt{85}$

5. 7.91^2 6. 2.57×3.7 7. $\sqrt{46.75}$ 8. $119 \div 31$

• *Your teacher will need to mark these.*

D2: Rounding to 2 d.p.

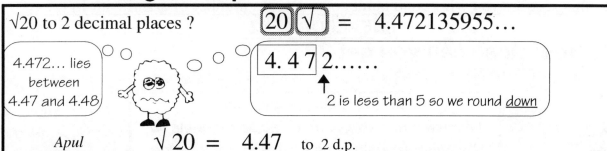

√20 to 2 decimal places ?   20 √ = 4.472135955…

4.472… lies between 4.47 and 4.48

4.4 7 2……

2 is less than 5 so we round *down*

Apul   √20 = 4.47   to 2 d.p.

Write to 2 d.p. :

1. √19   2. √315   3. √472   4. √21   5. √80   6. √71.6
7. √600   8. √421   9. √13.6   10. √59   11. √249   12. √336.9

• *Check your answers.*

D3: Rounding to 2 & 3 d.p.

√20 to 3 decimal places ?   20 √ = 4.472135955…

4.4 7 2 1 ……

1 is less than 5 so we round *down*

√20 = 4.472 to 3 d.p.

Work out each of these on your calculator. Write down the answer to 3 d.p.

1. 5.76 x 4.27   2. √89.6   3. 63.2 ÷ 35.61   4. 73.41 ÷ 2.9
5. √475   6. 37.6 x 3.872   7. √794   8. 7.113²

• *Check your answers.*

Round to 2 d.p.	
9. 9.78 x 3.12	10. 96.9 ÷ 2.42
11. √78.7	12. 82.4 x 7.32
13. √65.67	14. 45.6 x 8.58

Round to 3 d.p.	
15. √1005	16. 29.6 ÷ 13
17. √106.9	18. 24.58 x 5.34
19. √182	20. 37.6 ÷ 7.5

• *Check your answers.*

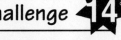

Star Challenge 14   7-8 correct = 1 star

Give the answers …

… to 1 d.p.	*… to 2 d.p.*	*… to 3 d.p.*	*… to 2 d.p.*
1. 47.43 x 0.51	3. 49.3 ÷ 8.7	5. 64.6 ÷ 6.6	7. 30.076 ÷ 2.97
2. √34.89	4. 72.1 x 9.9	6. 28.56 x 8.76	8. 5.76 x 3.8

• *Your teacher has the answers to these.*

Section 8: Significant figures

In this section, you will round numbers to a given number of significant figures.

DEVELOPMENT

D1: How close can <u>you</u> get ?

Modesto and Letmewin play a game.

Modesto chooses a number.
Letmewin has to get as close as possible to
that number using one digit and some zeros.

Modesto

Letmewin

Letmewin scores a point by getting as close as possible.
Modesto gets the point if Modesto can find a number that is closer
or if Letmewin uses more than one digit.

Letmewin gets it wrong
in rounds 3, 5, 7, 8, 10

Task 1: For each of these rounds:
 • give the correct number
 • explain what Letmewin did wrong

[The number was not close enough ?
—or more than one digit was used ?]

Round	Mod.	Let.	M's score	L's score
1	8	8	0	1
2	23	20	0	1
3	27	20	1	0
4	48	50	0	1
5	342	340	1	0
6	521	500	0	1
7	588	500	1	0
8	197	190	1	0
9	108	100	0	1
10	369	370	1	0

Task 2: *Now you play Modesto.*
Copy and complete this table:

Modesto's number	My number
4	
72	
48	
94	
75	
99	
108	
283	
2352	
4030	
0.23	
0.37	
0.061	
0.0079	

• *Check answers.*

This technique is called
'rounding to
1 significant figure'

Task 3: Now the rules are changed.

You can use <u>two</u> digits
and some zeros.

Copy and complete this table:

Modesto's number	My number
9	
38	
621	
839	
472	
122	
4712	
0.231	
0.0325	
378	
1571	

• *Check answers.*

This technique is called
'rounding to
2 significant figures'

D2: Significant figures

> The first significant figure is the first non-zero number.
>
> | 43.416 | = | 43 | to 2 significant figures | (2 s.f.) |
> | 43.416 | = | 43.4 | to 3 significant figures | (3 s.f.) |
> | 43.416 | = | 43.42 | to 4 significant figures | (4 s.f.) |

> Rounding rules are always the same. The instruction "... to 1 d.p." or "... to 2 s.f." just tells you how accurate you must be.

Write each number correct to 2 s.f.

1. 43.45
2. 5.213
3. 6.478
4. 25.2314
5. 33.25
6. 8.4528

Write each number correct to 3 s.f.

7. 26.721
8. 95.912
9. 3.692
10. 521.35
11. 45.788
12. 1.356

> | 5387 | = | 5000 | to 1 significant figure | (1 s.f.) |
> | 5387 | = | 5400 | to 2 significant figures | (2 s.f.) |
> | 5387 | = | 5390 | to 3 significant figures | (3 s.f.) |

Icee

Write each number correct to 1 s.f.

13. 4325
14. 67
15. 568
16. 371
17. 92
18. 108

Write each number correct to 2 s.f.

19. 6234
20. 875
21. 903
22. 1628
23. 3429
24. 4392

> | 0.0234 | = | 0.02 | to 1 significant figure | (1 s.f.) |
> | 0.574 | = | 0.57 | to 2 significant figures | (2 s.f.) |
> | 0.07188 | = | 0.719 | to 3 significant figures | (3 s.f.) |

> Start counting significant places at the first non-zero number !

Blurbl

Write each number correct to 1 s.f.

25. 0.023
26. 0.0047
27. 0.56
28. 0.047
29. 0.63
30. 0.00052

• *Check your answers.*

PRACTICE

P1: Mixed practice

Batch A:

Write to 1 s.f	Write to 2 s.f.	Write to 3 s.f.
1. 15 x 3.41	4. 745 ÷ 23	7. 143 x 2.51
2. 23.1 x 1.7	5. √137	8. 25.6 ÷ 0.24
3. 65 ÷ 19	6. 61.25 x 3.7	9. 3.9 ÷ 17

Batch B:

Write to 1 s.f	Write to 2 s.f.	Write to 3 s.f.
1. 57.8 ÷ 12	4. 43 ÷ 11	7. 478 x 0.35
2. 3.61 x 3.7	5. 239 x 0.16	8. √83.57
3. 1.68 x 1.69	6. 836 ÷ 29	9. 45.21 x 3.9

Star Challenge 15

Write to 1 s.f   8-9 correct = 1 star

1. 480 ÷ 31
2. √35.8
3. 7.68 x 1.3

    Write to 2 s.f.

4. √149
5. 275 ÷ 37
6. 569 ÷ 19

    Write to 3 s.f.

7. 258 ÷ 4.7
8. 67.9 ÷ 15.5
9. 47.8 x 3.2

• *Your teacher has the answers.*

Section 9: Changing fractions into decimals

In this section you will change fractions into decimals (with no rounding).

D1: Fractions into decimals

$$\frac{2}{5} = 2 \div 5 = 0.4$$

Change these fractions into decimals.
Copy and complete each statement.

Ruff

To change a fraction
into a decimal
divide the top number
by the bottom number

1. $\frac{1}{2}$ = ...
2. $\frac{1}{4}$ = ...
3. $\frac{3}{4}$ = ...
4. $\frac{1}{10}$ = ...
5. $\frac{7}{10}$ = ...

6. $\frac{3}{10}$ = ...
7. $\frac{2}{5}$ = ...
8. $\frac{1}{40}$ = ...
9. $\frac{3}{8}$ = ...
10. $\frac{7}{20}$ = ...

11. $\frac{4}{20}$ = ...
12. $\frac{9}{10}$ = ...
13. $\frac{4}{25}$ = ...
14. $\frac{5}{8}$ = ...
15. $\frac{11}{50}$ = ...

• *Check your answers.*

P1: Using decimals to search for equivalent fractions

Task 1: All these fractions, except one,
are equivalent to 0.5
Which one is the odd one out ?

$\frac{24}{48}$ $\frac{29}{58}$ $\frac{35}{70}$ $\frac{46}{89}$ $\frac{57}{114}$

Task 2: *Find the odd one out in each of these sets:*

Set A:

3	9	15
8	24	40
20	111	36
56	296	96

Set B:

18	54	450
24	72	608
132	63	249
176	84	332

Set C:

450	15	25
1440	48	80
30	55	95
128	176	304

• *Check your answers.*

Star Challenge ⭐16

22 correct = 2 stars
18–21 correct = 1 star

Sort these fractions into four sets of equivalent fractions:

| $\frac{80}{100}$ | $\frac{99}{132}$ | $\frac{7}{10}$ | $\frac{72}{100}$ | $\frac{468}{624}$ | $\frac{49}{70}$ | $\frac{4}{5}$ | $\frac{18}{25}$ | $\frac{3}{4}$ | $\frac{36}{45}$ | $\frac{90}{125}$ |

| $\frac{35}{50}$ | $\frac{150}{200}$ | $\frac{234}{325}$ | $\frac{16}{20}$ | $\frac{301}{430}$ | $\frac{200}{250}$ | $\frac{126}{175}$ | $\frac{84}{120}$ | $\frac{165}{220}$ | $\frac{119}{190}$ | $\frac{51}{68}$ |

• *Your teacher will need to mark these.*

P2: The fraction – decimal game   *A game for 2 players*

counters

0.9	0.44	0.12	0.375
0.625	0.2	0.5	0.4
0.21	0.125	0.65	0.3
0.25	0.01	0.1	0.75

THE GAME BOARD

$\frac{90}{100}$	$\frac{2}{5}$	$\frac{42}{200}$	$\frac{1}{10}$
$\frac{2}{10}$	$\frac{4}{8}$	$\frac{1}{100}$	$\frac{65}{100}$
$\frac{6}{8}$	$\frac{12}{100}$	$\frac{30}{80}$	$\frac{1}{8}$
$\frac{10}{16}$	$\frac{6}{20}$	$\frac{1}{4}$	$\frac{44}{100}$

For the 1st player only

Kooldood

$\frac{2}{16}$	$\frac{11}{25}$	$\frac{21}{100}$	$\frac{5}{8}$
$\frac{130}{200}$	$\frac{10}{100}$	$\frac{2}{4}$	$\frac{1}{5}$
$\frac{4}{10}$	$\frac{6}{50}$	$\frac{9}{10}$	$\frac{3}{4}$
$\frac{3}{8}$	$\frac{10}{40}$	$\frac{2}{200}$	$\frac{3}{10}$

For the 2nd player only

Each player, in turn:

- chooses one fraction from his/her board
- says which one has been chosen
- calculates the equivalent decimal
- places a counter on that decimal

> A calculator must not be used until the fraction has been chosen.

At the end of the game, a player gets one point for each counter on the board
PLUS one point for each row or column of three counters.

Section 10: Fractions into decimals again

In this section you will:
- change fractions into decimals rounded to 2 or 3 d.p.;
- review recurring decimals;
- change fractions into recurring decimals

DEVELOPMENT

D1: Changing fractions into decimals to 2 d.p.

$$^3/_7 = 3 \div 7 = 0.42857\ldots = 0.43 \text{ to 2 d.p.}$$

Change these fractions into decimals.
Write each answer to 2 d.p.

1. $\dfrac{1}{3}$ = ...

2. $\dfrac{3}{14}$ = ...

3. $\dfrac{5}{7}$ = ...

4. $\dfrac{1}{9}$ = ...

5. $\dfrac{2}{13}$ = ...

6. $\dfrac{2}{15}$ = ...

7. $\dfrac{7}{17}$ = ...

8. $\dfrac{3}{19}$ = ...

9. $\dfrac{7}{15}$ = ...

10. $\dfrac{9}{23}$ = ...

11. $\dfrac{4}{14}$ = ...

12. $\dfrac{5}{18}$ = ...

- *Check your answers.*

PRACTICE

P1: Practice in changing fractions into decimals

Change these fractions into decimals. Copy and complete each statement.

| Write down each answer to 3 d.p. |

At the end of each batch of questions, CHECK YOUR ANSWERS.

Batch A	Batch B	Batch C
1. $\dfrac{1}{8}$ = ...	1. $\dfrac{3}{25}$ = ...	1. $\dfrac{14}{20}$ = ...
2. $\dfrac{3}{8}$ = ...	2. $\dfrac{2}{3}$ = ...	2. $\dfrac{19}{31}$ = ...
3. $\dfrac{3}{7}$ = ...	3. $\dfrac{1}{15}$ = ...	3. $\dfrac{14}{35}$ = ...
4. $\dfrac{5}{13}$ = ...	4. $\dfrac{5}{8}$ = ...	4. $\dfrac{7}{16}$ = ...
5. $\dfrac{7}{17}$ = ...	5. $\dfrac{7}{18}$ = ...	5. $\dfrac{11}{25}$ = ...
6. $\dfrac{8}{13}$ = ...	6. $\dfrac{13}{18}$ = ...	6. $\dfrac{16}{29}$ = ...
7. $\dfrac{17}{23}$ = ...	7. $\dfrac{23}{28}$ = ...	7. $\dfrac{11}{19}$ = ...
8. $\dfrac{6}{15}$ = ...	8. $\dfrac{15}{16}$ = ...	8. $\dfrac{41}{57}$ = ...
9. $\dfrac{8}{14}$ = ...	9. $\dfrac{26}{29}$ = ...	9. $\dfrac{83}{27}$ = ...

Change these fractions into decimals.
Write down each answer to 3 d.p.

1. $\dfrac{9}{16}$ = ... 3. $\dfrac{23}{25}$ = ... 5. $\dfrac{17}{23}$ = ... 7. $\dfrac{27}{15}$ = ...

2. $\dfrac{7}{8}$ = ... 4. $\dfrac{12}{29}$ = ... 6. $\dfrac{19}{39}$ = ... 8. $\dfrac{13}{11}$ = ...

• Your teacher has the answers to these.

DEVELOPMENT

D2: Recurring decimals

$\dfrac{2}{9}$ = $2 \div 9$ = 0.22222... and this is written as $0.\dot{2}$

[the 2's go on for ever...]

$0.\dot{2}$ is shorthand for **0.222222...** $0.\dot{2}\dot{1}$ is shorthand for **0.212121...**

$0.\dot{3}1\dot{2}$ is shorthand for **0.312312312...** $0.\dot{3}45\dot{6}$ is shorthand for **0.3456345634...**

$0.12\dot{3}4\dot{5}$ is shorthand for **0.123453453...**

In recurring decimals, the dots go over the first and last of the repeating digits.

$0.\dot{2} = 0.22222...$

Write without dots:

1. $0.\dot{5}$ 2. $0.\dot{6}\dot{3}$ 3. $0.5\dot{6}\dot{3}$ 4. $0.\dot{5}6\dot{3}$ 5. $0.2\dot{5}6\dot{3}$

Write using dot notation :

6. **0.456456456...** 7. **0.4565656...**   8. **0.123454545...**

Write as recurring decimals, using dot notation:

9. $\dfrac{2}{9}$ 10. $\dfrac{1}{3}$ 11. $\dfrac{2}{3}$ 12. $\dfrac{5}{6}$

$\dfrac{2}{9} = 2 \div 9 = 0.\dot{2}$

13. $\dfrac{5}{11}$ 14. $\dfrac{8}{45}$ 15. $\dfrac{2}{111}$ 16. $\dfrac{5}{33}$

17. $\dfrac{387}{999}$ 18. $\dfrac{256}{1111}$ 19. $\dfrac{889}{999}$ 20. $\dfrac{345}{1110}$ • Check your answers.

Write these fractions as decimals. Write recurring decimals using dot notation

1. $\dfrac{3}{5}$ 2. $\dfrac{11}{20}$ 3. $\dfrac{5}{8}$ 4. $\dfrac{9}{50}$ 5. $\dfrac{1}{3}$

6. $\dfrac{8}{90}$ 7. $\dfrac{29}{45}$ 8. $\dfrac{17}{33}$ 9. $\dfrac{11}{13}$ 10. $\dfrac{13}{17}$

11. $\dfrac{2}{3}$ 12. $\dfrac{4}{20}$ 13. $\dfrac{3}{18}$ 14. $\dfrac{15}{18}$ 15. $\dfrac{15}{9}$

• Your teacher has the answers to these.

Section 11: Fractions, Decimals & Percentages

In this section you will:
* review equivalent decimals and percentages;
* change fractions into percentages exact and rounded).

D1: Decimals and percentages

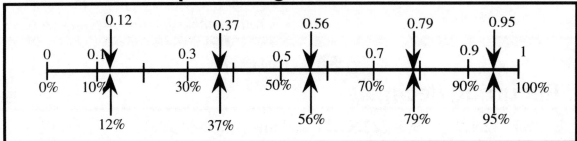

Copy and fill in this table of equivalent decimals and percentages:

Decimal	0.1	0.6	0.62					0.25	0.05
Percentage				73%	24%	15%			
Decimal			0.86	0.35		0.025			
Percentage	56%	40%			41%			10.5%	37.5%

• *Check your answers.*

D2: Changing fractions to percentages

Lubbly

$$\frac{37}{50} = 37 \div 50 = 0.74 \qquad\qquad 0.74 = 74\%$$

fractions —> decimals   decimals —> percentages

In the mid–course tests, Lubbly got $\frac{37}{50}$ for Bio Farming

The percentage mark was 74%.

The rest of Lubbly's marks are given below:

Space Navigation	$\frac{57}{60}$
Maths	$\frac{72}{75}$
Weapon Repairs	$\frac{60}{75}$
Communications	$\frac{51}{60}$

Task 1: Find the percentage mark for each test.

Task 2: Which was Lubbly's best subject?

Task 3: Which was Lubbly's worst subject?

Astronomy	$\frac{12}{15}$
Survival Skills	$\frac{15}{20}$
Galacto–Speak	$\frac{23}{25}$
Electronics	$\frac{32}{40}$

Task 4:

Calculate the mean percentage mark of these nine tests, to the nearest 1 d.p.

To pass, Lubbly must have a mean mark of at least 80%. Did Lubbly pass?

• *Check your answers*

D3: Percentage test marks

$$\frac{47}{62} \quad = \quad 47 \div 62 \quad = \quad 0.75806\ldots = 75.806\ldots\% \quad = 76\% \text{ to nearest }\%$$

Change these fractions into percentages. Write each answer to the nearest %

1. $\dfrac{17}{20}$ = ...%   2. $\dfrac{63}{74}$ = ...%   3. $\dfrac{25}{37}$ = ...%   4. $\dfrac{43}{96}$ = ...%

5. $\dfrac{37}{80}$ = ...%   6. $\dfrac{23}{53}$ = ...%   7. $\dfrac{28}{59}$ = ...%   8. $\dfrac{13}{21}$ = ...%

• *Check your answers.*

PRACTICE

P1: Practice in changing fractions into percentages

Change these test marks into percentages.
Write down each answer to the nearest whole percent.
At the end of each batch of questions, CHECK YOUR ANSWERS.
DO as many of these batches as you need.
STOP when you think you are good at the technique.

Batch A:

1. $\dfrac{17}{20}$ 2. $\dfrac{13}{18}$ 3. $\dfrac{22}{27}$ 4. $\dfrac{15}{25}$ 5. $\dfrac{12}{15}$ 6. $\dfrac{12}{20}$ 7. $\dfrac{17}{36}$ 8. $\dfrac{12}{35}$ 9. $\dfrac{21}{25}$ 10. $\dfrac{27}{38}$

Batch B:

1. $\dfrac{15}{20}$ 2. $\dfrac{24}{38}$ 3. $\dfrac{15}{19}$ 4. $\dfrac{43}{45}$ 5. $\dfrac{27}{36}$ 6. $\dfrac{29}{30}$ 7. $\dfrac{14}{33}$ 8. $\dfrac{57}{65}$ 9. $\dfrac{25}{44}$ 10. $\dfrac{19}{25}$

Batch C:

1. $\dfrac{26}{40}$ 2. $\dfrac{19}{46}$ 3. $\dfrac{18}{41}$ 4. $\dfrac{25}{32}$ 5. $\dfrac{17}{26}$ 6. $\dfrac{57}{67}$ 7. $\dfrac{92}{120}$ 8. $\dfrac{52}{145}$ 9. $\dfrac{37}{73}$ 10. $\dfrac{29}{88}$

Star Challenge ◄19

7 correct = 1 star

These Pan–Galactic students are comparing their best marks.

Didi's best mark was $^{22}/_{24}$

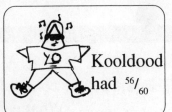
Kooldood had $^{56}/_{60}$

$^{21}/_{23}$ was the best Icee got

$^{12}/_{14}$ was Spottee's best mark

Idea's top mark was $^{47}/_{49}$

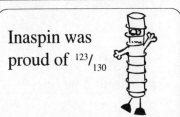
Inaspin was proud of $^{123}/_{130}$

Give each mark as a percentage to the nearest whole percent.
Who was the best overall ?

Section 12: Working with fractions, decimals and percentages

In this section you will use fractions and percentages to solve a variety of real–life problems.

DEVELOPMENT

D1: Percentage reasoning

EXAMPLE:

Q: It was the final Pan–Galactic Academy examination.
   67% of the Trainees passed.
   What percentage failed ?

   A: 33% failed

$100\% - 67\% = 33\%$

Blurbl

1. 41% of the members of a squash club are female.

    What percentage are male ?

2. 65% of a class like football.   **What percentage do not like football ?**

3. On the 8.00 am bus, 40% of the passengers are children and 35% are men.

    What percentage are women ?

4. For P.E. the pupils were given a choice of 4 activities:

24% chose to play Badminton
32% did Dance
33% did Gymnastics.
The rest went on a cross–country run.

    What percentage went on the run ?

5. In a school survey, pupils were asked to name their favourite subject.
    The results were:

Music 25%	Maths 21%	Science 16%	Technology 21%
English 6%	French 4%	PE ? %	

    What percentage chose PE ?

    • *Check your answers.*

Star Challenge 20

All correct = 1 star

1. Parents at the new High School voted on whether they wanted a school uniform.
    17% voted "No". 6% abstained (chose not to vote).

    What percentage voted "Yes" ?

2. Pupils at the new school voted on the colour of the school jumper.
    The results were:

Red 14%	Blue 16%	Green 6%	Navy ? %	Grey ? %
Equal numbers of pupils chose navy as chose grey.				

    What percentage chose Navy ?

    • *Your teacher will need to mark these.*

D2: Percentages of amounts

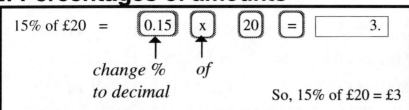

15% of £20 = | 0.15 | x | 20 | = | 3. |

change %   of
to decimal

So, 15% of £20 = £3

15% = 0.15
3% = 0.03
10% = 0.1

Ruff

Use this method to work out:

1. 10% of £40
2. 3% of £20
3. 5% of £15
4. 24% of £10
5. 70% of £64
6. 2% of £85
7. 34% of £80
8. 16% of £30
9. 7% of £82
10. 1% of £96
11. 9% of £11
12. 33% of £50

• *Check your answers.*

D3: Fractions of amounts

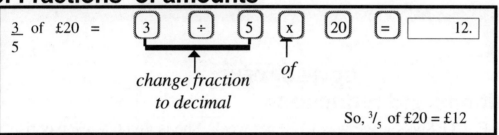

$\frac{3}{5}$ of £20 = | 3 | ÷ | 5 | x | 20 | = | 12. |

change fraction
to decimal

of

So, $\frac{3}{5}$ of £20 = £12

Use this method to work out:

1. $\frac{3}{4}$ of £80
2. $\frac{4}{5}$ of £16
3. $\frac{2}{7}$ of £35
4. $\frac{2}{3}$ of £18
5. $\frac{3}{8}$ of £20
6. $\frac{2}{5}$ of £36
7. $\frac{5}{16}$ of £36
8. $\frac{7}{8}$ of £30
9. $\frac{2}{9}$ of 45p
10. $\frac{2}{15}$ of 90p
11. $\frac{3}{20}$ of £1.60
12. $\frac{4}{7}$ of £42

• *Check your answers.*

PRACTICE

P1: Practice in finding percentages and fractions of amounts

Work out the following percentages and fractions of amounts.
At the end of each batch, CHECK YOUR ANSWERS.

Batch A:

1. 10% of £55
2. $\frac{2}{5}$ of £25
3. 5% of £21
4. $\frac{3}{4}$ of £36
5. 3% of £14
6. 7% of £19
7. $\frac{1}{3}$ of £27.60
8. 15% of £42
9. $\frac{3}{8}$ of £26
10. $\frac{2}{7}$ of £49
11. 12% of £43
12. $\frac{1}{4}$ of £25

Batch B:

1. 3% of £17
2. $\frac{3}{5}$ of £45
3. 45% of £60
4. $\frac{4}{7}$ of £63
5. 27% of £60
6. 4% of £28
7. $\frac{3}{16}$ of £48
8. 5% of £78
9. $\frac{4}{5}$ of £35
10. $\frac{3}{10}$ of £34
11. 6% of £22
12. $\frac{1}{3}$ of £24.90

Batch C:

1. 4% of £15
2. $^5/_6$ of £36
3. 3% of £46
4. $^1/_{10}$ of £25
5. 90% of £64
6. 80% of £125
7. $^3/_5$ of £95
8. 8% of £24.25
9. $^2/_5$ of £34.50
10. $^3/_8$ of £44
11. 17% of £23
12. $^5/_6$ of £30

DEVELOPMENT

D4: Additions and reductions

> **EXAMPLE:** Q: Sue's wage was £120 per week. She is given a 5% pay rise. How much is her new wage ?
>
> **Step 1:** 5% of £120 = [0.05] [x] [120] [=] [6.   ]
>
>   5% of
>
> Rise = £6
>
> **Step 2:** New wage = £120 + £6 = £126

1. Stephen's wage was £148 per week. He was given a 10% rise.
   What is his new wage ?

2. The price of a TV is £450. The sale reduction is 5%.
   What is the sale price ?

3. The restaurant bill came to £35.50. Bob added 10% to the bill as a tip.
   How much did he pay ?

4. A set of tables and chairs cost £300. The table is scratched.
   Mary is offered 15% off the usual price. **How much does she have to pay ?**

5. The bill in the café came to £15.80. Sally added a 10% tip to the bill.
   How much did she pay ?

6. Vera got a 7% pay rise. Before the rise, she had been earning £12,600 a year.
   How much did she get after the rise ?

7. The cost of the typewriter was £140 before VAT.
   Value Added Tax (VAT) at 15% needs to be added onto this price.
   What is the price of the typewriter to the customer ?

• *Check your answers.*

D5: Expressing one quantity as a percentage of another

EXAMPLE: Q: Taz scored 94 out of 200 in a test.
What percentage mark did he get ?

A: $\dfrac{94}{200}$ =   94   ÷   200   =   0.47 =   47%

$\uparrow$ *mark as a fraction of total* $\uparrow$ *mark as decimal* $\uparrow$ *mark as percentage*

Taz

Task 1: *Find the percentage mark in each case.*

Pow
24 out
of 80

Hoblin
54 out
of 60

Modesto
144 out
of 150

Task 2: *Find the percentage mark in each case.*
Give each mark to the nearest whole percentage.

Chyps
155 out
of 180

Driller
67 out
of 76

Frizzbang
34 out
of 75

EXAMPLE: Q: A bike was bought at £160 and sold at £120.
Find the percentage loss.

A: Loss = £160 – £120 = £40

Fractional loss   = $\dfrac{40}{160}$ ← loss
← original price

Percentage loss   = $\dfrac{40}{160}$ =   40 ÷ 160   = 0.25   =   25%

fraction   *decimal*   *percentage*

Task 3: £3.20 is rounded to £3.00
Calculate: (a) the error in rounding like this
(b) the error as a fraction of the exact amount
(c) the percentage error.

Task 4: A dealer bought a painting for £225 and sold it for £300
Calculate: (a) the profit
(b) the percentage profit.

• *Check your answers.*

E1: Do the words mean 'up' or 'down' ?

TV was £260 now £240	Hi–fi *now* £315 *next month* £325

Value of unit trust

April 1993	£2 000
October 1993	£1 600
April 1994	£1 800

Words used when value or price

goes up	goes down
gain	reduction
profit	loss
increase	decrease
service charge	discount

Value of car

1990	£15 000
1991	£10 000
1992	£8 000

Dave buys a bike for £80   He sells it to Mary for £60.
Mary later sells it to Bob for £70

1. What is the reduction in the price of the TV ?

2. What is the increase in the price of the Hi–fi ?

3. Does Dave make a gain or a loss, when he sells the bike ?

4. How much profit does Mary make when she sells the bike ?

5. Does the value of the unit trust increase between April and October 1993 ?

6. Does the value of the unit trust increase between October 1993 and April 1994 ?

7. What is the reduction in the value of the car between 1990 and 1991 ?

8. Does the car's value decrease more between 1990 and 1991 or between 1991 and 1992 ?

9. The price of a CD player is £440. Bob gets a discount of £20, How much does he pay ?

10. Sara buys a table for £30 and sells it for £25. Does she make a profit or a loss ?

11. Kriss buys £100 of shares. He later sells them for £115. Has their value increased or decreased since he bought them ?

12. If Asif can sell his CD player for £350, he will have made a £30 profit. How much did he buy it for ?

13. Ellen goes out for Sunday lunch. The meal costs £9.50. But, there is a discount of £1.50 if you eat after 1.30. Ellen eats at 2.00 pm. There is also a service charge of £1.00   How much does Ellen have to pay ?

• Check your answers.

1.

Coat £60	Sale Price 10% off

What is the sale price of the coat ?

2. On January 1st, the price of all Ruby cars goes up by 5%.
The price of the Ruby XL was £7540. What will its new price be ?

3. A restaurant adds 12% 'service charge' to its bills.
Copy each of these bills.   Work out the cost of each bill.

Starter	£3.50	Soup	£2.80	Paté	£3.20
Main course	£7.80	Steak + fries	£5.60	Fish	£6.70
Sweet	£2.70	Apple Pie	£2.40	Wine	£3.50
Wine/drinks	£4.50	Coffee	£1.20	Coffee	£1.20
subtotal	………	subtotal	………	subtotal	………
12% service	………	12% service	………	12% service	………
Total	………	Total	………	Total	………

4. In the 1981 census, the population of Merryweather was 3 540. In the next 10 years the population increased by 15%.   What was its population in 1991 ?

5. Derek bought a car for £2 500. During the next year its value falls by 14%. What is it worth after one year ?

• *Your teacher will need to mark these.*

Paul is comparing prices. He has the catalogues for two stores— SAVITT and EL CHEAPO. For each item they give the R.R.P. (recommended retail price) and the discount.   *For each item:*
* *calculate the price at each store;*
* *says which store sells it the cheapest;*
* *say what the difference in price is between the stores.*

	Item	R.R.P.	Savitt's Discount	El Cheapo's Discount
A	TV	£380	$\frac{1}{4}$	20%
B	CD player	£350	$\frac{1}{10}$	11%
C	Computer game	£15	$\frac{1}{5}$	25%
D	Video recorder	£240	$\frac{1}{3}$	30%
E	Camcorder	£550	$\frac{2}{5}$	35%
F	3 blank videos	£12	$\frac{1}{4}$	24%
G	Personal stereo	£21	$\frac{1}{3}$	35%
H	Computer	£1280	$\frac{2}{5}$	45%

• *Your teacher will need to mark these.*

Section 13: Putting it all together...

In this section you will put together equivalent fractions, decimals and percentages.

Star Challenge ⭐23 ⭐23 ⭐23

EXTENSION

| 32 correct fractions = 3 stars |
| 27–31 correct fractions = 2 stars |
| 21–26 correct fractions = 1 star |

Find the equivalent fractions for each decimal and percentage in the table below.

Write the equivalent fraction in the box below the decimal/percentage.

Each fraction $\frac{a}{b}$ is made by choosing a and b from the box on the right.

1	2	3
4	5	6
7	8	9

Choose a and b from here.

Big Edd

$0.\dot{3}$	0.2	$0.\dot{1}4285\dot{7}$	12.5%	0.5
	$^1/_5$			
0.375	25%	$0.\dot{6}$	0.75	$0.\dot{1}$
20%	$0.\dot{7}$	$0.\dot{2}$	0.875	50%
		$^2/_9$		
0.6	$0.1\dot{6}$	75%	$33^1/_3\%$	0.125
$0.\dot{8}$	37.5%	$0.8\dot{3}$	$0.\dot{4}2857\dot{1}$	60%
			$^3/_7$	
$0.\dot{5}7142\dot{8}$	$0.\dot{5}$	$0.\dot{2}8571\dot{4}$	0.8	$66^2/_3\%$
$0.\dot{8}5714\dot{2}$	$0.\dot{4}$	0.25	0.4	0.625

• *Your teacher has the answers to this.*

A SURESHOT GUIDE   page 44   *Developing Efficient* **EXTRA**
Calculator Techniques

THE NATIONAL CURRICULUM ...
... AND BEYOND ...

Sureshot

Understanding
Geometry

EXTRA

Part 1

Understanding Geometry EXTRA *Part 1*
Section 1: Mirror symmetry

In this section you will:
- find lines of symmetry;
- create symmetric shapes using given lines.

D1: Finding lines of symmetry

Task 1: *Draw in one line of symmetry for each shape:*

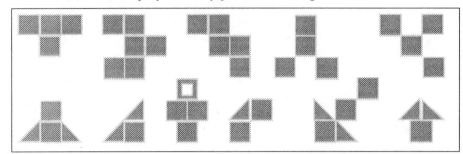

Task 2: *Draw as many lines of symmetry as you can find:*

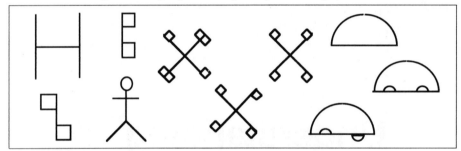

Task 3: *Draw as many lines of symmetry as you can find:*

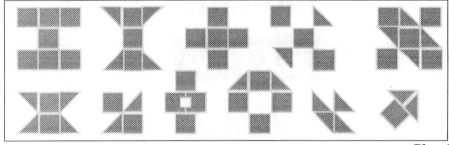

• *Check your answers.*

P1: How many lines of symmetry ?

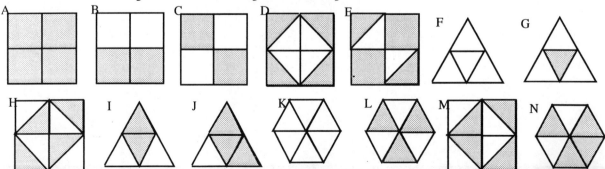

mirror

D2: Creating mirror symmetry

Reflect each shape in the mirror line(s) to create a symmetric pattern:

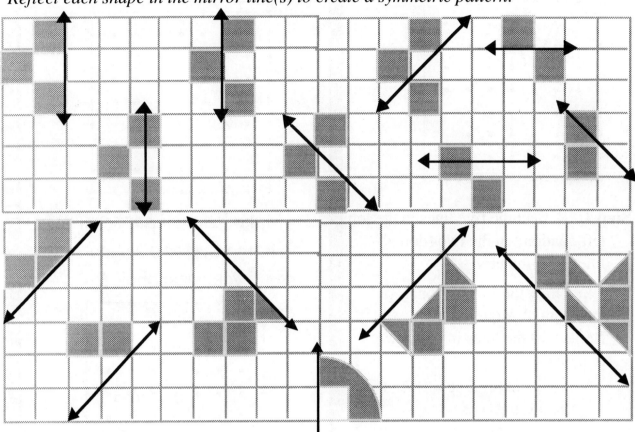

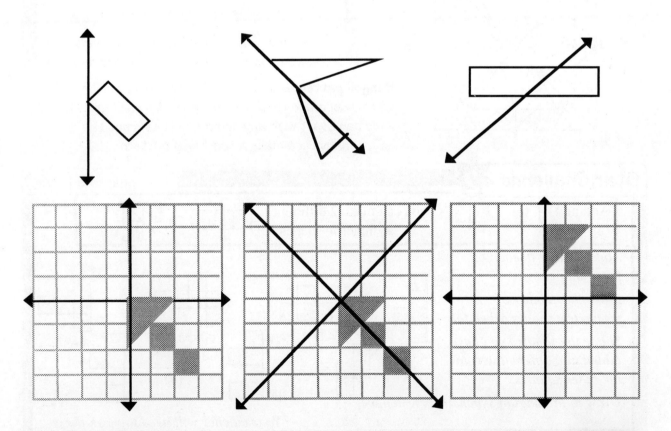

E1: Rangoli patterns

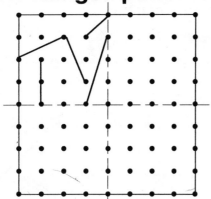

Step 1: Reflect the five lines in the top left quadrant in the two (dotted) lines of symmetry.

Step 2: Draw the two diagonals of the original, large square. Reflect all the lines in these two diagonals.

You should end up with the Rangoli pattern below.

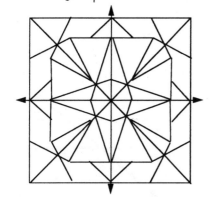

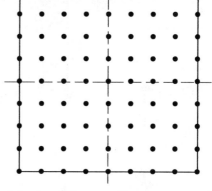

Make Rangoli pattern(s) using five or six lines of your own choice.

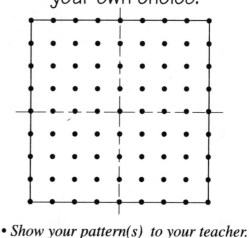

• *Show your pattern(s) to your teacher.*

Rangoli patterns are patterns that Hindu families make to decorate their homes for the Dirwali festival. You can start with any number of lines — but too many lines make a too-fussy pattern.

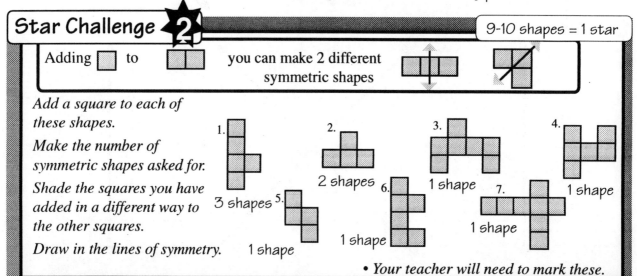

Adding ☐ to ☐☐ you can make 2 different symmetric shapes

Add a square to each of these shapes.

Make the number of symmetric shapes asked for.

Shade the squares you have added in a different way to the other squares.

Draw in the lines of symmetry.

1. 3 shapes
2. 2 shapes
3. 1 shape
4. 1 shape
5. 1 shape
6. 1 shape
7. 1 shape

• *Your teacher will need to mark these.*

Section 2: Rotational symmetry

In this section you will:
- review order of rotational symmetry;
- look at symmetries of polygons.

D1: Circle Patterns

pencil   compasses   eraser   tracing paper

Task 1: Circle Pattern A

- Draw a circle with radius 4 cm
- Draw a diameter
- Divide the diameter into four equal parts
- Draw the two semi-circles as shown
- Rub out the diameter to get Circle Pattern A

Task 2: Circle Pattern B

- Draw a circle with radius 4 cm
- Keep the compass distance 4 cm and use it to mark six points at equal distances round the circle
- Draw radii from three of the points (as shown)
- Draw semi-circles as shown
- Rub out the radii to get Circle Pattern B

Task 3: Circle Pattern C

- Draw another Circle Pattern A
- Rub out the diameter and half of the large circle to get Circle Pattern C

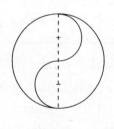

Task 4: Trace each circle pattern.
Work out the order of rotational symmetry of each.
Put your results into a table like this:

Circle Pattern	A	B	C
Order of rotational symmetry			

The order of rotational symmetry is the number of ways the tracing can be turned to fit onto the original shape.

- *Check your answers.*

D2: Rotational symmetry

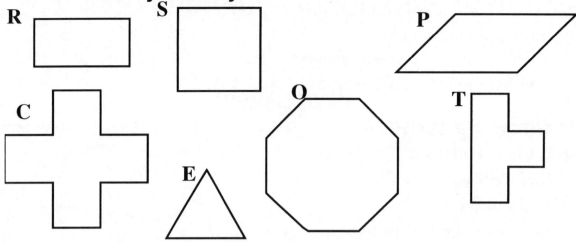

Task 1: *Trace one shape at a time.*
Count how many different ways the tracing will fit onto the original shape.
Do not turn the tracing paper over.
Put your results onto a table like this:

Shape	R	S	P	C	E	O	T
No. of ways							

Taz

It helps you keep count if you mark one corner of the shape on the tracing paper.

A tracing of this shape will fit on the shape in 3 different ways.
It has <u>rotational symmetry of order 3</u>.
[Or – its order of symmetry is 3]

Every shape has order of symmetry of at least 1.
[It will fit onto its own shape at least once]

We say that a shape has rotational symmetry if its order is more than 1.
The centre you rotate the shape around is called the <u>centre of rotation</u>.

Task 2: *For each of the following shapes, find:*
  • the order of rotational symmetry;
  • the number of lines of symmetry.
  Put your results into a table.

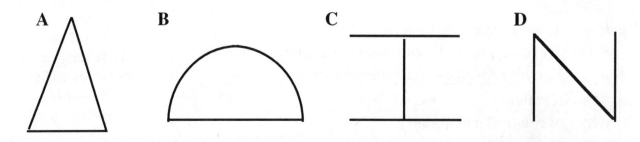

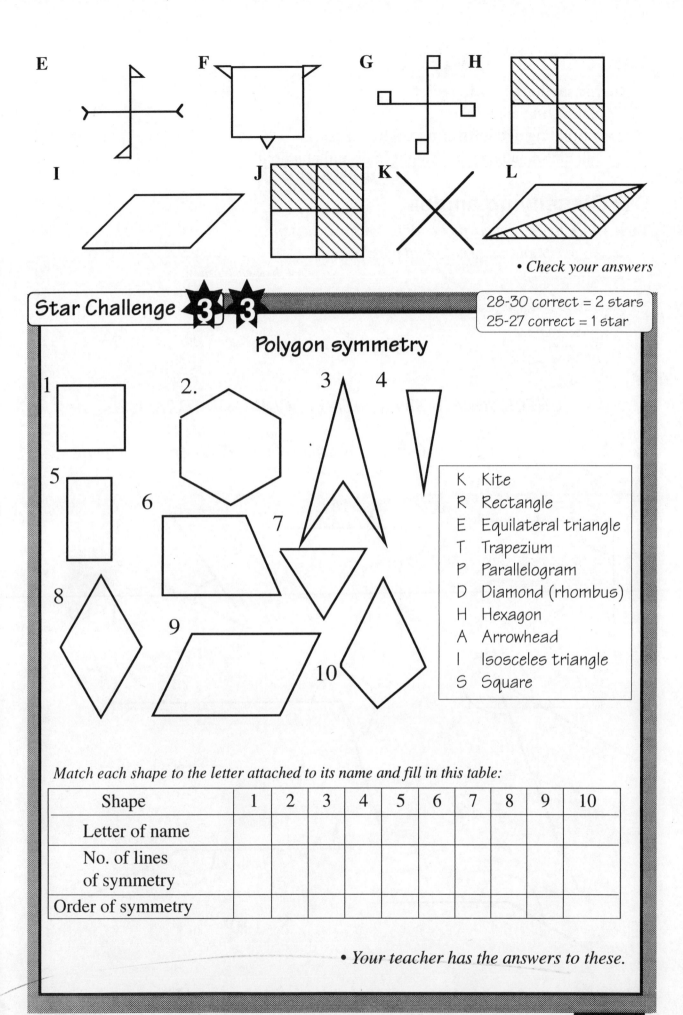

E   F   G   H

I   J   K   L

• *Check your answers*

28-30 correct = 2 stars
25-27 correct = 1 star

Polygon symmetry

1   2.   3   4

5   6   7

8   9   10

K	Kite
R	Rectangle
E	Equilateral triangle
T	Trapezium
P	Parallelogram
D	Diamond (rhombus)
H	Hexagon
A	Arrowhead
I	Isosceles triangle
S	Square

Match each shape to the letter attached to its name and fill in this table:

Shape	1	2	3	4	5	6	7	8	9	10
Letter of name										
No. of lines of symmetry										
Order of symmetry										

• *Your teacher has the answers to these.*

Section 3: Angle review

In this section you will review:
- classifying angles;
- estimating and measuring angles sizes;
- calculating angles on straight lines and at a point.

DEVELOPMENT

D1: Classifying angles

Task 1:   *Choose the correct ending for each sentence.*
Write out the whole sentence.

A right angle is ....

An acute angle is ....

A reflex angle is ....

An obtuse angle is ....

> *Choose from :*
> smaller than 90°
> 90°
> between 90° and 180°
> between 180° and 360°

CHECK YOUR ANSWERS BEFORE GOING ON TO TASK 2.

Task 2:   *For each angle, say whether it is acute, obtuse, reflex or a right angle.*

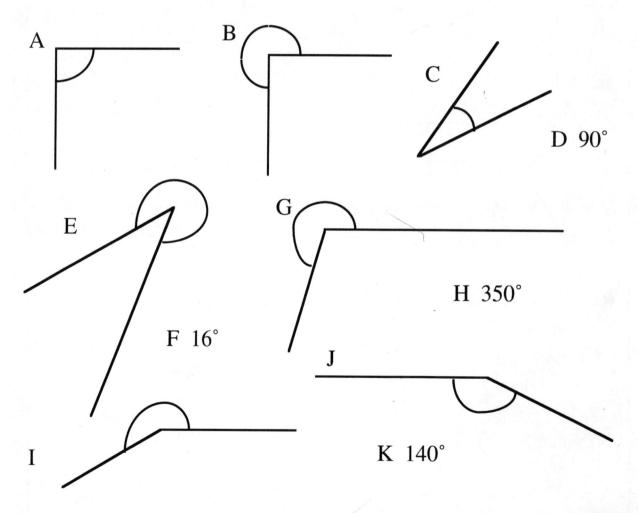

A

B

C

D 90°

E

F 16°

G

H 350°

I

J

K 140°

• *Check your answers.*

D2: Estimating angle sizes

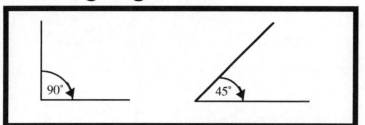

1.

The class were asked to estimate the size of this angle.
Letmewin's estimate was 30°
It was marked wrong.

Letmewin

Explain why the estimate should be between 45° and 90°

2. Apul and Crumbl also estimated the size of the angle in question 1.

Apul's estimate was 70°

Apul

Both were marked right.

Crumbl's estimate was 80°

Crumbl

Explain how both answers can be right.

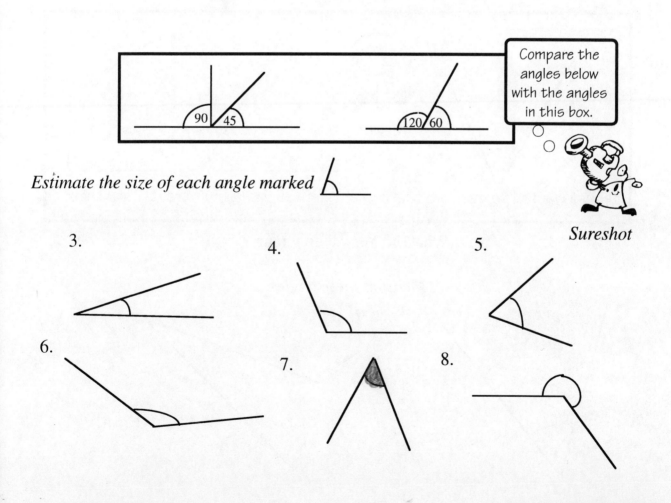

Compare the angles below with the angles in this box.

Estimate the size of each angle marked

Sureshot

3.

4.

5.

6.

7.

8.

• *Check your answers.*

D3: Measuring angles

Measure each angle as accurately as you can.

1.

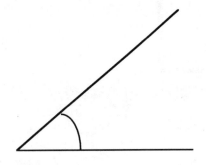

2.

3.

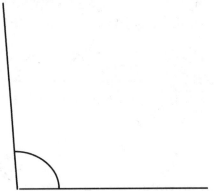

4.

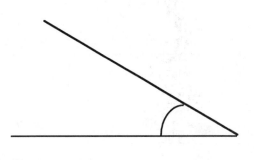

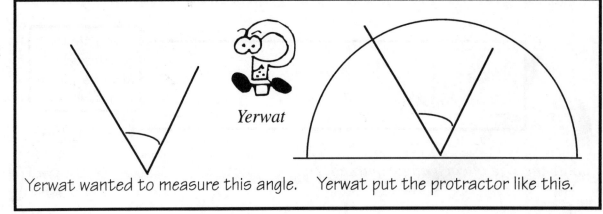

Yerwat

Yerwat wanted to measure this angle.   Yerwat put the protractor like this.

What did Yerwat do wrong ?

Measure these angles.

6.

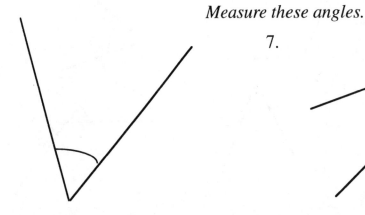

7.

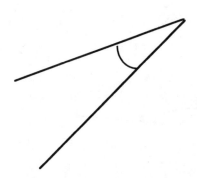

• *Check your answers.*

D4: Sets of angles

Task 1: *For each set of angles:*
- *copy the table*
- *estimate the size of each angle and put in the table*
- *measure the size of each angle and put in the table.*

Set A

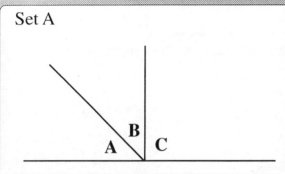

Angle	A	B	C
Estimate			
Measurement			
Sum of angles			

Set B

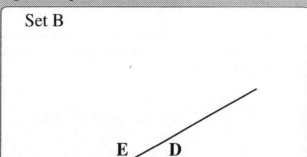

Angle	D	E
Estimate		
Measurement		
Sum of angles		

Set C

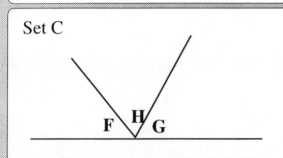

Angle	F	G	H
Estimate			
Measurement			
Sum of angles			

Set D

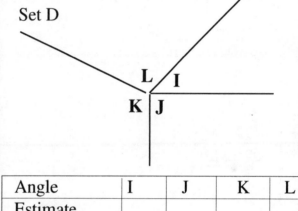

Angle	I	J	K	L
Estimate				
Measurement				
Sum of angles				

Task 2: *Sketch each diagram. Replace each letter by the correct angle size.*

1.

100° *a*

2.
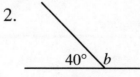
40° *b*

3.
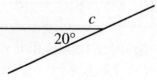
c
20°

4.
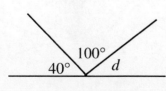
100°
40° *d*

5.
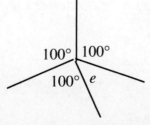
100° 100°
100° *e*

6.
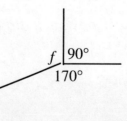
f 90°
170°

• *Check your answers.*

D5: Angles on straight lines

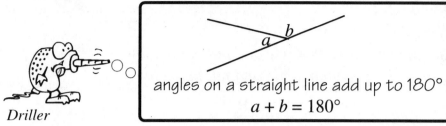

angles on a straight line add up to 180°

$a + b = 180°$

Driller

Copy each diagram. Replace the letters with the correct angle sizes.

1.

    $100°$
    c

2.

    d $30°$

3.

    $60°$ e

4.

    f
    $70°$

5.

This symbol means a right angle
The angle is 90°

k

What is the size of the angle marked k ?

Copy each diagram. Replace the letters with the correct angle sizes.

6.

    $160°$ m
    n

7.

    $150°$
    p

8.

    $120°$ r
    q $80°$

9.

    s $75°$
    t

10.

    u
    $30°$ $120°$

11.

    v
    $30°$

12.

    w $20°$

13.

    $165°$
    x

• *Check your answers.*

D6: Taking shortcuts

y $35°$

I know a shortcut

$180 - 35 = 145$

Spottee

$y = 145°$

1. Spottee thinks that $y = 145°$.
   (a) Does $145 + 35 = 180$?   (b) Does Spottee's shortcut work ?

   Copy each diagram. Replace the letters with the correct angle sizes.

2.

    z
    $58°$

3.

    a $16°$

4.

    b
    $115°$

5.

    $123°$ c

• *Check your answers.*

D7: More angles on lines

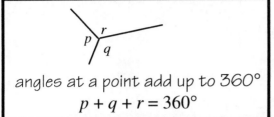

angles at a point add up to 360°

$p + q + r = 360°$

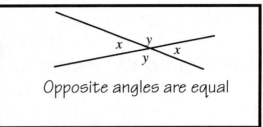

Opposite angles are equal

Copy each diagram. Replace the letters with the correct angle sizes.

1.
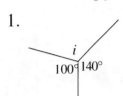

2.
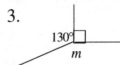

3.
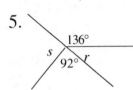

4.
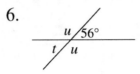

5.
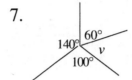

6.
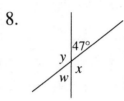

7.
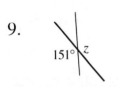

8.
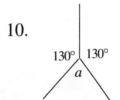

9.
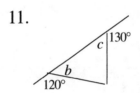

10.
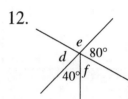

11.

12.
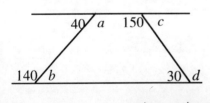

• *Check your answers.*

Star Challenge 4

All correct = 1 star

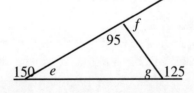

Star Challenge 5 5

9 letters correct = 2 stars

7-8 letters correct = 1 star

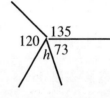

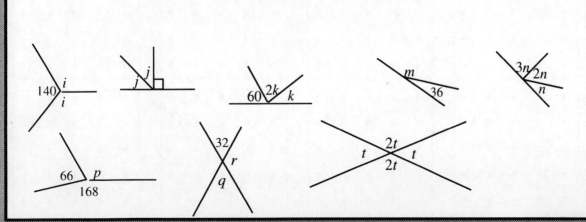

Section 4: Classifying triangles

In this section you will review triangle classification.

D1: Searching for triangles

A and B are fixed points. C is the third vertex (corner) of ΔABC.

ΔABC must be a right-angled triangle. There are 10 possible positions for C.

One of the right-angled triangles has been given.

Draw the other 9 right-angled triangles ABC

Check your answers.

Star Challenge 6 6

5 triangles = 2 stars
4 triangles = 1 star

A and B are fixed points. C is the third vertex of ΔABC.

ΔABC must be a right-angled triangle.

There are 5 possible positions for C that fit on this grid.   How many can you find ?

A and B are fixed points. C is the third vertex of ΔABC.
ΔABC must be an ISOSCELES triangle. There are 8 possible isosceles Δs.

How many can you find ?

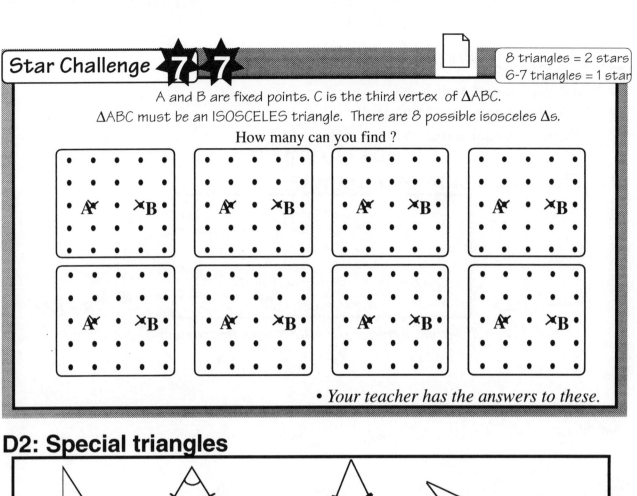

• *Your teacher has the answers to these.*

D2: Special triangles

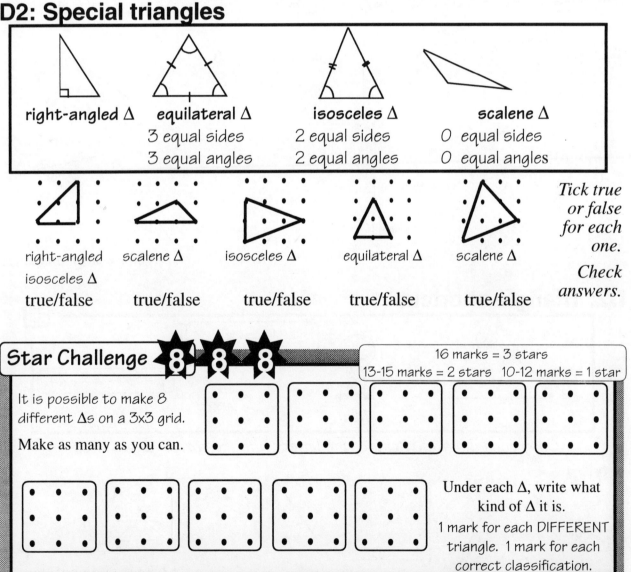

right-angled Δ   equilateral Δ   isosceles Δ   scalene Δ

                    3 equal sides   2 equal sides   0 equal sides
                    3 equal angles   2 equal angles   0 equal angles

right-angled   scalene Δ   isosceles Δ   equilateral Δ   scalene Δ
isosceles Δ

true/false   true/false   true/false   true/false   true/false

*Tick true
or false
for each
one.*

*Check
answers.*

It is possible to make 8
different Δs on a 3x3 grid.

Make as many as you can.

Under each Δ, write what
kind of Δ it is.

1 mark for each DIFFERENT
triangle. 1 mark for each
correct classification.

Section 5: Angles in triangles

In this section you will:
- calculate angles in a triangle;
- work with equilateral and isosceles triangles.

DEVELOPMENT

D1: The angle sum of a triangle

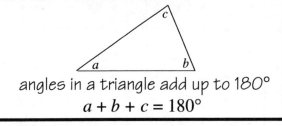

angles in a triangle add up to 180°

$$a + b + c = 180°$$

Big Edd

Copy each diagram. Replace the letters with the correct angle sizes.

1.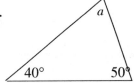

2.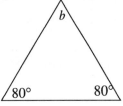

3.

4.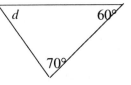

5.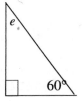

6.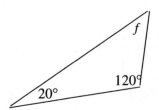

7.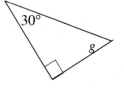

8.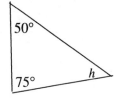

9.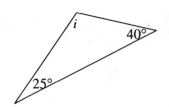

• *Check your answers.*

D2: Triangle shortcut

I know a shortcut for this !

$p = 180 - 84 - 44$

$p = 52°$

Idea

Copy each diagram. Replace the letters with the correct angle sizes.

1.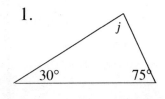

2.

3.

4.

• *Check your answers.*

A SURESHOT GUIDE   page 60   Understanding Geometry Part 1   **EXTRA**

P1: Angles in triangles practice

Copy each diagram. Replace the letters with the correct angle sizes.

1.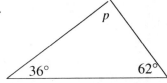

2.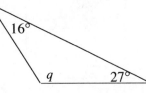

3.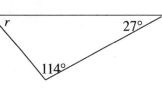

4.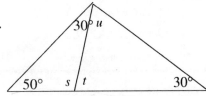

5.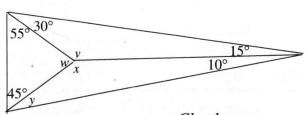

• *Check your answers.*

P2: Angles in triangles and on lines

Copy each diagram. Replace the letters with the correct angle sizes.

1.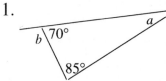

2.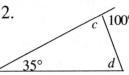

3.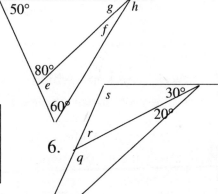

4.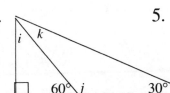

5.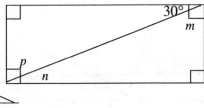

6.

• *Check answers.*

Star Challenge 9

12-13 correct = 1 star

Copy each diagram. Replace the letters with the correct angle sizes.

1.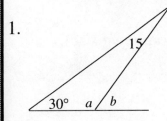

2.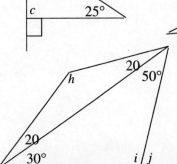

3.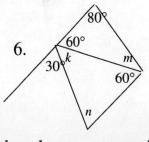

4.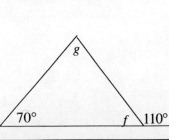

5.

6.

• *Your teacher has the answers to these.*

D3: Special triangles

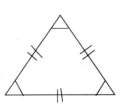

In ΔABC
AB = AC

A$\hat{B}$C = A$\hat{C}$B

Equal sides have the same markings.
Equal angles have the same markings.
If two angles have sizes given by the same letter, they are the same size.

An **equilateral** Δ has three equal sides and three equal angles

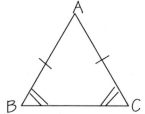

An **isosceles** Δ has two equal sides and two equal angles

Copy each diagram. Replace the letters with the correct angle sizes.

1.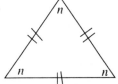

2.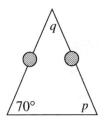

3.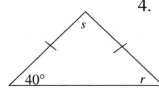

4.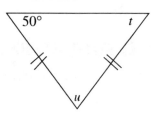

How do you know which are the two equal angles ?

The two equal angles are at the bottom of the two equal sides.

Spoton

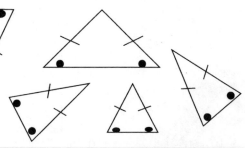

Which angles are the two equal angles ? [A&B, B&C or A&C ?]

5.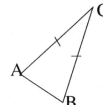

6.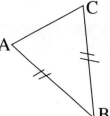

7.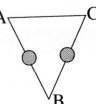

8.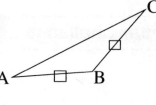

Copy each diagram. Replace the letters with the correct angle sizes.

9.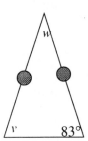

10.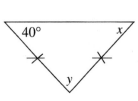

11.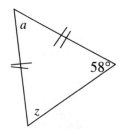

12.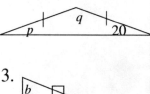

13.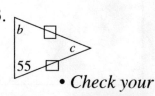

• *Check your answers.*

D4: Working out the base angles (the equal angles)

1. 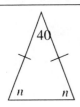 The equal angles are also called the 'base angles'.

Work out the size of each of the base angles.

• *If you cannot do this, talk to your teacher.*

Work out the size of the base angles in each triangle:

1.
2.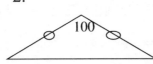
3.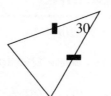
4.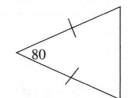

• *Check your answers.*

PRACTICE

P1: A mixture of isosceles triangles

Copy each diagram. Replace the letters with the correct angle sizes.

1.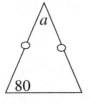
2.
3.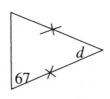
4.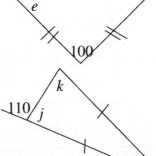

5.
6.
7.

• *Check your answers.*

Star Challenge ⭐10⭐10

| 8 correct = 2 stars |
| 6-7 correct = 1 star |

Copy each diagram. Replace the letters with the correct angle sizes.

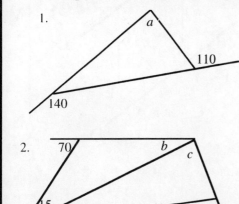

• *Your teacher has the answers to these.*

Section 6: Parallel and perpendicular lines

In this section you will:
- review parallel and perpendicular lines;
- calculate angles on parallel lines;
- find pairs of special angles on parallel lines.

DEVELOPMENT

D1: Naming and labelling

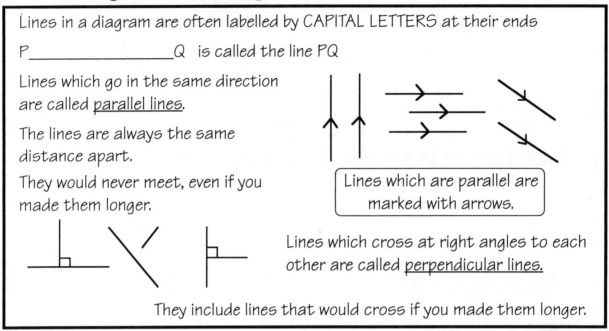

Lines in a diagram are often labelled by CAPITAL LETTERS at their ends

P_____Q   is called the line PQ

Lines which go in the same direction are called <u>parallel lines</u>.

The lines are always the same distance apart.

They would never meet, even if you made them longer.

Lines which are parallel are marked with arrows.

Lines which cross at right angles to each other are called <u>perpendicular lines</u>.

They include lines that would cross if you made them longer.

State whether each of the following is true or false:

1. EF is parallel to MN

2. AB is parallel to KL

3. KL is perpendicular to IJ

4. GH is parallel to CD

5. OP is perpendicular to EF

6. IJ is parallel to AB

7. CD is perpendicular to EF

8. OP is parallel to IJ

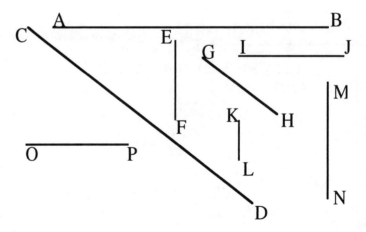

What are the missing words?

9. KL is ……… to MN

10. KL is ………… to OP

• *Check your answers.*

D2: Angles on parallel lines

A line that crosses two (or more) parallel lines is called a **transversal**

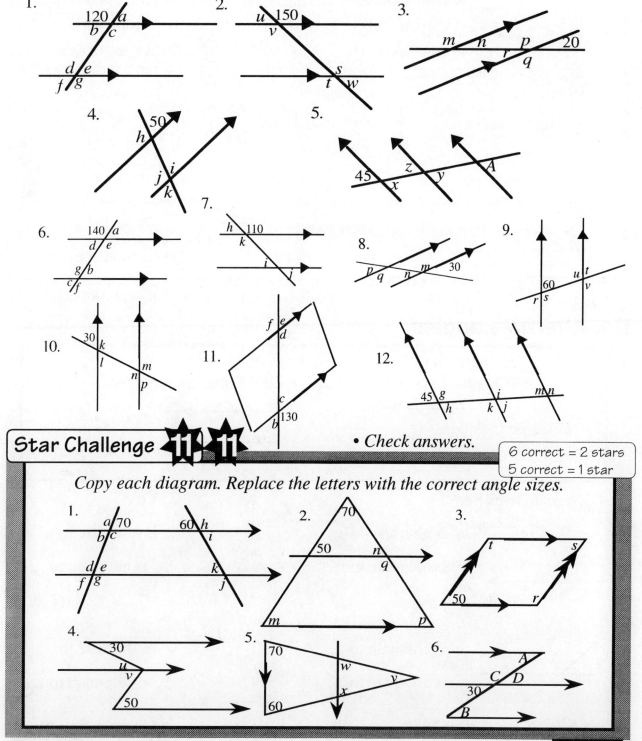

The acute angles along a transversal are all equal

The obtuse angles along a transversal are all equal

Copy each diagram. Replace the letters with the correct angle sizes.

Star Challenge 11 11

• *Check answers.*

6 correct = 2 stars
5 correct = 1 star

Copy each diagram. Replace the letters with the correct angle sizes.

D3: Corresponding angles

Corresponding angles lie in corresponding positions on the parallel lines.

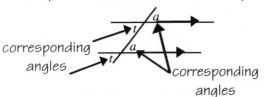

corresponding angles

corresponding angles

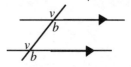

There are two pairs of corresponding angles here.

Copy and complete:

1.
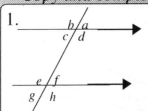

a corresponds to f

b corresponds to ......

c corresponds to ......

d corresponds to ......

2.
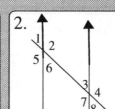

1 corresponds to ......

6 corresponds to ......

4 corresponds to ......

7 corresponds to ......

3. p corresponds to ......   q corresponds to ......

v corresponds to ......   w corresponds to ......

5 corresponds to ......   4 corresponds to ......

3 corresponds to ......   8 corresponds to ......

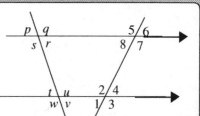

4.
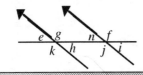

g corresponds to ......   k corresponds to ......

i corresponds to ......   n corresponds to ......

• *Check your answers.*

D4: Alternate angles

Alternate angles lie on alternate sides of the transversal
NOTE: alternate angles always lie INSIDE the parallel lines.

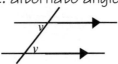
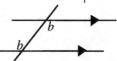

Here are two pairs of alternate angles.

Copy and complete:

1.
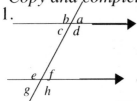

d is alternate to ...

f is alternate to ...

2.
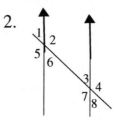

2 is alternate to ...

... is alternate to ...

3.
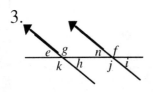

h is alternate to ...

j is alternate to ...

4.
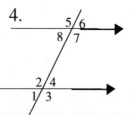

7 is alternate to ...

... is alternate to ...

• *Check your answers.*

D5: Corresponding, alternate and vertically opposite angles

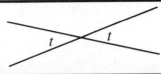 These two angles are vertically opposite angles.

Copy and complete:

1. *x* is vertically opposite to …

   y is vertically opposite to …

   r is vertically opposite to …

   p is vertically opposite to …

2. *x* corresponds to …

   y corresponds to …

   w is alternate to …

   z is alternate to …

3. *m* is vertically opposite to …

   d is vertically opposite to …

   p is vertically opposite to …

   p corresponds to …

4. *f* corresponds to …

   q corresponds to …

   q is alternate to …

   g is alternate to …

5. *v* is vertically opposite to …

   4 is vertically opposite to …

   7 is vertically opposite to …

   b is vertically opposite to …

   s corresponds to …

   3 corresponds to …

6. *n* corresponds to …

   7 corresponds to …

   t corresponds to …

   u is alternate to …

   7 is alternate to …

   s is alternate to …

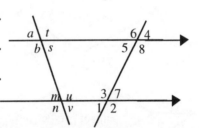

Star Challenge 12-12

• *Check your answers.*

19-20 correct = 2 stars
15-18 correct = 1 star

Copy and complete:

1. *w* corresponds to …

   e is alternate to …

   o corresponds to …

   a is alternate to …

2. *d* is vertically opposite to …

   h corresponds to …

   o is vertically opposite to …

   a corresponds to…

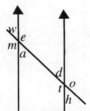

3. *n* corresponds to …

   m is alternate to …

   8 corresponds to …

   3 is alternate to …

   p corresponds to …

   p is alternate to …

4. *e* is vertically opposite to …

   e corresponds to …

   5 is vertically opposite to …

   6 corresponds to …

   6 is vertically opposite to …

   7 corresponds to…

• *Your teacher has the answers to these.*

Section 7: Quadrilaterals

In this section you will:
- find and classify quadrilaterals;
- use angle and symmetry properties of quadrilaterals to calculate angles.

A **quadrilateral** has 4 straight sides.   3G   3

It is possible to make 16 *different* quadrilaterals on a 3 by 3 geoboard.

Make as many as you can.

Draw them on 3 by 3 spotty paper.

- *Show your quadrilaterals to your teacher.*

D1: Classifying quadrilaterals

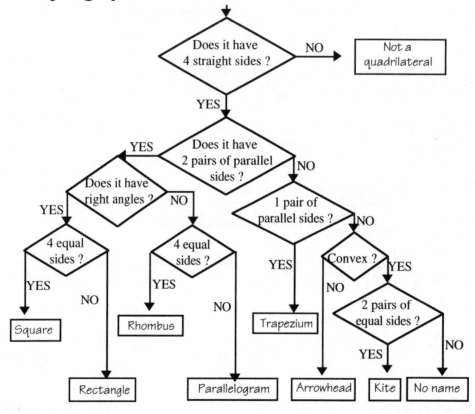

Work out what each shape is:

1. This shape has 2 pairs of parallel sides, all of which are equal, but no right angles.
2. This shape has 4 sides, only two of which are parallel.
3. This shape has no parallel sides and is convex.
4. This shape has no parallel sides, is not convex and has two pairs of equal sides.
5. This shape has 2 pairs of parallel sides, not all equal, and no right angles.

• *Check your answers*

Use the tree diagram to classify (name) each quadrilateral in Star Challenge 13.
Write the correct name under each of your quadrilaterals.

• *Your teacher will need to mark these.*

D2: Properties of named quadrilaterals

For each shape:
• draw the diagonals
• write yes (Y) or no (N) for each property

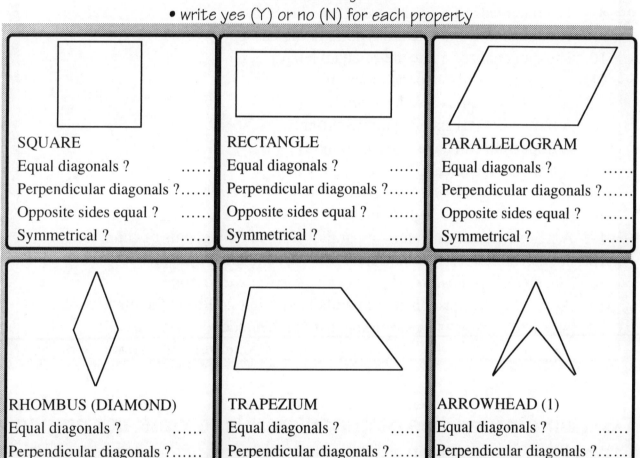

SQUARE

Equal diagonals ? ......
Perpendicular diagonals ?......
Opposite sides equal ? ......
Symmetrical ? ......

RECTANGLE

Equal diagonals ? ......
Perpendicular diagonals ?......
Opposite sides equal ? ......
Symmetrical ? ......

PARALLELOGRAM

Equal diagonals ? ......
Perpendicular diagonals ?......
Opposite sides equal ? ......
Symmetrical ? ......

RHOMBUS (DIAMOND)

Equal diagonals ? ......
Perpendicular diagonals ?......
Opposite sides equal ? ......
Symmetrical ? ......

TRAPEZIUM

Equal diagonals ? ......
Perpendicular diagonals ?......
Opposite sides equal ? ......
Symmetrical ? ......

ARROWHEAD (1)

Equal diagonals ? ......
Perpendicular diagonals ?......
Opposite sides equal ? ......
Symmetrical ? ......

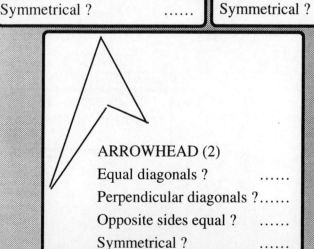

ARROWHEAD (2)

Equal diagonals ? ......
Perpendicular diagonals ?......
Opposite sides equal ? ......
Symmetrical ? ......

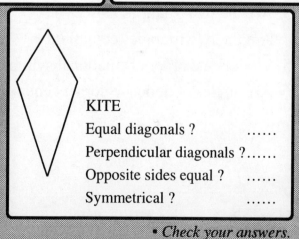

KITE

Equal diagonals ? ......
Perpendicular diagonals ?......
Opposite sides equal ? ......
Symmetrical ? ......

• *Check your answers.*

Say whether each of these statements is true or false. If it is false, say why.

1. A square has four right angles.
2. A parallelogram has diagonals of equal length.
3. A kite has two pairs of equal sides.
4. Only a kite has two pairs of equal sides.
5. The diagonals of a rhombus cross at right angles.
6. The diagonals of a rhombus are of equal length.
7. The diagonals of a square cross at right angles.
8. The diagonals of a square are of equal length.
9. The diagonals of a kite cross at right angles.
10. The diagonals of a kite are of equal length.
11. A rectangle is also a parallelogram.
12. A parallelogram is also a rectangle.
13. A trapezium is a special parallelogram.
14. A trapezium can have two right angles.
15. A trapezium can have just one right angle.

Say which TWO quadrilaterals could be defined in each case:

16. A .... has right angles.
17. A .... has 2 pairs of parallel sides and diagonals of equal length
18. A .... has 4 equal sides and perpendicular diagonals.

Say which ONE quadrilateral could be defined in each case:

19. A .... has 2 pairs of parallel sides but no lines of symmetry.
20. A .... has a pair of unequal parallel sides.

• *Your teacher has the answers to these.*

D3: Using properties of quadrilaterals to work out angles

Type 1   1.   Sketch this rectangle.
              Replace each letter with the size of the angle.

2. Are the two triangles right-angled ?

3. Are the two triangles isosceles ?

4. Are the two triangles congruent ?

5. What is the order of rotational symmetry ?

6. Are angles in opposite corners equal ?

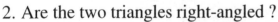

Shapes that are
congruent are identical
in shape and size.

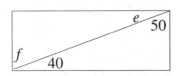

7. What are the values of *e* and *f* ?

8. What are the values of *m,n* and *p* ?

Type 2

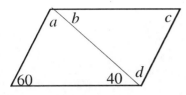

9. Sketch this parallelogram.
    Replace each letter with the size of the angle.
10. Are the two triangles right-angled ?
11. Are the two triangles isosceles ?
12. Are the two triangles congruent ?
13. What is the order of rotational symmetry ?
14. Are angles in opposite corners equal ?

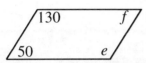

15. What are the values of *e* and *f* ?   16. What are the values of *m* and *n* ?

Type 3

17. Sketch this rhombus (diamond).
    Replace each letter with the size of the angle.
18. Are the two triangles right-angled ?
19. Are the two triangles isosceles ?
20. Are the two triangles congruent ?
21. What is the order of rotational symmetry ?
22. Are angles in opposite corners equal ?

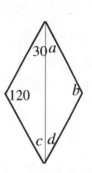

Type 4

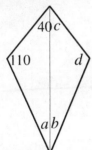

23. Sketch this kite.
    Replace each letter with the size of the angle.
24. Are the two triangles right-angled ?
25. Are the two triangles isosceles ?
26. Are the two triangles congruent ?
27. What is the order of rotational symmetry ?
28. Are angles in opposite corners equal ?

• *Check your answers.*

28 correctshapes = 3 stars
25-27 correct shapes = 2 stars
21-24 correct shapes = 1 star

Star Challenge 16·16·16

Make the following quadrilaterals on a 4 by 4 geoboard.   **4G** 4
Draw them on 4 by 4 spotty paper.

1. 4 different rectangles which are not squares
2. 5 different squares
3. 4 different kites
4. 4 different arrowheads
5. 5 different parallelograms which are not rectangles or squares
6. 6 different trapezia

                                    • *Show your shapes to your teacher.*

Section 8: Polygons

In this section you will:
- review and use the words used with polygons;
- tackle some puzzles involving polygons;
- review the properties of some polygons;
- construct regular polygons.

DEVELOPMENT

D1: Polygons – names and numbers

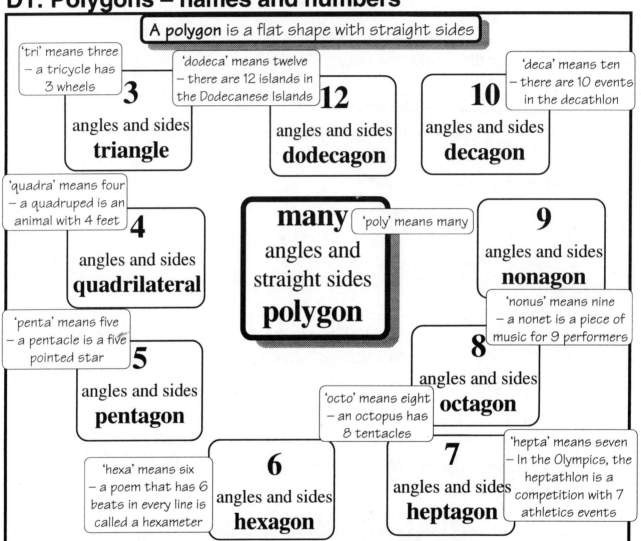

A **polygon** is a flat shape with straight sides

'tri' means three – a tricycle has 3 wheels

3 angles and sides **triangle**

'dodeca' means twelve – there are 12 islands in the Dodecanese Islands

12 angles and sides **dodecagon**

'deca' means ten – there are 10 events in the decathlon

10 angles and sides **decagon**

'quadra' means four – a quadruped is an animal with 4 feet

4 angles and sides **quadrilateral**

many angles and straight sides **polygon**

'poly' means many

9 angles and sides **nonagon**

'nonus' means nine – a nonet is a piece of music for 9 performers

'penta' means five – a pentacle is a five pointed star

5 angles and sides **pentagon**

'octo' means eight – an octopus has 8 tentacles

8 angles and sides **octagon**

'hexa' means six – a poem that has 6 beats in every line is called a hexameter

6 angles and sides **hexagon**

7 angles and sides **heptagon**

'hepta' means seven – In the Olympics, the heptathlon is a competition with 7 athletics events

Name each of these shapes:

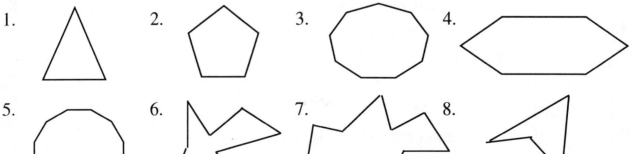

1.   2.   3.   4.

5.   6.   7.   8.

• *Check your answers.*

Star Challenge 17 17

Overlapping squares
You will need a piece of tracing paper.
Make a tracing of this square.

1. Move the tracing over this square until the overlap
   of the two squares is in the shape of a triangle.
   Draw the position of the two squares and colour
   the triangle.

Overlap the two squares until the overlap is in the shape of

2. a square   3. a pentagon   4. an octagon   5. a heptagon

For questions 2–5, draw the positions of the two squares and colour the overlap.

• Show your diagrams to your teacher.

Star Challenge 18 18 18

Make the following polygons on a 4 by 4 geoboard.
Draw them on 4 by 4 spotty paper.

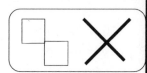

1. 5 different pentagons   2. 6 different hexagons

3. 8 different octagons   4. 1 dodecagon

• Show your diagrams to your teacher.

Star Challenge 19 19 19

Hexagon tangram

Trace this hexagon tangram onto
a piece of card.

Cut out the eight pieces
of the tangram.

Using two or more of the
tangram pieces make:

• 5 different triangles

• 8 different rectangles

• 6 parallelograms

• 2 kites

• 6 trapezia

Draw each of the shapes and show how they are made.

• Show your diagrams to your teacher.

D2: Properties of some polygons

A polygon is a flat shape with straight sides.

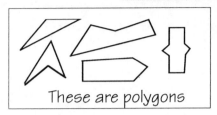

These are polygons

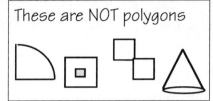

These are NOT polygons

1. Which of these are polygons ?

    Give the letters of the polygons.

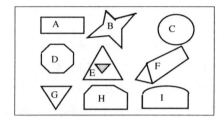

A regular polygon has equal sides and equal angles.

2.

Which of these polygons are regular ?

   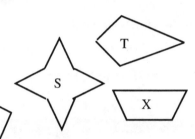

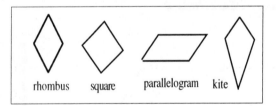

rhombus   square   parallelogram   kite

3. What is a regular quadrilateral called ?

4. Which quadrilateral has four equal sides but is <u>not</u> regular ?

5. What is a regular triangle called ?

• *Check your answers.*

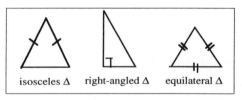

isosceles Δ   right-angled Δ   equilateral Δ

D3: Constructing regular polygons

1.

72 72
72 72
72

A regular pentagon is made from 5 congruent (identical) triangles.

(a) What kind of triangles are they ?

(b) Each triangle has one angle at the centre of the pentagon. The size of this angle is 72°. Why is it 72° ?

2. <u>Constructing a regular pentagon</u>

Step 1: Draw a circle of radius 6 cm.

Step 2: Construct five 72° angles at the centre of the circle.
   Extend the arms of each angle out to the circle.

Step 3: Join the ends of the arms to make a pentagon.

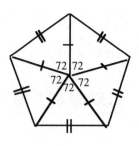

3. 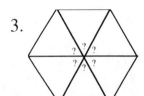 This is a regular hexagon.

(a) What is the size of each of the angles at the centre ?

(b) Construct a regular hexagon.

4. A regular nonagon has 9 equal sides and 9 equal angles.
    Construct a regular nonagon.

5. Construct a regular decagon (10 sided figure).

6. A regular octagon has 8 sides.

(a) Construct a regular octagon.

(b) Rub out all construction lines,
    leaving only the octagon.

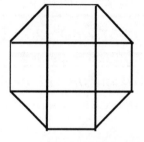

(c)   Draw horizontal and vertical lines in like this.

(d)   Are the five quadrilaterals inside this shape squares or rectangles ?

(e)   What kind of triangles are the four triangles ?

*7. What regular polygon has 18° angles at the centre ?

Star Challenge 20

Symmetries of regular polygons

1. Construct a regular triangle of side 4 cm.

2. Construct a regular quadrilateral of side 4 cm.

3. *Use these two diagrams and the regular polygons that you*
    made in D3 to complete this table:

Regular polygon	No. of equal sides	No. of equal angles	No. of lines of symmetry	Order of rotational symmetry
triangle	3	3		
square			4	
hexagon				
octagon				
pentagon				
decagon				
nonagon				

• *Your teacher will need to mark this.*

Section 9: Angles in polygons

In this section you will calculate angles in polygons.

DEVELOPMENT

D1: Exterior angles in a polygon

Imagine walking round the sides of a polygon
OABCD... until you get back to O.
At A you turn through the angle a
At B you turn through the angle b
At C ...

When you get back to O and are
facing in the direction OA, you
have turned through
one complete revolution.

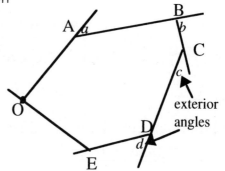

For any polygon the sum of the exterior angles is 360°

Task 1: *Work out the value of each letter.*
Any two angles with the same letter are the same size.

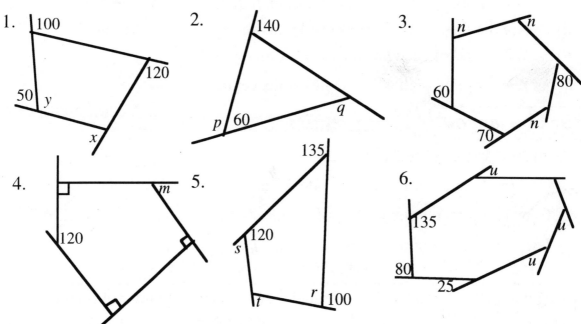

1. 100, 120, 50, y, x

2. 140, p, 60, q

3. n, n, 60, 80, 70, n

4. 120, m

5. 135, s, 120, r, 100, t

6. u, 135, u, 80, 25, u

Task 2: The rule should be

The sum of the exterior angles of any convex polygon is 360°

Explain why the rule does not work for concave polygons.

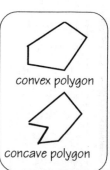

convex polygon

concave polygon

• *Check your answers.*

D2: The sum of the interior angles of a polygon

Task 1:

> The sum of the interior angles of any quadrilateral is 360°.

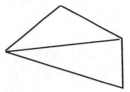

Explain how you can use the diagram to show this.

> Polygons can be divided into triangles, by drawing lines from one vertex to every other vertex.

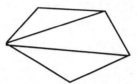 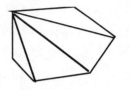

Task 2: *Copy and complete this table:*

No. of sides	No. of triangles	sum of interior angles
4		
5		
6		
7		
8		
20		
50		
n		

Task 3: S = sum of interior angles. Write S as a formula involving n.

• CHECK YOUR ANSWERS BEFORE GOING ON TO TASK 4.

Task 4: *Work out the value of each letter:*

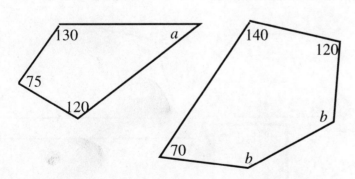 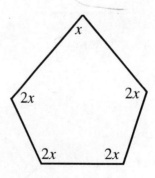

Task 5: To be exact, the rule should be written

> The sum of the interior angles of a convex polygon is $(n-2) \times 180°$

Explain how you know that the rule does not work for concave polygons.

• *Check your answers.*

D3: Angles in regular polygons

1.

   <u>Method 1</u>

A regular pentagon has 5 equal interior angles and 5 equal exterior angles.

   (a) Calculate the size of an exterior angle of a regular pentagon.

   (b) Use the answer from (a) to work out the size of an interior angle of a regular pentagon.

2. <u>Method 2</u>

   (a) Use the formula (from D2) to work out the sum of the interior angles of a regular pentagon.

   (b) Use the answer from (a) to work out the size of one interior angle of a regular pentagon.

   Calculate the interior angles of each of these regular polygons.

   Use method 1   3. regular hexagon   4. regular octagon

   Use method 2   5. regular decagon (10 sides)   • *Check your answers.*

1. Use method 1 to work out the interior angle of a regular dodecagon (12 sides)

2. Use method 2 to work out the interior angle of a regular icosagon (20 sides)

3. How many sides has a regular polygon, if one <u>exterior</u> angle is 15° ?

4. How many sides has a regular polygon, if one <u>interior</u> angle is 175° ?

   • *Your teacher has the answers to these.*

Work out the value of x in each case.
The polygons are not drawn accurately.

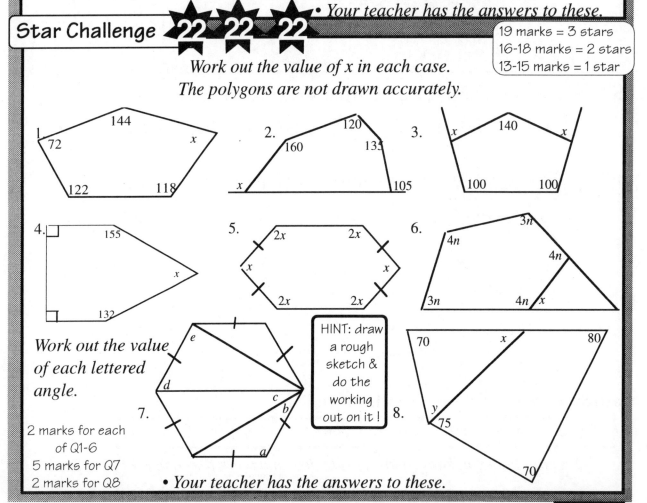

Work out the value of each lettered angle.

7.

HINT: draw a rough sketch & do the working out on it !

2 marks for each of Q1-6
5 marks for Q7
2 marks for Q8

• *Your teacher has the answers to these.*

Section 10: Drawing shapes with a computer

In this section you are going to devise sets of instructions to make a computer draw the shapes you want.

D1: Right-angled shapes

'Meet Pen–y Pen–y carries a pen.

She follows sets of instructions to draw shapes.

At the start of any set of instructions she is always ready to move in this direction.

Instructions
FORWARD 40
RIGHT 90
FORWARD 40
RIGHT 90
FORWARD 40
RIGHT 90
FORWARD 40

Using this set of instructions Pen–y drew this square. The arrows show the direction Pen–y travelled in.

Write the instructions to get Pen–y to draw each of these shapes:

1.
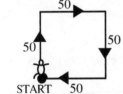

2.
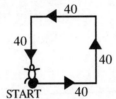

Hint: you need to turn Pen–y before moving her.

3.
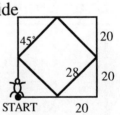

4.
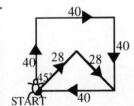

5.
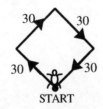

6. Pen–y draws the outside square first, then the inside square. She always moves clockwise.

Two new instructions

To get Pen–y to move without writing use PEN UP ......

To get Pen–y to start writing again, use PEN DOWN ......

---

7. Give instructions to get Pen–y to draw this shape.
Do the outer rectangle first.

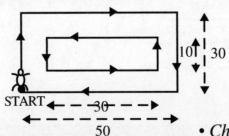

• *Check your answers.*

D2: Drawing different angles

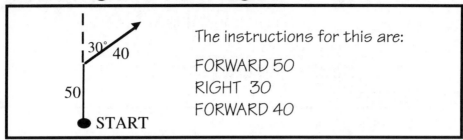

The instructions for this are:

FORWARD 50
RIGHT 30
FORWARD 40

Write the instructions to get Pen–y to draw each of these shapes:

1.
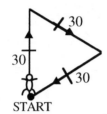

2.
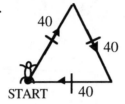

3.
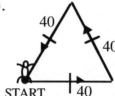

4.
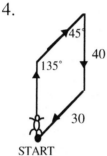

*5.
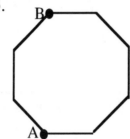

Give instructions to draw
      this regular octagon:
(a) starting at A and going
    clockwise
(b) starting at A and going
    anti–clockwise
(c) starting at B and going
    clockwise

• Check your answers.

Star Challenge 23 23

1 star for each correct
set of instructions

1.   Give the instructions to draw a
    regular hexagon with edge 30.
    Move clockwise and start from C.

2.   Give instructions to get Pen–y to
    draw this shape.
    Do the outer rectangle first.

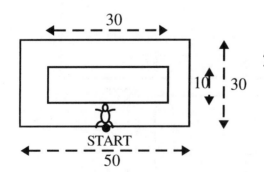

• Your teacher has the answers to these.

THE NATIONAL CURRICULUM ...
... AND BEYOND ...

Sureshot

Developing Efficient
Non-Calculator Techniques

EXTRA

Part 1

Developing Efficient Non-Calculator Techniques EXTRA
Section 1: Multiples and divisibility

In this section you will review multiples of numbers, primes and rules for divisibility.

D1: From multiples to primes

1	**2**	3	4	5	6	7	8	9	10
11	12	13	14	15	16	17	18	19	20
21	22	23	24	25	26	27	28	29	30
31	32	33	34	35	36	37	38	39	40
41	42	43	44	45	46	47	48	49	50
51	52	53	54	55	56	57	58	59	60
61	62	63	64	65	66	67	68	69	70
71	72	73	74	75	76	77	78	79	80
81	82	83	84	85	86	87	88	89	90
91	92	93	94	95	96	97	98	99	100

Task 1: Shade in all the multiples of **2**

Task 2: Describe any patterns you get :

....

1	2	**3**	4	5	6	7	8	9	10
11	12	13	14	15	16	17	18	19	20
21	22	23	24	25	26	27	28	29	30
31	32	33	34	35	36	37	38	39	40
41	42	43	44	45	46	47	48	49	50
51	52	53	54	55	56	57	58	59	60
61	62	63	64	65	66	67	68	69	70
71	72	73	74	75	76	77	78	79	80
81	82	83	84	85	86	87	88	89	90
91	92	93	94	95	96	97	98	99	100

Task 3: Shade in all the multiples of **3**

Task 4: Describe any patterns you get :

....

1	2	3	4	**5**	6	7	8	9	10
11	12	13	14	15	16	17	18	19	20
21	22	23	24	25	26	27	28	29	30
31	32	33	34	35	36	37	38	39	40
41	42	43	44	45	46	47	48	49	50
51	52	53	54	55	56	57	58	59	60
61	62	63	64	65	66	67	68	69	70
71	72	73	74	75	76	77	78	79	80
81	82	83	84	85	86	87	88	89	90
91	92	93	94	95	96	97	98	99	100

Task 5: Shade in all the multiples of **5**

Task 6: Describe any patterns you get :

....

1	2	3	4	5	6	**7**	8	9	10
11	12	13	14	15	16	17	18	19	20
21	22	23	24	25	26	27	28	29	30
31	32	33	34	35	36	37	38	39	40
41	42	43	44	45	46	47	48	49	50
51	52	53	54	55	56	57	58	59	60
61	62	63	64	65	66	67	68	69	70
71	72	73	74	75	76	77	78	79	80
81	82	83	84	85	86	87	88	89	90
91	92	93	94	95	96	97	98	99	100

Task 7: Shade in all the multiples of **7**

Task 8: Describe any patterns you get :

....

Task 9: In this grid, circle all the numbers that have NOT been shaded in any of the other grids.

	2	3	4	5	6	7	8	9	10
11	12	13	14	15	16	17	18	19	20
21	22	23	24	25	26	27	28	29	30
31	32	33	34	35	36	37	38	39	40
41	42	43	44	45	46	47	48	49	50
51	52	53	54	55	56	57	58	59	60
61	62	63	64	65	66	67	68	69	70
71	72	73	74	75	76	77	78	79	80
81	82	83	84	85	86	87	88	89	90
91	92	93	94	95	96	97	98	99	100

The numbers you have circled are **prime numbers.**

Stick this worksheet in your book. **You will need the prime numbers here in Sections 2 and 3.**

• *Check your answers.*

D2: Multiples and divisibility

Use the tables in D1 to help you answer these questions:

1. Is 36 a multiple of 2 ?
2. Is 36 a multiple of 3 ?
3. Is 36 a multiple of 5 ?
4. Is 36 a multiple of 7 ?
5. How can you use the tables to tell you that 37 is not a multiple of 7 ?

Copy and complete:

6. The multiples of 2 between 21 and 31 are ....
7. The multiples of 3 between 25 and 40 are ....
8. The multiples of 5 between 36 and 71 are ....
9. The multiples of 7 between 10 and 50 are ....
10. Between 20 and 50 there are five numbers which are multiples of both 2 and 3.
    These are ....

> 12 is a multiple of 2, 3, 4, 6, and 12
>
> This also means that
>
> **12 is divisible by 2, 3, 4, 6, and 12**

EXAMPLE   Q: Use one of the tables to find out if 15 is divisible by 3.

A: The second table shows us that 15 is a multiple of 3   So, 15 is divisible by 3

Idea   Yes – 15 is divisible by 3

38	53	67	73	85	56	87	95

Use the tables in D1 to help you answer these questions:

11. Which of these numbers are divisible by 2 ?
12. Which of these numbers are divisible by 3 ?
13. Which of these numbers are divisible by 5 ?
14. Which of these numbers are divisible by 7 ?   • *Check your answers.*

Star Challenge 1

18-22 marks = 1 star

1. Four of these numbers are multiples of 2. Find them.
2. Four of these numbers are multiples of 3. Find them.
3. Which of these numbers are divisible by 3 ?
4. Which of these numbers are divisible by 5 ?
5. Which of these numbers are divisible by 7 ?
6. Five of these numbers are prime numbers. Find them.

27	15	70
43	36	
73	63	37
91	19	
64	82	79

1 mark for each correct answer   • *Your teacher has the answers to these.*

D3: Simple rules for divisibility

> A number is divisible by 2 if it ends in 0, 2, 4, 6 or 8
> A number is divisible by 5 if it ends in 5 or 0
> A number is divisible by 10 if it ends in 0

125	64	92
340		28
83	566	65
27		7248
356	4791	890

1. List the numbers here that are divisible by 10

2. List the numbers here that are divisible by 5

3. List the numbers here that are divisible by 2

• *Check your answers.*

D4: Digit sums

> To find **the final digit sum** of 482
>
>   The digit sum of 482 is 4 + 8 + 2 = 14
>
>   The digit sum of 14   is 1 + 4 = 5
>
>   The final digit sum of 482 is 5
>
> *You stop when there is just one digit left !*
>
> *Sureshot*

1. *Work out the final digit sum of each of these numbers.*
   Write down both the number <u>and</u> its final digit sum.

   439   **357**   **5112**   **73289**   **31569**

> There is special rule for numbers that are divisible by 3
>
> > If a number has a final digit sum equal to 3, 6 or 9,
> >   then the number is divisible by 3

2. Which of the numbers in question 1 are divisible by 3 ?

3.   **742**   **1473**   **6382**   **21444**   **7935**
          Work out which of these numbers is divisible by 3.

These numbers are divisible by 9

90   **189**   **279**
4356   **316593**

4. Work out the final digit sums of each of the numbers in the box.

5. There is a special rule for numbers divisible by 9. Explain the rule.

• *Check your answers.*

Star Challenge ⭐2⭐2

23 correct answers = 2 stars   19-22 correct = 1 star

1. List the numbers that are divisible by 2
2. List the numbers that are divisible by 5
3. List the numbers that are divisible by 10
4. List the numbers that are divisible by 3
5. List the numbers that are divisible by 9

342	435	65
600		243
423	555	230
6741		12345

• *Your teacher has the answers to these.*

Section 2: Multiples, factors and primes

In this section you will:
* multiply and divide using a table square;
* find factors using a table square;
* work with factors and primes.

D1: Using a table square

x	2	3	4	5	6	7	8	9	10	11	12	13	14	15
2	4	6	8	10	12	14	16	18	20	22	24	26	28	30
3	6	9	12	15	18	21	24	27	30	33	36	39	42	45
4	8	12	16	20	24	28	32	36	40	44	48	52	56	60
5	10	15	20	25	30	35	40	45	50	55	60	65	70	75
6	12	18	24	30	36	42	48	54	60	66	72	78	84	90
7	14	21	28	35	42	49	56	63	70	77	84	91	98	105
8	16	24	32	40	48	56	64	72	80	88	96	104	112	120
9	18	27	36	45	54	63	72	81	90	99	108	117	126	135
10	20	30	40	50	60	70	80	90	100	110	120	130	140	150
11	22	33	44	55	66	77	88	99	110	121	132	143	154	165
12	24	36	48	60	72	84	96	108	120	132	144	156	168	180
13	26	39	52	65	78	91	104	117	130	143	156	169	182	195
14	28	42	56	70	84	98	112	126	140	154	168	182	196	210
15	30	45	60	75	90	105	120	135	150	165	180	195	210	225

Multiplication   13

5 ———————— (65) $5 \times 13 = 65$

Ruff

Copy and complete each of these multiplication sums:

1. $12 \times 3 = ...$ 2. $14 \times 5 = ...$ 3. $7 \times 9 = ...$ 4. $13 \times 4 = ...$ 5. $13 \times 14 = ...$

6. $9 \times 8 = ...$ 7. $7 \times 12 = ...$ 8. $8 \times 8 = ...$ 9. $11 \times 13 = ...$ 10. $6 \times 14 = ...$

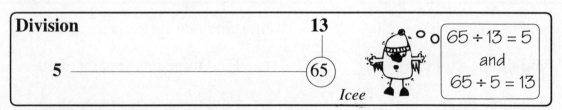

Division   13

5 ———————— (65) $65 \div 13 = 5$
and
$65 \div 5 = 13$

Icee

Copy and complete each of these division sums:

11. $32 \div 4 = ...$ 12. $63 \div 7 = ...$ 13. $108 \div 9 = ...$ 14. $91 \div 7 = ...$ 15. $42 \div 6 = ...$

16. $24 \div 4 = ...$ 17. $24 \div 6 = ...$ 18. $96 \div 8 = ...$ 19. $96 \div 12 = ...$ 20. $72 \div 8 = ...$

21. $72 \div 9 = ...$ 22. $54 \div 9 = ...$ 23. $54 \div 6 = ...$ 24. $210 \div 15 = ...$ 25. $98 \div 7 = ...$

• *Check your answers.*

D2: What are factors ?

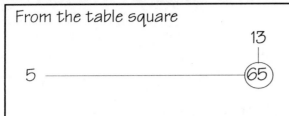

From the table square

13
|
5 ——————————————(65)

This tells us that 5 divides into 65
and 13 divides into 65

We say that:
5 is a **factor** of 65
& 13 is a **factor** of 65

Pow

Say whether each statement is true (T) or false (F):

1. 3 is a factor of 30
2. 7 is a factor of 35
3. 9 is a factor of 46
4. 3 is a factor of 15
5. 4 is a factor of 20
6. 15 is a factor of 95
7. 6 is a factor of 30
8. 1 is a factor of 7
9. 7 is a factor of 15
10. 1 is a factor of 12
11. 12 is a factor of 12
12. 20 is a factor of 20

13. 1 is a factor of every number
14. Any number is a factor of itself

15. 8 has four factors.   Find all four factors of 8.
16. 14 has four factors.   Find all the factors of 14.
17. 25 has three factors.   Find all the factors of 25.
18. 16 has five factors.   Find all the factors of 16.
19. 12 has six factors.   Find all the factors of 12.

• *Check your answers.*

D3: Factor pairs

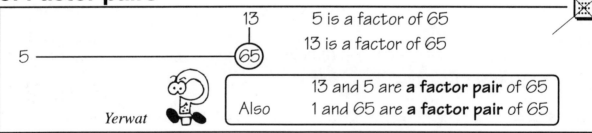

13
|
5 ——————————————(65)

5 is a factor of 65

13 is a factor of 65

Yerwat

Also

13 and 5 are **a factor pair** of 65
1 and 65 are **a factor pair** of 65

1. Find two factor pairs of 6
2. Find two factor pairs of 10

3. Find three factor pairs of 18
4. Find three factor pairs of 20

5. Find three factor pairs of 28
6. Find three factor pairs of 12

7. Find two factor pairs of 15
8. Find two factor pairs of 21

9. Find three factor pairs of 60
10. Find three factor pairs of 50
    (two of them are not on the table square)

• *Check your answers.*

P1: Connect–five

A game for 2–5 players

You will need :   two ordinary dice of different colours
a set of counters in one colour for each player

Rules

1. You are going to make a 2-digit number by throwing the two dice.
    First decide which dice will give you the units digit and which will give
    you the tens digit.

2. The first player throws the two dice. The player covers ONE number on
    the board that is a factor of the 2-digit number that has been thrown

3. Each player takes it in turn to throw the dice and cover any factors of the
    number made.

4. The winner is the first player to get five counters in a row, across, down
    or diagonally.

CONNECT–FIVE Game board

2	1	4	5	6	9	3	1	2
3	5	9	1	7	11	8	4	6
4	11	8	3	6	4	5	1	7
6	4	1	7	9	2	4	5	1
7	8	3	11	5	1	4	6	9
11	2	4	5	1	9	7	3	8
2	7	6	8	4	3	5	2	11
1	3	5	7	9	11	8	6	4
6	1	2	4	8	5	2	7	9

D4: Factor diagrams

1.

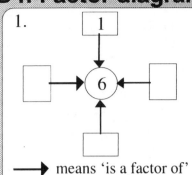

⟶ means 'is a factor of'

Copy and complete
this factor diagram for 6

2.

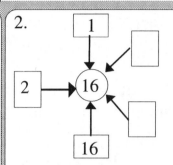

⟶ means 'is a factor of'

Copy and complete
this factor diagram for 16

3.

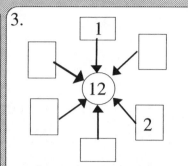

⟶ means 'is a factor of'

Copy and complete
this factor diagram for 12

4.

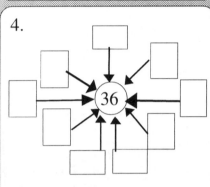

Copy and complete
this factor diagram for 36

5.

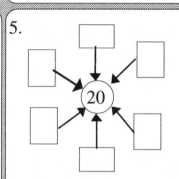

Copy and complete
this factor diagram for 20

6.

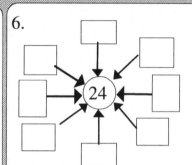

Copy and complete
this factor diagram for 24

Star Challenge 3

Prime numbers have exactly two factors – 1 and the number itself.

1. There are two prime numbers between 30 and 40.
   List them.   (2 marks)

2. An **emirp** is a prime number which is also prime when reversed.
   13 and 31 are emirps.
   There are 9 emirps between 10 and 100 (including 13 and 31)
   Find them.   (7 marks)

• *Your teacher has the answers to these.*

You met **prime numbers** in Section 1, D1

Big Edd

Check your answers

Star Challenge 4 4

The factors of 6 are 1, 2, 3, 6
2 & 3 are prime numbers

We say that 2 & 3 are
prime factors of 6

1. The factors of 12 are 1, 2, 3, 4, 6, 12
   What are the prime factors of 12 ?

2. The factors of 15 are 1, 3, 5, 15
   What are the prime factors of 15 ?

3. What are the prime factors of 18 ?

4. What are the prime factors of 20 ?

5. What are the prime factors of 24 ?

• *Your teacher has the answers to these.*

Emirp is prime written backwards !

E1: The factor grid game *A game for small groups – or the whole class*

This game is excellent for the last 10 minutes of any maths lesson.
The only equipment needed is an ordinary dice.

Each player draws a copy of this grid.

	9	20	36	Score
18				
24				
10				
Score				

Rules

1. The teacher throws the dice and gives out the number on the dice.
2. Each player puts that number in one of the nine middle spaces.

> The scores are not counted until the end of the game , BUT …
>
> … you will score 1 point if the number is a factor of the number at the head of that row/column.
>
> … you will score 2 points if the number is a factor of the number at the head of the row <u>and</u> a factor of the number at the head of the column

	9	20	36
18		(3)	

a 3 here earns 1 point
– it is a factor of 18
but not of 20

Spottee

	9	20	36
18	(3)		

BUT – a 3 here earns
2 points – it is a
factor of 18 and of 9

3. The dice is thrown and the dice numbers are placed on the grid until all nine spaces are filled.

4. **Once a number has been placed in a box, it cannot be changed.**

5. When the nine spaces have been filled, the total score is calculated.

Here is an example of how the score is calculated.

	9	20	36	Score
18	3	5	6	2
24	2	1	3	3
10	5	3	2	2
Score	1	2	3	13

← 2 numbers in this row are factors of 18, so the score is 2

↑ only 1 number in this column is a factor of 9, so the score is 1

Chyps

Section 3: Square and cube numbers

In this section you will:
• review square and cube numbers;
• work with squares, cubes and primes.

D1: Square and cube review

Table square

The story so far …

$$4^2 = 4 \times 4 = 16$$

4^2 is read as | 4 to the power of 2
or | 4 squared
or | the square of 4

16 is a square number

To square a number, you multiply it by itself.

EXAMPLE
The square of 3 is 9

Sureshot

Copy these. Use the table square to fill in the values.

1. The square of 5 is …
2. 10 squared is …
3. 6 to the power of 2 is …
4. $12^2 = …$
5. the square of 13 is …
6. 9 to the power of 2 is …
7. the square of 8 is …

8. $7^2 = …$
9. the square of 11 is …
10. 13 squared is …
11. 14 to the power of 2 is …
12. the square of 15 is …
13. 4 squared is …
14. $9^2 = …$

$4 \times 4 = 16$ *so*   16 is a square number

15. How can you tell from the table that 169 is a square number ?

16. Which of these numbers are square numbers ?

| 25 | 36 | 50 | 144 | 81 | 9 | 65 | 121 |

Use your table square from Section 2

17. *Copy and complete:*

The first 15 square numbers are 1 4 9 16 …………………………

$$2^3 = 2 \times 2 \times 2 = 8$$

2^3 is read as | 2 to the power of 3
or | 2 cubed
or | the cube of 2

8 is a cube number

Chyps

You will need these square numbers for Star Challenge 5 !

18. *Copy and complete:*

$$1^3 = 1 \times 1 \times 1 = …   3^3 = … \times … \times … = …$$

19. $4^3 \neq 12$ What is the value of 4^3 ?

20. $5^3 \neq 15$ What is the value of 5^3 ?   • *Check your answers.*

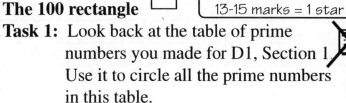
1	2	3	4
5	6	7	8
9	10	11	12
13	14	15	16
17	18	19	20
21	22	23	24
25	26	27	28
29	30	31	32
33	34	35	36
37	38	39	40
41	42	43	44
45	46	47	48
49	50	51	52
53	54	55	56
57	58	59	60
61	62	63	64
65	66	67	68
69	70	71	72
73	74	75	76
77	78	79	80
81	82	83	84
85	86	87	88
89	90	91	92
93	94	95	96
97	98	99	100

19 marks = 3 stars
16-18 marks = 2 stars
13-15 marks = 1 star

The 100 rectangle

Task 1: Look back at the table of prime numbers you made for D1, Section 1. Use it to circle all the prime numbers in this table.

Task 2: Every prime number in column 1 can be written as the <u>sum</u> of two square numbers.

Complete this: (11 marks)

$$5 = \ldots\ldots + \ldots\ldots$$
$$13 = \ldots\ldots + \ldots\ldots$$
$$\ldots\ldots = \ldots\ldots + \ldots\ldots$$
$$\ldots\ldots = \ldots\ldots + \ldots\ldots$$
$$\ldots\ldots = \ldots\ldots + \ldots\ldots$$
$$\ldots\ldots = \ldots\ldots + \ldots\ldots$$
$$\ldots\ldots = \ldots\ldots + \ldots\ldots$$
$$\ldots\ldots = \ldots\ldots + \ldots\ldots$$
$$\ldots\ldots = \ldots\ldots + \ldots\ldots$$
$$\ldots\ldots = \ldots\ldots + \ldots\ldots$$
$$\ldots\ldots = \ldots\ldots + \ldots\ldots$$

Remember:
You made a list of
square numbers in
D1 question 17

Hukka

Task 3: Every prime number in column 3 can be written as the <u>difference</u> of two square numbers.

Complete these: (6 marks)

$$3 = \ldots\ldots - \ldots\ldots$$
$$7 = \ldots\ldots - \ldots\ldots$$
$$11 = \ldots\ldots - \ldots\ldots$$
$$19 = \ldots\ldots - \ldots\ldots$$
$$23 = \ldots\ldots - \ldots\ldots$$
$$31 = \ldots\ldots - \ldots\ldots$$

Task 4: Why is there only one prime number in column 2 ?

....
....
....
....
....
....
....

(2 marks)

WARNING !
One of the squares that you will need is bigger than the squares you found in D1, Q17 !

Idea

E1: Digit cube chains

Number	1	2	3	4	5	6	7	8	9	10
Cube	1	8	27	64	125	216	343	512	729	1000

You are going to make chains of numbers by finding the sums of the cubes of the digits of each number.

The numbers in the boxes are to show you how each number is made. You don't need to put them in.

EXAMPLE $\boxed{5^3 + 7^3}$ $\boxed{4^3 + 6^3 + 8^3}$

57 —> 468   —> 792 —> 1080—> 513 —> 153

The chain stops here because 153 —> 153 ...

Taz

Task 1 : *Copy and complete this digit cube chain for 12*

12 —> 9 — > ……

Task 2 : *Make digit cube chains for each of these numbers*

13   14   15   16   17   18

• *Check your answers.*

Star Challenge ⬢ 6 ⬢ 6 ⬢ 6

1 star for each correct Task

Task 3 : Hypothesis : "For digit cube chains, all multiples of 3 end up with the same set of digits."

Investigate the truth of this hypothesis.
You must use at least four examples to justify your conclusion.

Task 4 : Investigate digit cube chains of numbers which are multiples of 3 minus 1 (eg $14 = 5 \times 3 - 1$)
Find a rule for these chains.
You must use at least four examples to justify your conclusion.

Task 5: Hypothesis : "For digit cube chains, all numbers which are multiples of 3 plus 1 (eg 16) end up with either the digits 3,7,0 or 2,5,0 "

Investigate the truth of this hypothesis.
You must use at least *nine* examples to justify your conclusion.

• *Show the results of your investigations to your teacher.*

Section 4: Index notation

In this section you will:
- review index notation;
- work with powers and indices.

D1: Review of powers

$$5^2 = 5 \times 5 = 25 \quad \text{(read as "5 squared")}$$
$$2^3 = 2 \times 2 \times 2 = 8 \quad \text{(read as "2 cubed")}$$
$$3^4 = 3 \times 3 \times 3 \times 3 = 81 \quad \text{(read as "3 to the power of 4")}$$

The value of 3^4 is 81

Work out the value of each of these. Copy and complete each expression.

1. $4^2 = \ldots$
2. $5^3 = \ldots$
3. $7^2 = \ldots$
4. $10^3 = \ldots$
5. $2^5 = \ldots$
6. $3^3 = \ldots$
7. $4^3 = \ldots$
8. $2^4 = \ldots$
9. $8^2 = \ldots$
10. $6^2 = \ldots$

Copy and complete each expression:

11. $2^{\cdots} = 16$
12. $3^{\cdots} = 81$
13. $7^{\cdots} = 49$
14. $9^{\cdots} = 81$
15. $2^{\cdots} = 64$

Note: To work out 5×2^3, work out 2^3 first, then multiply by 5

Note: Work out any brackets first $\quad (3^2 + 1)^2 = 10^2 = 100$

Copy and complete:

16. $3 \times 4^2 = \ldots$
17. $4 \times 3^3 = \ldots$
18. $2 \times 10^2 = \ldots$
19. $(4^2 - 13)^2 = \ldots$
20. $(2^2 + 3)^3 = \ldots$
21. $5 \times (3^2 + 2) = \ldots$
22. $5^2 - (3 \times 2^2) = \ldots$
23. $(2^2)^3 = \ldots$

- *Check your answers.*

Star Challenge 7

All correct = 1 star

Find the value of each letter:

1. $8 = 2^a$
2. $3^2 = b$
3. $4^c = 64$
4. $5^d = 125$
5. $10^e = 1000$
6. $2^3 \times 3 = f$
7. $10^g - 3^2 = 91$
8. $4^2 + 3^3 = h$
9. $5^i = 25$
10. $2^j \times 3 = 12$
11. $5 \times 2^k = 20$
12. $3^2 + 3^3 = m$

- *Your teacher has the answers to these.*

Star Challenge 8

All correct = 1 star

Order of operations	B	I	D M	A S
Work out	brackets first	indices (powers)	division & multiplication	addition & subtraction

Match these expressions and their values:

Expressions $\quad 3 \times 2^2 \quad\quad 3 + 2^2$

$(3 \times 2)^2 \quad (3 + 2)^2 \quad 3^2 \times 2 \quad 3^2 + 2$

$3^2 \times 2^2 \quad 3 + 5 \times 2 \quad 3 \times 5 + 2 \quad (5 + 3) \times 2$

Values

36   25   12

11   7   16

13   17   18   36

- *Your teacher has the answers to these.*

Section 5: Techniques for addition & multiplication

In this section you will review pencil-and-paper techniques for addition and multiplication

DEVELOPMENT

D1: Addition review

Copy and complete:

```
1.      1  3  4      2.   2  4  1      3.        7  2      4.   3  5  4
   +       5  5         + 1  7  6         + 2  1  9           + 1  4  8
   _____         +    2  2         _____         + 2  3  0
                       _____                           _____


5.      2  4  2      6.   4  7  0      7.  8  7  5
   +    3  4  5         + 3  6  1               2  5
   _____         + 2  1  7         + 1  0  2
                       _____         _____
```

WHEN ADDING, you must stack numbers with units under units, tens under tens …

Write each addition sum as in questions 1–7. Work out each answer.

8.   23 + 14   9.   45 + 65   10.   16 + 8 + 55

11. 125 + 46   12. 471 + 35 + 2   13.   239 + 65

14. 401 + 23 + 17   15. 542 + 261 + 48   16.   748 + 256 + 42

• *Check your answers.*

Hukka

D2: Multiplication review

```
   4  3
   x  4
   1 7 2
     1
```

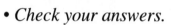

Modesto

```
      4  3
      x  4
       2
      1
```

Step 1
4 x 3 = 12
2 down, carry 1

```
   4  3
   x  4
   1 7 2
     1
```

Step 2
4 x 4 = 16
add 1 = 17

Driller

Remember
you can use the table square in Section 2 !

Copy and complete the following multiplication sums:

```
1.   1  4      2.   2  5      3.   3  7      4.   4  3      5.   7  4      6.   9  2
     x  3           x  3           x  2           x  5           x  6           x  7
     _____          _____          _____          _____          _____          _____


7.   2  1  4   8.   2  3  1   9.   4  4  6   10.  5  8  7
        x  3         x  8          x  7          x  6
     _____        _____       _____       _____
```

• *Check your answers.*

EXTRA

P1: Basic multiplication practice

Table square

Do the following multiplication sums.
Set out working as in D2.
CHECK ANSWERS AT THE END OF EACH BATCH.
Do as many batches as you need.

Batch A
1. 21 x 4	2. 64 x 3	3. 52 x 5	4. 36 x 7	5. 123 x 8
6. 152 x 3	7. 412 x 9	8. 351 x 6	9. 63 x 9	10. 572 x 8

Batch B
1. 48 x 2	2. 44 x 7	3. 49 x 6	4. 71 x 9	5. 510 x 3
6. 36 x 5	7. 824 x 6	8. 637 x 9	9. 452 x 3	10. 125 x 7

Batch C
1. 37 x 3	2. 65 x 4	3. 84 x 7	4. 49 x 5	5. 130 x 6
6. 29 x 7	7. 317 x 6	8. 711 x 9	9. 532 x 6	10. 259 x 5

P2: Different totals

1. You can make 6 different multiplication sums like this □□
using **3, 4** and **5**   x □

   Here are two of them :

   $$\begin{array}{r} 3\ 4 \\ \underline{x\ \ 5} \\ 1\ 7\ 0 \end{array} \qquad \begin{array}{r} 4\ 3 \\ \underline{x\ \ 5} \\ 2\ 1\ 5 \end{array}$$ These give totals **170** and **215**

   Find the other four multiplication sums. Work out their totals.

2. Make 6 multiplication sums like this □□
using **3, 4** and **7**   x □

   How many different totals can you get ?   Write down the totals.

3. How many different totals can you get using **5, 4** and **4** and □□ ?

   Show all working. What totals do you get ?   x □

• *Check answers.*

Star Challenge ⭐ 9

6-8 correct = 1 star

Make multiplication sums like   □□□

using the digits **3, 5, 8, 9**   x 9

Find six different totals.   ─── ───   (6 marks)

What is the *largest* total that you can get ?   (2 marks)

• *Your teacher will need to mark these.*

D3: Multiplication by 10, 100, 1000

To multiply a whole number by 10,	you add 0
To multiply a whole number by 100,	you add 00
To multiply a whole number by 1000,	you add 000

| 2 x 10 = 20 | 3 x 100 = 300 | 5 x 1000 = 5 000 |
| 23 x 10 = 230 | 35 x 100 = 3500 | 47 x 1000 = 47000 |

This method only works for whole numbers. It does not work for decimals.
1.5 x 10 does not equal 1.50
There is another rule that works for whole numbers and decimals. You will meet it later.

Copy and complete each of these multiplication sums:

1. 5 x 10 = ...
2. 13 x 10 = ...
3. 5 x 100 = ...
4. 17 x 100 = ...

5. 9 x 1000 = ...
6. 15 x 10 = ...
7. 27 x100 = ...
8. 62 x 10 = ...

9. 34 x 1000 = ...
10. 11 x 10 = ...
11. 68 x 100 = ...
12. 7 x 1000 = ...

13. 85 x 1000 = ...
14. 46 x 100 = ...
15. 57 x 10 = ...
16. 14 x 100 = ...

• *Check your answers*

D4: Multiplication by 20, 30, ... 200, 300, ...

EXAMPLE 1	Q: Work out 3 x 40	Remember 40 = 4 x 10
A:	3 x 40 = 3 x 4 x 10	
	= 12 x 10	
	= 120	*Kooldood*

Work out these multiplications.

1. 4 x 20
2. 5 x 30
3. 3 x 200
4. 9 x 300

5. 6 x 2000
6. 8 x 40
7. 4 x 500
8. 7 x 60

9. 8 x 300
10. 9 x 50
11. 5 x 700
12. 11 x 500

EXAMPLE 2	Q: Work out 300 x 60		*Idea*
A:	300 x 60 = 3 x 100 x 6 x 10	**LOOK!**	
	= 18 x 100 x 10	100 x 10 has 3 zeros	
	= 18000	& the answer has 3 zeros !	

Work out these multiplications.

13. 30 x 20
14. 50 x 30
15. 30 x 30
16. 700 x 30

17. 600 x 40
18. 70 x 50
19. 800 x 50
20. 80 x 20

21. 40 x 300
22. 90 x 40
23. 600 x 30
24. 40 x 50

• *Check your answers*

14-16 correct = 1 star

Work out these multiplications:

1.	17 x 4	2.	35 x 10	3.	7 x 30	4.	231 x 5
5.	6 x 20	6.	47 x 100	7.	9 x 500	8.	300 x 40
9.	24 x 3	10.	67 x 6	11.	4 x 1000	12.	632 x 4
13.	60 x 40	14.	2 x 600	15.	52 x 100	16.	16 x 7
17.	22 x 5	18.	200 x 80	19.	45 x 3	20.	6 x 200

• *Your teacher has the answers to these.*

D5: Another method of multiplication

This method can also be used to work out more difficult multiplications

EXAMPLE 3   Q: Work out 54 x 6

x	50	4
6	300	24

$$\begin{array}{r} 300 \\ + \ \ 24 \\ \hline 324 \end{array}$$

So, 54 x 6 = 324

Use this method to work out these multiplications:

1.	13 x 4	2.	27 x 5	3.	36 x 3	4.	92 x 5
5.	68 x 3	6.	37 x 8	7.	55 x 7	8.	82 x 9

• *Check your answers.*

D6: Multiplying larger numbers

EXAMPLE 4   Q: Work out 54 x 26

x	50	4
20	1000	80
6	300	24

$$\begin{array}{r} 1000 \\ + \ \ 300 \\ + \ \ \ \ 80 \\ + \ \ \ \ 24 \\ \hline 1404 \\ {\scriptstyle 1} \end{array}$$

So, 52 x 26 = 1404

Use this method to work out these multiplications:

1.	24 x 13	2.	36 x 25	3.	27 x 52	4.	18 x 21
5.	36 x 51	6.	65 x 43	7.	26 x 71	8.	84 x 92

• *Check your answers. If you need more practice, do questions 9 – 16.*

Use this method to work out these multiplications:

9.	72 x 14	10.	53 x 15	11.	39 x 28	12.	16 x 16
13.	33 x 21	14.	34 x 45	15.	85 x 37	16.	39 x 93

• *Check your answers.*

D7: Multiplying a 3-digit number by a 2-digit number

1. Letmewin was asked to multiply 354 x 26.

   Letmewin started with this table:

Letmewin

x	300	50	4
20	6000	1000	80
6	1800	300	24

   Copy the table and work out the answer to the multiplication.

   Use this method to work out the following sums:

2. 131 x 27   3. 225 x 23   4. 346 x 43   5. 594 x 78

• *Check your answers.*

PRACTICE

P3: Multiplication practice

Work out each sum. Show all your working.
At the end of each batch, CHECK YOUR ANSWERS.
Do as many batches as you need.
Then do the Star Challenge !

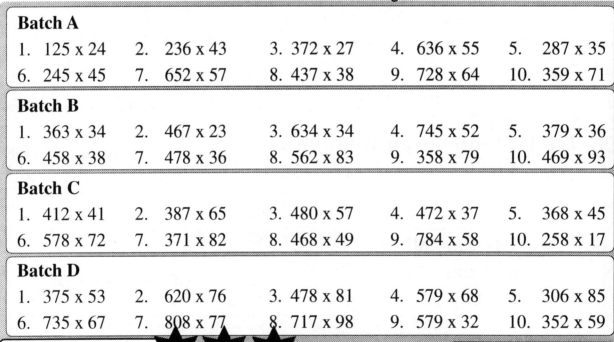

Batch A

1. 125 x 24   2. 236 x 43   3. 372 x 27   4. 636 x 55   5. 287 x 35
6. 245 x 45   7. 652 x 57   8. 437 x 38   9. 728 x 64   10. 359 x 71

Batch B

1. 363 x 34   2. 467 x 23   3. 634 x 34   4. 745 x 52   5. 379 x 36
6. 458 x 38   7. 478 x 36   8. 562 x 83   9. 358 x 79   10. 469 x 93

Batch C

1. 412 x 41   2. 387 x 65   3. 480 x 57   4. 472 x 37   5. 368 x 45
6. 578 x 72   7. 371 x 82   8. 468 x 49   9. 784 x 58   10. 258 x 17

Batch D

1. 375 x 53   2. 620 x 76   3. 478 x 81   4. 579 x 68   5. 306 x 85
6. 735 x 67   7. 808 x 77   8. 717 x 98   9. 579 x 32   10. 352 x 59

Star Challenge **11 11 11**

15-16 correct = 3 stars
10-14 correct = 2 stars
8-9 correct = 1 star

Work out these multiplications. Show all your working.

1. 58 x 5   2. 9 x 20   3. 12 x 34   4. 476 x 51
5. 295 x 2   6. 95 x 31   7. 495 x 74   8. 217 x 5
9. 605 x 12   10. 240 x 15   11. 15 x 15   12. 23 x 32
13. 567 x 23   14. 538 x 49   15. 271 x 8   16. 444 x 82

• *Your teacher has the answers to these.*

Section 6: Techniques for division

In this section you will review and practise non-calculator techniques for division.

D1: Sharing with counters

14 counters

EXAMPLE 1   Q: Share 12 counters between 3 people.
How many counters does each person get ?

A:

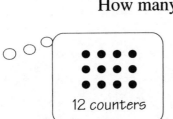

12 counters

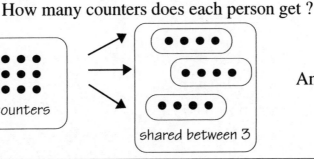

shared between 3

Ans: 4

Sureshot

Work out how many counters each person gets:

1. Share 6 counters between 2 people.   2. Share 6 counters between 3 people.

3. Share 8 counters between 2 people.   4. Share 8 counters between 4 people.

5. Share 10 counters between 5 people.   6. Share 12 counters between 4 people.

• *Check answers.*

EXAMPLE 2   Q: Share 14 counters between 3 people.
(a) How many counters does each person get ?
(b) How many counters are left over ?

A:

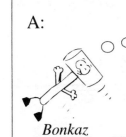

Bonkaz

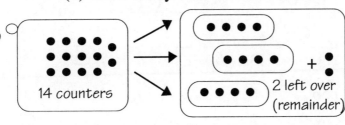

14 counters

2 left over
(remainder)

Ans: (a) 4
(b) 2 left over

In questions 7 – 12 (a)   Work out how many counters each person gets.
(b)   How many counters are left over ?

7. Share 7 counters between 2 people.   8. Share 10 counters between 3 people.

9. Share 9 counters between 2 people.   10. Share 8 counters between 3 people.

11. Share 11 counters between 5 people.   12. Share 14 counters between 4 people.

• *Check answers.*

EXAMPLE 3   Q: Work out $6 \div 3$

A:

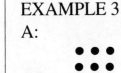

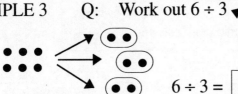

$6 \div 3 = $ 2

$6 \div 3$ is shorthand for
'share 6 between 3 people'

Icee

Copy and complete:

13. $15 \div 3 = \ldots$ 14. $12 \div 4 = \ldots$ 15. $20 \div 5 = \ldots$ 16. $8 \div 4 = \ldots$

17. $12 \div 2 = \ldots$ 18. $16 \div 4 = \ldots$ 19. $18 \div 6 = \ldots$ 20. $21 \div 3 = \ldots$

• *Check your answers.*

D2: Division using the table square

Use the table square in Section 2 D1

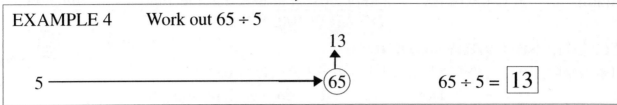

EXAMPLE 4   Work out $65 \div 5$

13

5 ————————————→ (65) $65 \div 5 = \boxed{13}$

Copy and complete:

1. $16 \div 2 = \ldots$ 2. $12 \div 4 = \ldots$ 3. $15 \div 5 = \ldots$ 4. $18 \div 6 = \ldots$

5. $28 \div 4 = \ldots$ 6. $24 \div 3 = \ldots$ 7. $24 \div 6 = \ldots$ 8. $42 \div 7 = \ldots$

9. $64 \div 8 = \ldots$ 10. $66 \div 11 = \ldots$ 11. $54 \div 9 = \ldots$ 12. $75 \div 15 = \ldots$

13. $143 \div 13 = \ldots$ 14. $81 \div 9 = \ldots$ 15. $35 \div 5 = \ldots$ 16. $32 \div 4 = \ldots$

17. $45 \div 9 = \ldots$ 18. $72 \div 8 = \ldots$ 19. $91 \div 7 = \ldots$ 20. $210 \div 15 = \ldots$

• *Check your answers.*

D3: Setting out division sums

table square

EXAMPLE 5   Work out $2 \overline{)\,14}$ ←

A: $\dfrac{7}{2 \overline{)\,14}}$ ← answer   This means $14 \div 2$

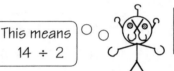

Use the table square !

Hukka

Copy and complete:

1. $3 \overline{)\,15}$ 2. $5 \overline{)\,30}$ 3. $6 \overline{)\,48}$ 4. $7 \overline{)\,28}$ 5. $6 \overline{)\,36}$

6. $4 \overline{)\,36}$ 7. $8 \overline{)\,56}$ 8. $9 \overline{)\,72}$ 9. $11 \overline{)\,99}$ 10. $12 \overline{)\,48}$

• *Check your answers.*

D4: More difficult division sums

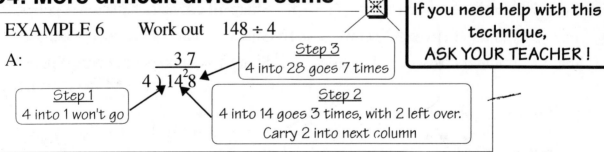

EXAMPLE 6   Work out $148 \div 4$

A: $\dfrac{3\ 7}{4\,)\,14^2 8}$

Step 3
4 into 28 goes 7 times

If you need help with this technique,
ASK YOUR TEACHER !

Step 1
4 into 1 won't go

Step 2
4 into 14 goes 3 times, with 2 left over.
Carry 2 into next column

Work out :

1. $5 \overline{)\,95}$ 2. $4 \overline{)\,96}$ 3. $5 \overline{)\,255}$ 4. $3 \overline{)\,222}$ 5. $7 \overline{)\,616}$

6. $5 \overline{)\,525}$ 7. $6 \overline{)\,270}$ 8. $272 \div 2$ 9. $368 \div 4$ 10. $276 \div 6$

11. $5 \overline{)\,675}$ 12. $3 \overline{)\,243}$ 13. $357 \div 7$ 14. $138 \div 6$ 15. $126 \div 9$

• *Check your answers*

PRACTICE

P1: Division practice

table square

You must be good at these before you can go on to D5

Do as many batches as you need.

At the end of each batch, CHECK YOUR ANSWERS.

Batch A: *Work out :*

1. $474 \div 2$ 2. $615 \div 5$ 3. $665 \div 7$ 4. $104 \div 8$ 5. $168 \div 7$

6. $750 \div 5$ 7. $232 \div 8$ 8. $276 \div 6$ 9. $153 \div 9$ 10. $428 \div 4$

Batch B: *Work out :*

1. $144 \div 3$ 2. $357 \div 3$ 3. $574 \div 7$ 4. $159 \div 3$ 5. $762 \div 6$

6. $496 \div 8$ 7. $370 \div 5$ 8. $628 \div 2$ 9. $540 \div 4$ 10. $296 \div 4$

Batch C: *Work out :*

1. $471 \div 3$ 2. $416 \div 8$ 3. $635 \div 5$ 4. $954 \div 3$ 5. $477 \div 9$

6. $448 \div 7$ 7. $102 \div 6$ 8. $385 \div 7$ 9. $468 \div 6$ 10. $390 \div 5$

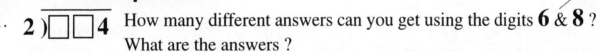

Star Challenge 12-12

10 correct = 2 stars
8-9 correct = 1 star

1. $544 \div 2$ 2. $228 \div 6$ 3. $366 \div 3$ 4. $328 \div 4$ 5. $189 \div 7$

6. $414 \div 9$ 7. $268 \div 4$ 8. $520 \div 8$ 9. $203 \div 7$ 10. $342 \div 6$

• *Your teacher has the answers to these.*

P2: Division puzzles

1. $2\overline{)\Box\Box 4}$ How many different answers can you get using the digits **6 & 8** ?
What are the answers ?

2. $3\overline{)\Box\Box\Box}$ How many different answers can you get using the digits **6, 9 & 9** ?
What are the answers ?

3. $3\overline{)\Box\Box\Box}$ You can get six different answers using the digits **5, 6 & 7** ?
     What are the answers ?   • *Check your answers.*

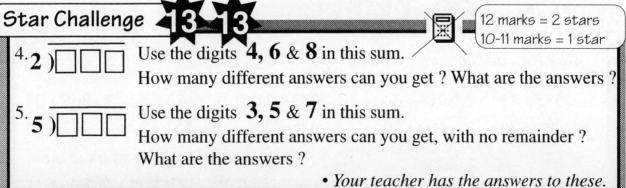

Star Challenge 13-13

12 marks = 2 stars
10-11 marks = 1 star

4. $2\overline{)\Box\Box\Box}$ Use the digits **4, 6 & 8** in this sum.
How many different answers can you get ? What are the answers ?

5. $5\overline{)\Box\Box\Box}$ Use the digits **3, 5 & 7** in this sum.
How many different answers can you get, with no remainder ?
What are the answers ?

• *Your teacher has the answers to these.*

A SURESHOT GUIDE   *page 101*   *Developing Efficient*
Non-Calculator Techniques

EXTRA

D5: Dividing 3-digit numbers by 2-digit numbers

EXAMPLE 7   Work out $345 \div 23$

A:
$$23 \overline{) 3\ 4\ ^{11}5}\ ^{1\ 5}$$

The method is the same as in D4, BUT you can't use the table square

Sureshot

Writing out a table like this helps.

Make this table by adding 23 each time.

$1 \times 23 = 23$
$2 \times 23 = 46$
$3 \times 23 = 69$
$4 \times 23 = 92$
$5 \times 23 = 115$
...

Work out the answer to each of these. Show your working.

1. $11 \overline{) 187}$ 2. $14 \overline{) 322}$ 3. $435 \div 15$ 4. $504 \div 12$ 5. $896 \div 16$

6. $989 \div 23$ 7. $837 \div 31$ 8. $441 \div 21$ 9. $957 \div 11$ 10. $756 \div 21$

11. $480 \div 15$ 12. $208 \div 16$ 13. $793 \div 13$ 14. $999 \div 27$ 15. $612 \div 12$

• *Check your answers.*

PRACTICE

P3: Large number division practice

Do as many batches as you need.

Show all working.

At the end of each batch, CHECK YOUR ANSWERS.

Batch A: *Work out :*
1. $165 \div 15$ 2. $782 \div 17$ 3. $462 \div 21$ 4. $156 \div 13$ 5. $630 \div 14$
6. $957 \div 33$ 7. $473 \div 11$ 8. $572 \div 22$ 9. $306 \div 18$ 10. $732 \div 61$

Batch B: *Work out :*
1. $663 \div 13$ 2. $624 \div 24$ 3. $731 \div 17$ 4. $923 \div 13$ 5. $667 \div 23$
6. $406 \div 29$ 7. $897 \div 69$ 8. $1008 \div 14$ 9. $954 \div 53$ 10. $851 \div 37$

Star Challenge ◄14·14·14

20 marks = 3 stars
18-19 marks = 2 stars
13-17 marks = 1 star

Work each division sum out. Show all working.

1. $585 \div 15$ 2. $918 \div 34$ 3. $693 \div 11$ 4. $676 \div 52$ 5. $868 \div 31$
6. $494 \div 26$ 7. $400 \div 16$ 8. $475 \div 25$ 9. $552 \div 12$ 10. $702 \div 54$

• *Your teacher has the answers to these.*

2 marks for each question :
1 for the answer and 1 for the working

Section 7: Checking calculations

In this section you will use approximation methods to check calculations.

DEVELOPMENT

D1: Using approximations to check multiplication

1.

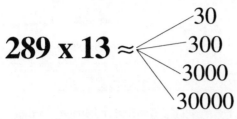

$$289 \times 13 \approx \begin{cases} 30 \\ 300 \\ 3000 \\ 30000 \end{cases}$$

≈ means
'approximately equal to'

Which of these is the most reasonable approximation the answer ?
Explain how you know.

2.

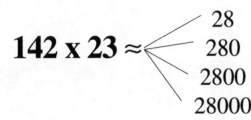

$$142 \times 23 \approx \begin{cases} 28 \\ 280 \\ 2800 \\ 28000 \end{cases}$$

Which of these is the most reasonable approximation the answer ?
Explain how you know.

3. Which is the best estimate of the number of bricks in this wall ?

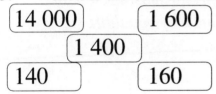

| 14 000 | | 1 600 |
| 1 400 |
| 140 | | 160 |

Explain how you know.

18 bricks

74 bricks

4. Four Pan–Galactic Trainee Explorers are using approximations to check answers
to the sum 18 x 36. *Do not work out the answer to this sum.*

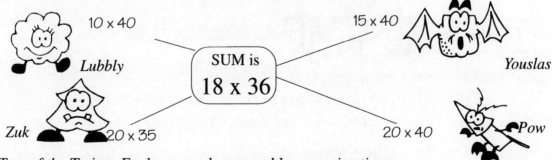

10 x 40

Lubbly

Zuk

20 x 35

SUM is

18 x 36

15 x 40

Youslas

20 x 40

Pow

(a) Two of the Trainee Explorers made reasonable approximations.
     Which two were they ?

(b) For the same sum, Dwork tried to use the approximation 18 x 35
     Why is this not much use as a check ?

Dwork

• *Check your answers*

D2: Using approximations to check division

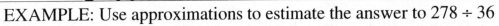

> EXAMPLE: Use approximations to estimate the answer to $278 \div 36$
>
> Method 1: $278 \div 36 \approx \dfrac{300}{40} = \dfrac{30}{4} = 7\frac{1}{2}$
>
> Method 2: $278 \div 36 \approx \dfrac{280}{40} = \dfrac{28}{4} = 7$
>
> Method 3: $278 \div 36 \approx \dfrac{280}{35} = \dfrac{40}{5} = 8$
>
>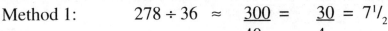
>
> *Fission*
>
> Each of these methods give reasonable estimates.

1. > Pan–Galactic Academy Space Navigational Mathematics Exam
    >
    > Q23. The Early Warning satellite orbits round the planet Elsinor once every 47 minims. How many orbits does it make in one day ?
    > [An Elsinor day is 1653 minims long.]

    All these four trainees chose the right sum : $1653 \div 47$
    But they got four different answers.

    Spottee
    3.5 orbits

    Stripee
    350 orbits

    Burga
    97 orbits

    Didi
    35 orbits

    Use approximations to decide which answer seems the most reasonable.
    Explain who you think has the right answer and why you think so.

2. ## SUM: $357 \div 62$

    Possible answers (to 1 d.p.)

    | 58.1 | | 85.3 | | 5.8 | | 582.4 | | 853.7 |

    Use approximations to decide which answer seems the most reasonable.
    Explain which you think is the most likely answer and why .

Star Challenge ⭐15 ⭐15 ⭐15

• *Check answers.*

33-36 marks = 3 stars
28-32 marks = 2 stars
24-27 marks = 1 star

For each sum: • *work out the answer* (2 marks)
• *use approximations to check your answer* (1 mark)
• *show all the working for both sum and check*

1. 435×59	2. $3204 \div 89$	3. 705×75	4. $6562 \div 17$
5. $754 \div 29$	6. 454×69	7. 920×37	8. $888 \div 24$
9. 317×46	10. 365×89	11. $1566 \div 29$	12. $4009 \div 19$

• *Your teacher has the answers to these.*

THE NATIONAL CURRICULUM ...
... AND BEYOND ...

Sureshot

How Likely
Is It ?
EXTRA

How Likely Is It ?   EXTRA
Section 1: Warming up to probability

In this section you will:
- play a guessing game under several different sets of instructions;
- devise strategies for guessing the number in as few guesses as possible;
- review probability ideas and terminology and use them to explain why some strategies work better than others.

DEVELOPMENT   *Class activity*

D1: Methods for guessing the number

Game 1:   Straight guessing

Teacher chooses a number from

1, 2, 3, 4, 5, 6, 7, 8, 9, 10, 11, 12, 13, 14, 15, 16

The class has to guess the number.

You can only ask "Is the number __ ?"

Each guess is written on the classroom board.

How many guesses did it take ?

Play the game twice.

Yerwat

Game 2 :   Reducing the possibilities

Teacher chooses a number from | 1, 2, 3, 4, 5, 6, ... 62, 63, 64 |

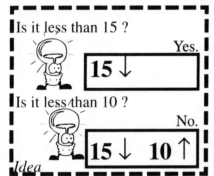

Is it less than 15 ?

Yes.

15 ↓

Is it less than 10 ?

No.

15 ↓ 10 ↑

Idea

The class has to guess the number.

Why would you NOT use the straight guessing method ?

You may ask   "Is the number less than or equal to__?"
                        or   "Is the number __ ?"

The results are written on the classroom board.

How many guesses did it take ?

Play the game several times.

Find a strategy that will reduce the number of guesses needed.

Game 3 :   Reducing the possibilities as much as you can

Teacher chooses a number from | 1, 2, 3, 4, 5, 6, ... 126, 127, 128 |

The class has to guess the number.

You can only ask   "Is the number less than or equal to__?"
                        or   "Is the number __ ?"

The results are written on the classroom board.

At the end, record the number of guesses that it took.

Play the game several times.

There is a strategy that will always give you the answer in 8 guesses.
Find this strategy.

D2: Strategies and probabilities

> **Game 1:** **Straight guessing**
> Teacher chooses a number from
> | 1, 2, 3, 4, 5, 6, 7, 8, 9, 10, 11, 12, 13, 14, 15, 16 |
> The class has to guess the number.

For the first guess, there are 16 possibilities.
The chance of getting it right is 1 in 16.
The probability of getting it right is $\frac{1}{16}$

1. If the first guess is wrong, there are 15 possibilities for the second guess.

   (a) What is the chance of getting the second guess right ?

   (b) What is the probability of getting the second guess right ?

2. If the first two guesses are wrong :

   (a) how many possibilities are there for the third guess ?

   (b) what is the probability of getting the third guess right ?

Icee

3. This strategy will always give you the answer in 16 guesses of less. **True or false ?**

> **Straight guessing**
> Teacher chooses a number from | 1, 2, 3, 4, 5, 6, ... 62, 63, 64 |
> The class has to guess the number.

4. For the first guess, there are 64 possibilities.

   (a) What is the chance of getting the first guess right ?

   (b) What is the probability of getting the first guess right ?

   (c) If the first guess is wrong, what is the probability of getting the second guess right ?

   (d) What is the maximum number of guesses that it could take.

> **Halving the previous number of possibilities**
> Teacher chooses a number from | 1, 2, 3, 4, 5, 6, ... 62, 63, 64 |
>
> The class has to guess the number.
> Strategy: Halve the number of possibilities each time.
> First question : Is the number less than or equal to 32 ?

For the first question, there are 2 possibilities.
The chance of getting it right is 1 in 2.
The probability of getting it right is $\frac{1}{2}$

5. If the first answer is "yes", then the second question is
   "Is the number less than or equal to 16 ? "
Sureshot

   (a) If the first answer is wrong, what should the second question be ?

   (b) What is the probability of getting a "yes" for the second question ?

   (c) What is the number of guesses needed, using this method ?

A SURESHOT GUIDE   page 107   *How Likely Is It ?* **EXTRA**

Section 2: Improving your estimates

In this section you will:
- use sampling to estimate the unseen contents of a bag;
- see how the estimates change as the number of samples increases.

Class activity

D1: How many of each colour are there ?

Game 1: Teacher has an opaque bag with 12 coloured cubes in it. (or 12 counters) There are no more than 3 different colours.

Teacher walks round the class, getting students to pick out a cube/counter, without looking in the bag. The result is recorded.

The bag is shaken and another selection made. The result is recorded. ……

After 12 selections, the class guess how many there are of each colour in the bag. After 24 selections, the class is asked if they want to change their guess. The sampling is continued until the class is convinced that they have the right numbers.

The class finds out if it is right.

Class discussion points:
- *does it get easier to guess if you have more results (samples) ?*
- *how many samples did you need to make before you were confident you were right ?*
- *were you right ?*

Game 2:   Teacher has a second bag with 12 coloured cubes in it. (or 12 counters) There are no more than 3 different colours.
Game 1 is repeated with a different bag of cubes/counters.

Game 3:   Teacher has a third bag with 12 coloured cubes in it. (or 12 counters) There are no more than 3 different colours.
Game 1 is repeated with a third bag of cubes/counters.

Game 4:   Students work in pairs.
One student makes up his/her own bag of cubes/counters.
There must be no more than 3 different colours.

The second student samples and records the results. …
The second student guesses how many there are of each colour.

The students then reverse their roles and repeat the experiment.

Optymistic

Big Edd

Pesymistic

Pow

Section 3: Probability lines

In this section you will:
- make estimates of probability;
- use the probability scale 0 to 1.

All individual work

D1: The probability line

The probability of an event says how likely the event is.
Probability is given as a number between 0 and 1.

How likely ⟶ Impossible   Even chance   Certain

Probability ⟶ 0 $\frac{1}{2}$ 1

If an event is impossible, its probability is 0

If an event is certain, its probability is 1

Task 1:

There are 3 sweets on this dish.

2 toffees
1 chocolate

Alan is given one of these sweets.

Copy this probability line.

Put these labels into the correct boxes on the probability line.

toffee or chocolate		toffee

fruit drop

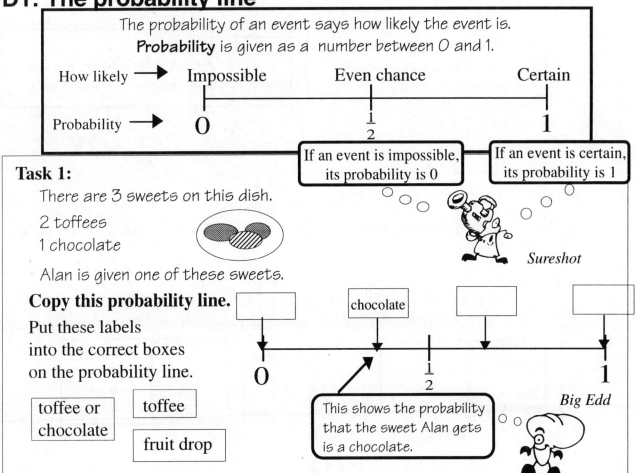

chocolate

0        $\frac{1}{2}$ 1

Sureshot

Big Edd

This shows the probability that the sweet Alan gets is a chocolate.

Task 2:

There are 4 sweets on this dish.
2 toffees
1 chocolate
1 fruit drop

Emily is given one of these sweets.

Copy this probability line.

Put these labels into the correct boxes on the probability line.

toffee or chocolate	fruit drop

toffee, fruit drop or chocolate	toffee

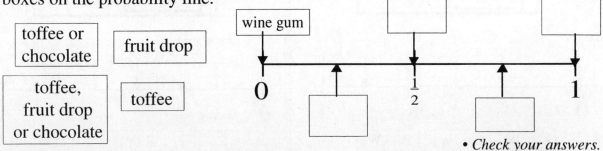

wine gum

0        $\frac{1}{2}$ 1

- *Check your answers.*

P1: Counter probability

Do one question at a time.

CHECK YOUR ANSWERS **AFTER EACH QUESTION.**

The questions get more difficult as you go on.

Ask if you do not understand.

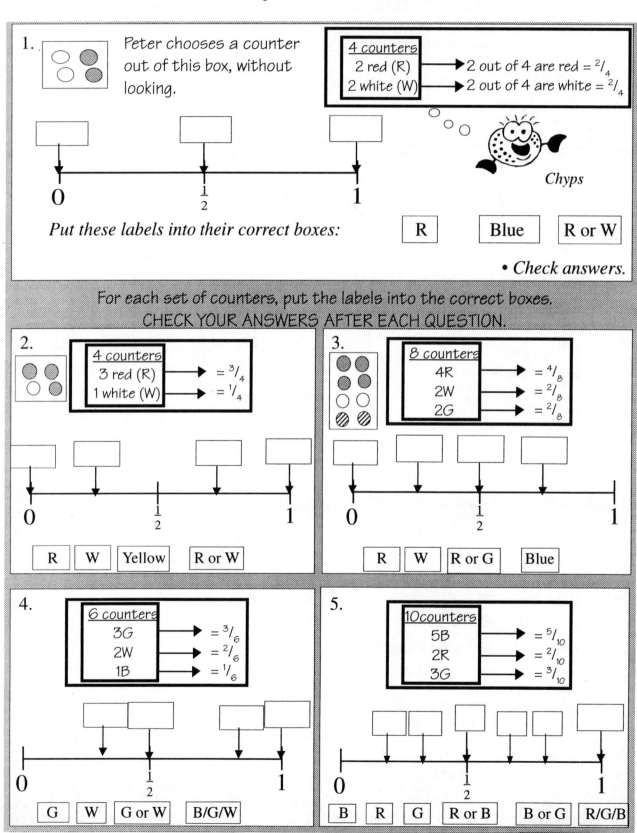

1. Peter chooses a counter out of this box, without looking.

4 counters	
2 red (R)	→ 2 out of 4 are red = $^2/_4$
2 white (W)	→ 2 out of 4 are white = $^2/_4$

Chyps

0     $\frac{1}{2}$ 1

Put these labels into their correct boxes: R   Blue   R or W

• *Check answers.*

For each set of counters, put the labels into the correct boxes.

CHECK YOUR ANSWERS AFTER EACH QUESTION.

2.

4 counters	
3 red (R)	→ = $^3/_4$
1 white (W)	→ = $^1/_4$

0    $\frac{1}{2}$ 1

R   W   Yellow   R or W

3.

8 counters	
4R	→ = $^4/_8$
2W	→ = $^2/_8$
2G	→ = $^2/_8$

0    $\frac{1}{2}$ 1

R   W   R or G   Blue

4.

6 counters	
3G	→ = $^3/_6$
2W	→ = $^2/_6$
1B	→ = $^1/_6$

0    $\frac{1}{2}$ 1

G   W   G or W   B/G/W

5.

10 counters	
5B	→ = $^5/_{10}$
2R	→ = $^2/_{10}$
3G	→ = $^3/_{10}$

0    $\frac{1}{2}$ 1

B   R   G   R or B   B or G   R/G/B

6.

16 counters		
8R	→	$= \frac{8}{16}$
4G	→	$= /$
2B	→	$= /$
2Y	→	$= /$

Liam chooses one of these counters without looking.

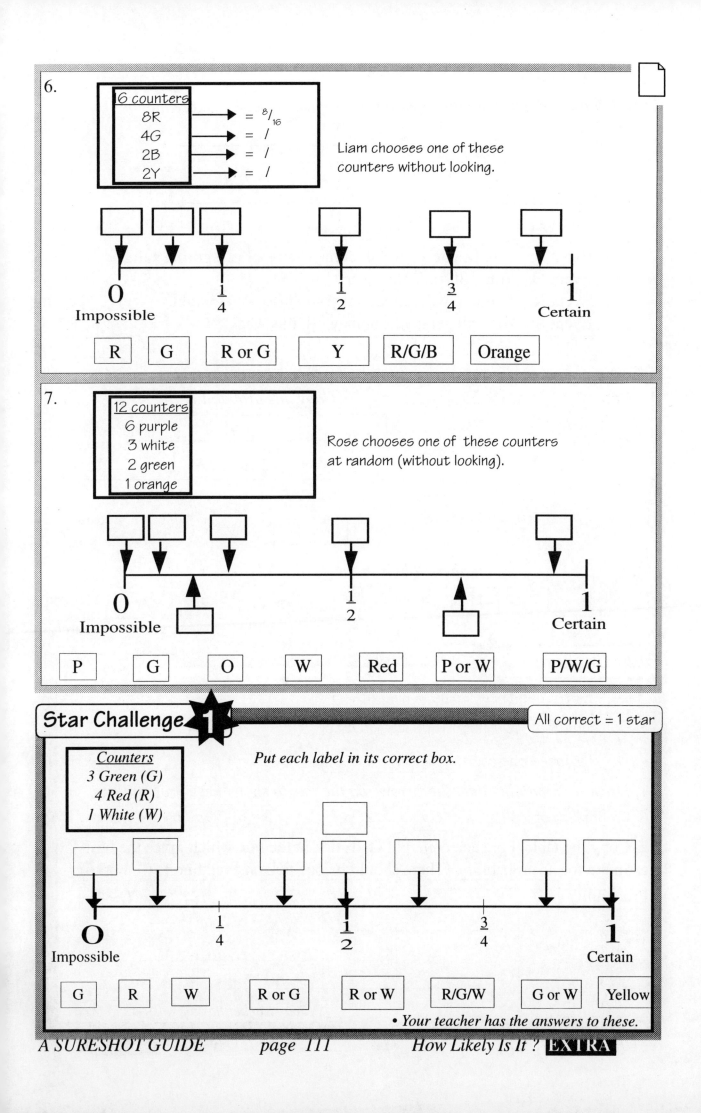

0 — Impossible $\frac{1}{4}$ $\frac{1}{2}$ $\frac{3}{4}$ 1 — Certain

| R | G | R or G | Y | R/G/B | Orange |

7.

12 counters
6 purple
3 white
2 green
1 orange

Rose chooses one of these counters at random (without looking).

0 — Impossible $\frac{1}{2}$ 1 — Certain

| P | G | O | W | Red | P or W | P/W/G |

Star Challenge 1

All correct = 1 star

Counters
3 Green (G)
4 Red (R)
1 White (W)

Put each label in its correct box.

O — Impossible $\frac{1}{4}$ $\frac{1}{2}$ $\frac{3}{4}$ 1 — Certain

| G | R | W | R or G | R or W | R/G/W | G or W | Yellow |

• *Your teacher has the answers to these.*

P2: Estimating probabilities

1. *Match these events with the probabilities shown on each of these number lines:*

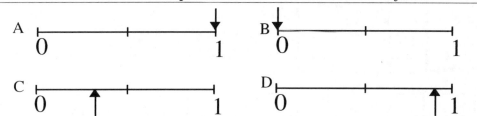

Event P: Your headteacher will come to school in a gorilla suit.
Event Q: You will smile this year.
Event R: A mouse will run across your classroom tonight.
Event S: You will get maths homework this week.

2.

Colour of cars in car park	
Red (R)	20
White (W)	15
Grey (G)	10
Other colours (O)	15

A car is driven out of this car park

Copy this probability line:

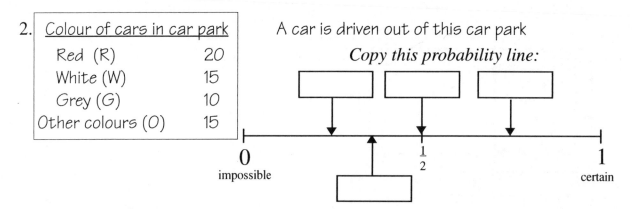

Put these labels in their correct boxes:

R		R or G		R, G or W		W

• *Check your answers.*

Star Challenge 2

7-8 marks = 1 star

Erroll has these coins in his pocket:

(5p) (5p) (5p) (10p) (10p) (10p) (10p) (20p)

He loses one coin.

1. *Draw a probability line. Put arrows on the line to show these probabilities.*

Probability of losing | 10p | | 20p | | 5p | | 50p | (4 marks)

2. Copy the table. For each coin, put ONE tick in the box which gives the best estimate for its probability. [There should be one tick on each line.] (4 marks)

Probability	0	$0 - \frac{1}{4}$	$\frac{1}{4}$	$\frac{1}{4} - \frac{1}{2}$	$\frac{1}{2}$	$\frac{1}{2} - \frac{3}{4}$	$\frac{3}{4}$	$\frac{3}{4} - 1$
5p								
10p								
20p								
50p								

• *Your teacher has the answers to these.*

Section 4: Experimental probabilities

In this section you will:
- do experiments to estimate some probabilities;
- decide whether the outcomes of each experiment are equally likely.

EXPERIMENTS

EXP 1: Tossing a coin   *Class activity*   scientific calculator

Task 1: Each student tosses a coin 20 times and records the number of heads.

OR

Each student uses the random number button on the calculator to simulate tossing a coin.
When pressed, the random number button produces a 3 digit decimal, say 0.328
If the last digit is odd, count this as a head.
If the last digit is even, count this as a tail.

Task 2: This table is drawn on the class board and the results of all the students' experiments are put into the first 2 columns.

Student	Running total of throws (T)	Number of heads	Running total of heads (RTH)	RTH ÷ T (to 2 d.p.)
1	20			
2	40			
3	60			
4				
...				

This is called the **experimental probability**.

Each student copies the table and completes the last 2 columns.

Task 3:

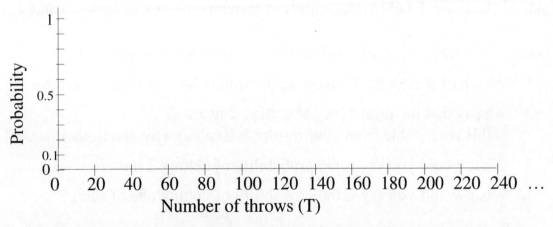

Draw a graph of the probability (last column) against the number of throws (T)
Draw a straight line across the graph through probability = 0.5.

Task 4:   Class discussion

What happens to the graph as the number of throws gets larger ?

Estimate how many heads would you expect to get after 2 000 throws..

We say that the probability of getting a head is ½.
Is this reasonable from this experiment ?

What would be the probability of getting a tail ?

Are 'getting a head' and 'getting a tail' equally likely outcomes ?

EXP 2: Two coins

Working in pairs

Task 1:   Two different coins are tossed 20 times

OR

Each student uses the random number button on the calculator to simulate tossing a coin.
When pressed, the random number button produces a 3 digit decimal, say 0.328
If the last digit is odd, count this as a head. If the last digit is even, count this as a tail.
A pair of random numbers gives the results of tossing the 2 coins.

You should record the results in two different ways.
Copy both these tables and record the results on both tables.

Table 1: Two coins   (20 throws)

Result	Tally	Frequency
HH		
HT		
TH		
TT		

Table 2: Two coins   (20 throws)

Result	Tally	Frequency
2 heads		
2 tails		
one of each		

Task 2: Collect the results from each pair of students. Put them into these two tables.

Table 3: Two coins   (whole class)

Result	Tally	Frequency
HH		
HT		
TH		
TT		

Table 4: Two coins   (whole class)

Result	Tally	Frequency
2 heads		
2 tails		
one of each		

Task 3: Draw and label two bar charts to show the results in Tables 3 and 4.

Task 4: *Use the bar charts and tables to answer each of these questions:*

1. Which of these sets of outcomes is equally likely (Table 3 or Table 4) ?

2. We say that the probability of getting 2 heads is $\frac{1}{4}$.
   Is this reasonable from your results ? Explain why you think it is or it isn't.

3. What would you say is the probability of getting 2 tails ?

4. What would you say is the probability of getting one of each ?

If you tossed two coins 4000 times, estimate …

5. … how many times you would get 2 heads.

6. … how many times you would get 2 tails.

7. … how many times you would get one head and one tail.

8. Why do we look at the results of the whole class, instead of just the results
   of one group ?

• *Check your answers.*

EXP 3: Dropping a drawing pin

Task 1: Drop a drawing pin 20 times.
Record whether it lands point up ⊥ or point down ✗

Task 2: Record the class results in this table.

Student Pair	Running total of drops (T)	Number of 'points up' ⊥	Running total of 'points up' (UP)	UP ÷ T (to 2 d.p.)
1	20			
2	40			
3	60			
4				
...				

> This is called the **experimental probability**.

Task 3:

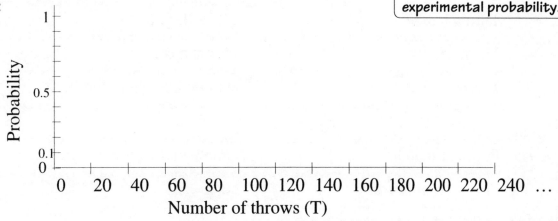

Draw a graph of the probability (last column) against the number of throws (T)

As the number of throws gets bigger, the probability should settle down to a fairly steady value. Estimate this value.

• *Your teacher will need to check this.*

EXTENSION

E1: Experimental cheats

Three sets of results are shown for each experiment. One group is either cheating or has made a mistake. Which one? Explain why you think so.

Experiment 1 : Tossing a coin

Group A	H	497
	T	503

Group B	H	240
	T	260

Group C	H	135
	T	65

Experiment 2 : Choosing counters (unseen) from 2R, 1B and 1W

Group P	R	143
	B	69
	W	66

Group Q	R	500
	B	250
	W	250

Group R	R	481
	B	255
	W	239

• *Check answers.*

Section 5: Equally likely outcomes

In this section you will decide whether outcomes are equally likely;

DEVELOPMENT

D1: Equally likely or not ?

For each situation state whether the outcomes are equally likely (Y) or not (N).

	Situation	Outcomes
1.	Toss a coin	H, T
2.	Choose one from 5 boys, 3 girls	boy, girl
3.	Choose one from 5 boys, 5 girls	boy, girl
4.	Drop a glass	break, bounce
5.	Throw a dice	1, 2, 3, 4, 5, 6
6.	Throw a dice	six, not a six
7.	Throw a dice	odd number, even number
8.	Choose a card from a full pack	red, black
9.	Football match	home win, away win, draw
10.	Pick a counter from (red) (red) (red) (green)	red, green
11.	Pick a counter from R_1 R_2 R_3 G	R_1 R_2 R_3 G
12.	Get home late	mother cross, mother not cross
13.	Fail exams	get a job, not get a job
14.	Toss two coins	HH, HT, TH, TT
15.	Toss two coins	HH, TT, one of each
16.	Weather tomorrow	wet, dry
17.	Drop a drawing pin	lands ⊥ lands ⟍
18.	Throw dart at dartboard	hit board, miss board
19.	Bowl cricket ball at batsman	hit wicket, not hit wicket
20.	Penalty shot at goal	goal, miss

• *Check your answers.*

Section 6: Working out probabilities

In this section you will work out probabilities of events with equally likely outcomes.

D1: Simple probabilities

What do we know ?   We know that...

... if an event is impossible, its probability is 0.

... if an event is certain, its probability is 1

... if an event is uncertain, its probability is a number between 0 and 1.

EXAMPLE 1

probability of getting a black counter is 1

or   prob(black) = 1   [shorthand]

probability of getting a white counter is 0

or   prob(white) = 0   [shorthand]

EXAMPLE 2

chance of getting a white counter is 2 out of 5

or   prob(white) = $^2/_5$ [shorthand]

chance of getting a black counter is 3 out of 5

or   prob(black) = $^3/_5$ [shorthand]

Fill in the gaps:

1.

chance of getting a white counter is …… out of ………

prob (white) =

………

chance of getting a black counter is …… out of ………

prob (black) =

………

2.

chance of getting a white counter is …… out of ………

prob (white) =

………

chance of getting a black counter is …… out of ………

prob (black) =

………

3.

chance of getting a white counter is …… out of ………

prob (white) =

………

chance of getting a black counter is …… out of ………

prob (black) =

………

4.

prob (white) =

………

prob (black) =

………

5.

prob (white) =

………

prob (black) =

………

6.

prob (white) =

………

prob(black) =

………

D2: More difficult probabilities

Fill in the gaps:

1.

prob(white) = ...

prob(black) = ...

prob(striped) = ...

2.

prob(white) = ...

prob(black) = ...

prob(striped) = ...

3.

prob(white) = ...

prob(black) = ...

prob(striped) = ...

4.

prob(white) = ...

prob(black) = ...

prob(striped) = ...

You have been choosing counters at random.
"At random" means that each counter is equally likely to be chosen.
Now you will choose letters at random.

Fill in the gaps:

5.   **S U P E R B**   chance of getting an E is ...... out of ......

prob(E) = ...   prob(B) = ...   prob (U) = ...

6. I N S A N I T Y   chance of getting an A is ...... out of ......

prob(A) = ...   prob(N) = ...   prob(I) = ...   prob (I or T) = ...

7.   A R I T H M E T I C

prob(A) = ...   prob (T) = ...   prob (I) = ...   prob (T or M) = ...   prob (C or I) = ...

• *Check your answers*.

Star Challenge ⭐3

Fill in the gaps:

All correct = 1 star

1.   **E L E P H A N T**

prob(P) = ...   prob(L) = ...   prob(C) = ...   prob(E) = ...   prob(E or L) = ...

2.   **O U T S T A N D I N G**

prob(A) = ...   prob(T) = ...   prob(N) = ...   prob(I or N) = ...   prob(Z) = ...

P1: One dice probabilities

> One dice is tossed.
> The possible outcomes are 1 2 3 4 5 6

The chance of getting 2 is 1 out of 6.	The chance of getting 3 or 5 is 2 out of 6.
prob(2) = $^1/_6$	prob(3 or 5) = $^2/_6$

What is the probability of getting …

1. … 4 ?
2. … 3 ?
3. … an even score ?
4. … 1 or 5 ?
5. … a score less than 3 ?
6. … a score more than 3 ?
7. … 8 ?
8. … 1, 3 or 5 ?
9. … more than 4 ?

• *Check your answers.*

P2: Two dice probabilities

1. This table shows the <u>sum of the scores</u> when two dice are thrown. It is not complete.

		1	2	3	4	5	6
	6	7	8	9	10	11	12
	5	6					
first dice	4				8	9	10
	3						
	2						
	1	2	3	4	5	6	7
		\multicolumn{6}{c}{second dice}

Each entry in the table is an outcome.

Copy and complete this table of outcomes.

Pow

2. How many outcomes are there altogether ?

prob (12) = $^1/_{36}$	prob (11) = $^2/_{36}$	prob (11 or 12) = $^3/_{36}$

Copy and complete these probabilities:

3. prob (4) = ………
4. prob (2) = ………
5. prob (6) = ………
6. prob (7) = ………
7. prob (8) = ………
8. prob (2, 4 or 6) = ………
9. prob (5 or less) = …
10. prob (8 or more) = ……
11. prob(multiple of 5) = ……

• *Check your answers.*

Star Challenge ★4 4★

10 correct = 2 stars
9 correct = 1 star

Use the table for two dice. Copy and complete these probabilities:

1. prob (3) = ……
2. prob (3 or 4) = ……
3. prob (7 or 8) = ……
4. prob (10) = ……
5. prob (15) = ……
6. prob (more than 7) = ……
7. prob (a multiple of 3) = ……
8. prob (less than 4) = ……
9. prob (an even score) = ……
10. prob (an odd score) = ……

• *Your teacher has the answers.*

P3: Probabilities with a pack of cards

												Court Cards		
RED	Hearts	Ace	2	3	4	5	6	7	8	9	10	Jack	Queen	King
	Diamonds	Ace	2	3	4	5	6	7	8	9	10	Jack	Queen	King
BLACK	Clubs	Ace	2	3	4	5	6	7	8	9	10	Jack	Queen	King
	Spades	Ace	2	3	4	5	6	7	8	9	10	Jack	Queen	King

PACK OF CARDS

Thinking about the pack.   How many …

1.   … cards are there in the pack ?
2.   … clubs are there in the pack ?
3.   … diamonds are there ?
4.   … red cards are there ?

5.   … 5s are there ?
6.   … Queens are there ?
7.   … court cards are there ?
8.   … black court cards are there ?

$$\text{prob (black card)} = {}^{26}/_{52} \text{ or } {}^1/_2$$

$$\text{prob (black Queen)} = {}^2/_{52} \text{ or } {}^1/_{26}$$

CHECK YOUR ANSWERS TO THE FIRST 8 QUESTIONS.
Copy and complete these probabilities.
CHECK YOUR ANSWERS AT THE END OF EACH BATCH.

Batch A:

1. prob (black card)   = ……
2. prob (a spade)   = ……
3. prob (a 2 of clubs)   = ……
4. prob (a 5)   = ……
5. prob (a red 5)   = ……

6.   prob (Jack)   = ……
7.   prob (King or Queen) = ……
8.   prob (5 or 6)   = ……
9.   prob (5, 6 or 7)   = ……
10. prob (a court card)   = ……

Batch B:

1. prob (an ace)   = ……
2. prob (ace of hearts)   = ……
3. prob (a red ace)   = ……
4. prob (3, 4, 5 or 6)   = ……
5. prob (Queen)   = ……

6.   prob (a red King)   = ……
7.   prob (a black Jack)   = ……
8.   prob (Jack of Hearts) = ……
9.   prob (a black 3)   = ……
10. prob (5 or 6 of hearts) = ……

Star Challenge ⭐ 5

9–10 correct = 1 star

Copy and complete these probabilities:

1. prob (10 or Jack)   = ……
2. prob (10, Jack or Queen)   = ……
3. prob (a red 10)   = ……
4. prob (black Jack or black Queen) = …
5. prob (black Queen)   = ……

6.   prob (2,3,4 or 5)   = ……
7.   prob (red 2 or 3)   = ……
8.   prob (black 3, 4, or 5) = ……
9.   prob (black 5)   = ……
10. prob (the 5 of spades) = ……

• *Your teacher has the answers.*

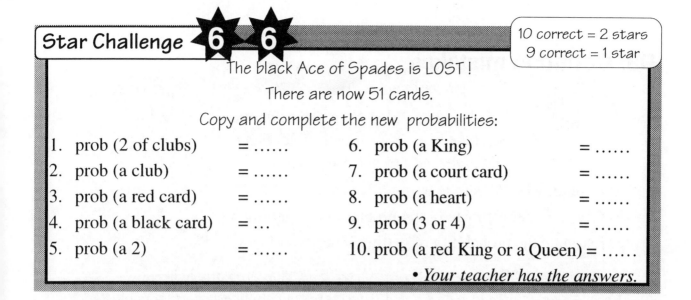

The black Ace of Spades is LOST !
There are now 51 cards.
Copy and complete the new probabilities:

1. prob (2 of clubs)   = ...
2. prob (a club)   = ...
3. prob (a red card)   = ...
4. prob (a black card)   = ...
5. prob (a 2)   = ...

6. prob (a King)   = ...
7. prob (a court card)   = ...
8. prob (a heart)   = ...
9. prob (3 or 4)   = ...
10. prob (a red King or a Queen) = ...

• *Your teacher has the answers.*

P4: Mixed practice

1. You throw a dice. What is the probability that you get either a 5 or a 6 ?

2. Your choose a letter from the word S I L L Y.
    What is the probability that you choose an L ?

3. You choose a counter from these (R) (R) (G) (B)
    What is the probability that you get:
    (a) a green counter   (b) a red counter   (c) a white counter ?

4. What is the probability that tomorrow is 24 hours long ?

5. You want to choose someone from Pat, Pete, Mick and Mary.
    You put their names into a hat and choose one at random.
    What is the probability that Pete is chosen ?

6. What is the probability that your teacher will give you a sweet in the next five
    minutes ?

7. What is the probability that you will learn Japanese today ?

8. You buy a raffle ticket. 80 tickets have been sold.
    What is the probability that you win ?

9. You buy 5 raffle tickets. 80 tickets have been sold.
    What is the probability that you win ?

10. You have five cards : King, Queen, Jack, 10, 9. You choose one card at random.
    What is the probability that you choose a picture card ?

11. A letter is chosen from the word F E R R E T.
    What is the probability that you choose (a) an R (b) an R or and E (c) an F ?

12. You buy this 'scratch card'. You can only scratch one square.
    There are two winning squares.
    What is the probability of winning ?

• *Check your answers.*

D3: Common mistakes

1. This spinner is spun.

Youslas says "There are two colours, so there is a 1 in 2 chance of getting red. The probability of getting red is $\frac{1}{2}$."

Youslas

(a) Explain why Youslas is wrong.

(b) Give a better estimate of the probability of getting red.

(c) Estimate the probability of getting blue.

2. Letmewin says "The three outcomes, red, blue, blue are equally likely. There is one chance of getting red. There are two chances of getting blue. So the probability of getting red is $\frac{1}{2}$."

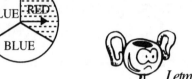

(a) Explain why Letmewin is wrong.

(b) Estimate the probability of getting red.

(c) Estimate the probability of getting blue.

Letmewin

3. W W B W W W

Meedy Oker says "The probability of getting black is $\frac{1}{5}$ because there are 5 white and 1 black."

Meedy Oker

Modesto
Modesto says "The probability of getting black is $\frac{1}{6}$ because there are 6 beads and 1 of them is black"

Who is correct?

4.  Write down the probability of getting each colour?

• *Check your answers.*

Star Challenge 7 7

8 correct = 2 stars
7 correct = 1 star

1. A counter is chosen from these: **R   G   R**
   What is the probability that it is (a) a red counter (b) a green counter?

2. There are 6 red socks, 4 black socks and 3 white socks in a drawer.
   A sock is taken out at random.
   What is the probability that it is :   (a) white (b) red (c) black?

3. At the end of the disco, these packets of crisps are left:

   | 2 smokey bacon | 2 prawn cocktail | 4 kipper | 1 plain |

   Carl takes one without looking. Write down the probability of getting:
   (a) plain   (b) kipper   (c) smokey bacon or kipper.

   • *Your teacher has the answers to these.*

D4: Sums of probabilities

1. These black and white counters are shaken in a bag.
   One counter is taken at random.

   Write down the probability of getting

   (a) a black counter   (b) a white counter

2. The probability of getting a black or a white counter is 1. Explain why.

> For any one event, the sum of all probabilities is 1

> prob (something NOT happening) = 1 − prob (it happens)

3. Another bag has only red and green counters in it.
   The probability of getting a red counter is $\frac{1}{4}$.
   What is the probability of getting a green counter ?

4. A cup is dropped. The probability it will break is $\frac{2}{3}$.
   What is the probability it will not break ?

5. The probability that it will rain tomorrow is 0.6.
   What is the probability it will not rain ?

6. There are traffic lights at the end of my road.
   The probability that I will have to stop at these lights is 0.7.
   What is the probability that I will get through the lights without stopping ?

7. A drawer has blue, white and grey socks in it. One sock is taken out at random.
   The probability of getting a blue sock is 0.3.
   The probability of getting a grey sock is 0.1.
   What is the probability of getting a white sock ?   • *Check your answers.*

Star Challenge ✦8✦8

> 10 correct = 2 stars
> 8-9 correct = 1 star

1. I often come home late. When I am late, the probability that my mother will
   moan at me is $\frac{3}{4}$ What is the probability that she will *not* moan at me ?

2. A box contains these snooker balls:

6 red balls
4 yellow balls
3 green balls
1 black ball

   A ball is taken out at random.

   Write down the probability that it is:

   (a) a red ball   (b) a green or yellow ball   (c) a black ball
   (d) a pink ball   (e) not a yellow ball   (f) a red, black or green ball

3. Six boxes of matches are found to contain 45, 48, 46, 47, 48, 47 matches.
   A box is chosen at random. What is the probability that it contains:
   (a) 47 matches   (b) less than 50 matches   (c) more than 46 matches
   • *Your teacher has the answers to these.*

Section 7: Methods of estimating probability

In this section you will look at several methods of estimating probabilities.

DEVELOPMENT

D1: Choose the right method

Here are four different ways of estimating probabilities.

> METHOD O: <u>Use equally likely outcomes</u>
> The probability of getting a '5' when throwing a dice is one sixth.
> This is because there are six equally likely outcomes.

> METHOD D: <u>Look at statistical data</u>
> If I wanted to know the probability of a pupil at my school passing 10 GCSEs
> I could look at the school's exam records.

> METHOD E: <u>Do an experiment to collect data</u>
> If I wanted to know the probability that a dropped piece of bread will land butter
> side up, I could do an experiment.

> METHOD S: <u>Carry out a survey to collect data</u>
> If I wanted to estimate the probability that any pupil in Y11 has a computer at
> home, I could do a survey.

Look at each of the following situations.
For each, say which of these methods you could use to estimate the probability.

1. The probability that any girl chosen at random in Y11 is left handed.

2. The probability that the referee will get 'head' when a coin is tossed.

3. The probability that we will have a hailstorm in June this year.

4. The probability that a hockey team could win six games in a row.

5. The probability that a new box of matches will have exactly 47 matches in it.

6. The probability that the next car that I see will have two people in it.

7. The probability that any Y11 student chosen at random has never been absent from school this year.

8. The probability that it will snow on Christmas Day.

9. The probability that I will win in a raffle.

10. The probability that I will live to be 90.

11. The probability that there will be an earthquake in Europe this year.

12. The probability that the favourite colour of students in a class is red.

13. The probability that a 'shatter-resistant' ruler will break when dropped.

14. The probability that I will get more than 60% in my next maths test.

• *Check your answers*

Section 8: Listing equally likely outcomes

In this section you will:
- develop systematic ways of getting all equally likely outcomes of an event;
- calculate probabilities for these outcomes.

DEVELOPMENT

D1: Lu-Lu

Lu-Lu is a game payed in Hawaii. It is played with four flat pieces like this.

Each piece is plain on the other side.   The four pieces are usually made from volcanic rock.

The four pieces are thrown and the total score is recorded.

1. What total scores is it possible to get ?

2. *Copy and complete this list of all the equally likely outcomes:*

Score	Outcomes
0	◯ ◯ ◯ ◯
1	⊕ ◯ ◯ ◯
2	⊕ ◯ ◯ ◯
3	⊕ ⊕ ◯ ◯ ⊕ ◯ ◯ ◯
4	
...	

3. How many equally likely outcomes are there ?

4. What is the probability that you score 10 ?

5. *Copy and complete this table of probabilities:*

Score	0	1	2	3	...
Probability	$\frac{1}{16}$	$\frac{1}{16}$		$\frac{2}{16}$	

6. What is the probability of getting a score that is:

   (a) more than 8   (b) 8 or more (c) less than 4 (d) a multiple of 3 ?

• *Check your answers.*

Rules of the game of Lu-Lu

One player throws the four stones. The total score is recorded. Any stones lying plain–side up are thrown once more. Their scores are added to the previous score. However, if you get 1 + 2 + 3 + 4 with just one throw, you score 10 and get a second throw. Players take turns to throw and score. First player to 100 wins !

D2: Dominoes

There are 28 dominoes in a standard 'double-six' set of dominoes.
One domino is drawn from this set at random.

1. *Copy and complete this set of equally likely outcomes:*

Total Score	Outcomes
12	[6 6]
11	[6 5]
10	[6 4] [5 5]
9	[6 3] [5 4]
8	
7	
6	[6 0]
5	—
4	— — [4 0]
3	
2	
1	
0	

> Check that you have 28 dominoes !

2. How many ways are there of getting :

   (a) 10   (b) 5   (c) 6   (d) 0   ?

3. The probability of getting a score of zero is $\frac{1}{28}$

   What is the probability of getting a total score of:

   (a) 10   (b) 7   (c) 1   (d) 10 or more   (e) more than 10

   (f) 0   (g) 3 or 4   (h) 5 or less (i) less than 4   (j) an even score

   • *Check your answers.*

> 19 correct = 2 stars
> 16-18 correct = 1 star

Star Challenge ⭐9 ⭐9

A 'double-six' set of dominoes has all dominoes from double six downwards to double zero. You are going to work with a double-four set of dominoes. One domino is to be drawn at random from this set.

1. Make a table showing the 'Total Score' and 'Outcomes' for a double-four set of dominoes.   (5 marks)

2. *Copy and complete this table of probabilities:*   (9 marks)

Total score	0	1	2	3	4	5	6	7	8
Probability									

3. What is the probability of getting a total score of: (5 marks)

   (a) 8   (b) 4   (c) 10   (d) 5 or more   (e) less than 6

   • *Your teacher has the answers to these.*

P1: Systematic methods of getting all outcomes

1. Listing | Two coins, 10p and 5p, are tossed.

The outcomes can be listed like this:
(H, H)   (H, T)   (T, H)   (T, T)

These three coins are tossed.
There are 8 possible outcomes.

(a) *Complete this list of outcomes:*

(HHH), ...

When 3 coins are tossed, what is the probability of getting:

(b) 3 heads   (b) 2 heads   (c) no heads   (d) at least 1 tail

2. Tommy has two pairs of shorts: 1 white and 1 black
He has three different coloured T-shirts: red, green, blue
He wears a T-shirt with his shorts.

(a) List all the possible combinations of colours.

(b) He chooses T–shirt and shorts at random.
What is the probability he chooses a red T–shirt with black shorts ?

3. Diagram | Kooldood has tops and jeans in three colours.

TOPS

	Black	Silver	Purple
Black	(black, black)		
Blue		(blue, silver)	
Grey			

JEANS

(a) *Copy and complete this diagram*
of colour combinations.

Kooldood

(b) Kooldood chooses top and jeans at random.
What is the probability he is dressed all in black ?

4.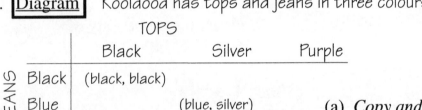

Harry has the choice of 4 drinks.
Cola | Orange | Lemon | Raspberry

He has the choice of 3 crisp flavours.
Dead Rat | Squashed Fly | Dried Toad

He chooses one drink and one packet of crisps.

Show all the possible combinations in a diagram like that in Q3.

5. Table of results | These two spinners are spun and the outcomes are recorded.

⊕		
1	(1,7) (1,8) (1,9)
2	(2,7)
3	
4	

Copy and complete this table of results.
• *Check answers.*

E1: Beat the teacher

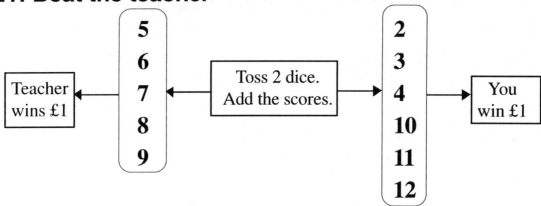

Task 1

Play this game several times. Explain how you can tell that the game is not fair. Who is more likely to win ?

Task 2

Copy and complete this table of equally likely outcomes:

Total score	Outcomes
2	(1,1)
3	(1,2) (2,1)
4	
5	
6	
7	
8	
9	
10	
11	
12	

There should be 36 outcomes altogether

Task 3

Work out the probability of getting each score.

Task 4

Work out the probability of the teacher winning.

• *Check your answers.*

Star Challenge ⭐10⭐10

Correct game and explanation = 2 stars

Devise a version of "Beat the Teacher" which is fair.

The probability of the Teacher winning must be $\frac{1}{2}$ and the probability of you winning must be $\frac{1}{2}$

Koodood

Show how you know that your game is fair.

Letmewin

• *Show your game to your teacher.*

THE NATIONAL CURRICULUM ...
... AND BEYOND ...

Sureshot

Developing Efficient Non-Calculator Techniques

EXTRA

Part 2

Developing Efficient Non-Calculator Techniques EXTRA *Part 2*

Section 1: Fractions are easy

In this section you will review basic fraction techniques.

Star Challenge ⭐1-1⭐

14-16 correct = 2 stars
10-13 correct = 1 star

1. Divide this rectangle into four parts. Each part must be a different size. Shade each one a different colour.

   On each colour, write what fraction of the rectangle it covers. *(4 marks)*

2.

   Shade $\frac{1}{6}$ of this rectangle.

   How many squares have you shaded ? .... *(2 marks)*

3. Shade $\frac{2}{9}$ of this rectangle. How many squares have you shaded ? ....
   (2 marks)

4. (a) Shade $\frac{1}{2}$ of this square with one colour.

   (b) Shade $\frac{1}{3}$ of the square with a second colour.

   (c) Shade $\frac{1}{6}$ of the square with a third colour.

   (d) What is $\frac{1}{2} + \frac{1}{3} + \frac{1}{6}$? ....
   (4 marks)

5. (a) Shade $\frac{1}{2}$ of this rectangle with one colour.

   (b) Shade $\frac{1}{3}$ of the rectangle with a second colour.

   (c) Shade $\frac{1}{6}$ of the rectangle with a third colour.

   (d) What is $\frac{1}{2} + \frac{1}{3} + \frac{1}{6}$? .... *(4 marks)*

   • Your teacher will need to check these.

D1: What fraction is ... ?

1. What fraction is shaded ?

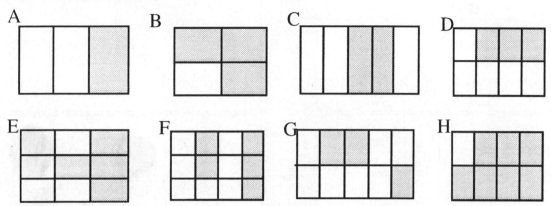

2. What fraction is *not* shaded in each diagram in question 1?

3. If $\dfrac{2}{7}$ of a shape is shaded, what fraction is not shaded ?

4. If $\dfrac{4}{11}$ of a shape is *not* shaded, what fraction is shaded ?

Questions 5, 6 and 7 are based on these diagrams.

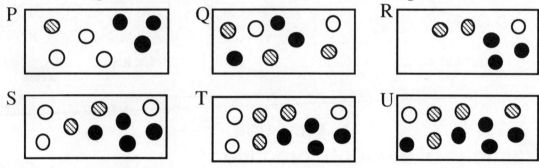

5. What fraction of each set of counters is black ?   [*6 answers are needed*]

6. What fraction of each set of counters is white ?

7. What fraction of each set of counters is striped ?

8. If I eat $\dfrac{1}{5}$ of a bar of chocolate, what fraction do I have left ?

9. I slept for $\dfrac{2}{3}$ of the journey. For what fraction of the journey was I awake ?

10. Last week I spent $\dfrac{3}{4}$ of my allowance. What fraction did I have left ?

11. $\dfrac{4}{5}$ of my friends prefer Indie groups. What fraction do not ?

12. I like $\dfrac{25}{28}$ of my tutor group. What fraction of the group do I not like ?

• *Check your answers.*

D2: Fractions of amounts

Copy and complete:

1.
   $\frac{1}{4}$ of 8 smarties = ...smarties

2.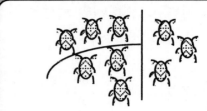
   $\frac{1}{3}$ of 9 beetles = ... beetles

3.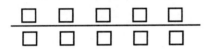
   $\frac{1}{5}$ of 15p = ... p

4.
   $\frac{1}{4}$ of £12 = £ ......

5.
   $\frac{1}{2}$ of 10 toffees = ... toffees

6.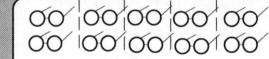
   $\frac{1}{7}$ of 14 cm = ... cm

7.
   $\frac{1}{3}$ of 6 marbles = ... marbles

8.
   $\frac{1}{5}$ of 10 spectacles = ... spectacles

• *Check your answers.*

PRACTICE

P1: Fractions of amounts practice

Counters

Copy and complete:

1. $\frac{1}{2}$ of 6p = ...
2. $\frac{1}{4}$ of 12 lorries = ...
3. $\frac{1}{3}$ of £15 = ...
4. $\frac{1}{7}$ of 14 cm = ...
5. $\frac{1}{5}$ of 20p = ...
6. $\frac{1}{9}$ of 27 boys = ...
7. $\frac{1}{4}$ of 20 sweets = ...
8. $\frac{1}{6}$ of 12 lemons = ...
9. $\frac{1}{5}$ of 15 apples = ...
10. $\frac{1}{8}$ of £24 = ... • *Check*
11. $\frac{1}{10}$ of 20 horses = ...
12. $\frac{1}{3}$ of 21 m = ... *answers.*

Star Challenge 2

14-16 correct = 1 star

Work out:

1. $\frac{1}{3}$ of £30
2. $\frac{1}{2}$ of 40p
3. $\frac{1}{4}$ of 16 toffees
4. $\frac{1}{6}$ of 24 bottles
5. $\frac{1}{7}$ of £21
6. $\frac{1}{3}$ of 12 cm
7. $\frac{1}{8}$ of 24 apples
8. $\frac{1}{5}$ of 10p
9. $\frac{1}{6}$ of 30 cm
10. $\frac{1}{2}$ of 20 m
11. $\frac{1}{4}$ of 28 smarties
12. $\frac{1}{3}$ of 9 matches
13. $\frac{1}{4}$ of 12 girls
14. $\frac{1}{5}$ of £25
15. $\frac{1}{10}$ of 50p
16. $\frac{1}{6}$ of £30

• *Your teacher has the answers to these.*

D3: More complex fractions of amounts

1. (a) What is $\frac{1}{5}$ of 10 ?

   (b) What is $\frac{2}{5}$ of 10 ?

   (c) What is $\frac{3}{5}$ of 10 ?

   (d) What is $\frac{4}{5}$ of 10 ?

$\frac{2}{5} = 2 \times \frac{1}{5}$
   or 2 lots of $\frac{1}{5}$

Sureshot

2. (a) What is $\frac{1}{3}$ of 9 ?   (b)   What is $\frac{2}{3}$ of 9 ?

3. (a) What is $\frac{1}{4}$ of 12 ?   (b)   What is $\frac{3}{4}$ of 12 ?

• *Check your answers.*

P2: More complex fraction practice

Do as much practice as you need. Check your answers at the end of each batch.

Batch A: *Work out:*

1. (a) $\frac{1}{3}$ of £6   (b) $\frac{2}{3}$ of £6   2. (a) $\frac{1}{4}$ of £20   (b) $\frac{3}{4}$ of £20

3. (a) $\frac{1}{7}$ of £21   (b) $\frac{2}{7}$ of £21   (c) $\frac{4}{7}$ of £21   (d) $\frac{5}{7}$ of £21

4. (a) $\frac{1}{5}$ of £20   (b) $\frac{4}{5}$ of £20   (c) $\frac{3}{5}$ of £20

5. $\frac{2}{3}$ of 6 toffees   6. $\frac{3}{4}$ of £8   7. $\frac{2}{5}$ of 15 boys

8. $\frac{2}{3}$ of 15 girls   9. $\frac{4}{5}$ of 15 white mice   10. $\frac{2}{7}$ of 21 sticky buns

11. $\frac{3}{10}$ of £40   12. $\frac{5}{8}$ of 32 matches   13. $\frac{5}{6}$ of £24

Batch B: *Work out:*

1. $\frac{2}{3}$ of £15   2. $\frac{3}{5}$ of £15   3. $\frac{3}{4}$ of 16 boys   4. $\frac{2}{7}$ of 21 girls

5. $\frac{3}{8}$ of 40 cm   6. $\frac{4}{5}$ of £100   7. $\frac{3}{7}$ of 35 sweets   8. $\frac{5}{8}$ of 16 cars

9. $\frac{7}{10}$ of £50   10. $\frac{2}{11}$ of 44 cm   11. $\frac{7}{8}$ of 16 kittens   12. $\frac{2}{9}$ of 18 flowers

Star Challenge 3 3

15-16 correct = 2 stars
12-14 correct = 1 star

Work out:

1. $\frac{2}{3}$ of £30   2. $\frac{2}{5}$ of 20p   3. $\frac{3}{4}$ of 12 apples   4. $\frac{5}{6}$ of 12 cars

5. $\frac{3}{7}$ of £35   6. $\frac{2}{3}$ of 30 cm   7. $\frac{3}{8}$ of £24   8. $\frac{4}{5}$ of 20p

9. $\frac{5}{6}$ of 30 cm   10. $\frac{5}{8}$ of 40 m   11. $\frac{3}{4}$ of 36 cm   12. $\frac{2}{3}$ of 18 matches

13. $\frac{3}{4}$ of 12 men   14. $\frac{2}{5}$ of 15 mm   15. $\frac{3}{10}$ of 40p   16. $\frac{3}{7}$ of £35

• *Your teacher has the answers to these.*

Section 2: Words and fractions

In this section you will:
 • meet and work with words that are used with fractions;
 • change improper fractions into mixed numbers;
 • change mixed numbers into improper fractions.

DEVELOPMENT

D1: Getting the words right

Terminology

$\dfrac{3}{5}$ ← **numerator** (or top number)
  ← **denominator** (or bottom number)

$\dfrac{3}{7}$ is a **proper fraction** (or **vulgar fraction**)
   Its numerator is less than its denominator.

$\dfrac{9}{7}$ is an **improper** or **top–heavy fraction.**

$3\dfrac{2}{7}$ is a **mixed number**

3 is a **whole number**

'vulgar fractions' are 'common fractions'

Fission

1. In the fraction $\dfrac{7}{9}$ what is (a) the denominator (b) the numerator ?

   (c) Is this fraction a proper fraction or an improper fraction ?

2. In the fraction $\dfrac{8}{5}$ what is (a) the numerator (b) the denominator?

   (c) Is this fraction a vulgar fraction or a top heavy fraction ?

$$\dfrac{3}{4} \qquad 3 \qquad \dfrac{4}{3} \qquad 3\dfrac{3}{5} \qquad \dfrac{2}{9} \qquad \dfrac{12}{5} \qquad \dfrac{15}{9} \qquad \dfrac{40}{33}$$

$$1\dfrac{1}{3} \qquad \dfrac{2}{7} \qquad 2 \qquad 4\dfrac{6}{7} \qquad \dfrac{19}{23} \qquad \dfrac{13}{15} \qquad \dfrac{12}{7}$$

3. List the numbers in the box that …
   (a) … are whole numbers   (b) …are mixed numbers
   (c) …are proper fractions   (d) …are improper fractions
   (e) … have a numerator which is less than 4
   (f) … have a denominator which is more than 20

4. $2\dfrac{1}{4}$ is a mixed number.

   $\dfrac{9}{4}$ is a top heavy fraction.

   $2\dfrac{1}{4} = \dfrac{9}{4}$

   Find a mixed number and a top heavy fraction in the box (before Q3) that equal each other.

   • *Check your answers.*

D2: Changing improper fractions into mixed numbers

EXAMPLE: $\dfrac{14}{3} = \dfrac{12}{3} + \dfrac{2}{3}$

So, $\dfrac{14}{3} = 4\dfrac{2}{3}$

Change into mixed numbers or whole numbers:

1. $\dfrac{3}{2}$ 2. $\dfrac{4}{3}$ 3. $\dfrac{5}{2}$ 4. $\dfrac{7}{3}$ 5. $\dfrac{6}{5}$ 6. $\dfrac{10}{5}$ 7. $\dfrac{10}{9}$ 8. $\dfrac{20}{3}$ 9. $\dfrac{21}{4}$

• Check your answers.

D3: Changing mixed numbers into improper fractions

EXAMPLE: $2\dfrac{2}{3} = \dfrac{6}{3} + \dfrac{2}{3}$

So, $2\dfrac{2}{3} = \dfrac{8}{3}$

Change into improper fractions:

1. $2\dfrac{1}{2}$ 2. $1\dfrac{5}{8}$ 3. $2\dfrac{1}{3}$ 4. $3\dfrac{2}{3}$ 5. $1\dfrac{4}{5}$ 6. $3\dfrac{3}{10}$ 7. $4\dfrac{8}{9}$ 8. $3\dfrac{5}{6}$

• Check your answers

PRACTICE

P1: Mixed number practice
Check answers at end of each batch.

Batch A: *Change into mixed numbers or whole numbers:*

1. $\dfrac{9}{2}$ 2. $\dfrac{5}{3}$ 3. $\dfrac{9}{2}$ 4. $\dfrac{7}{4}$ 5. $\dfrac{8}{5}$ 6. $\dfrac{12}{4}$ 7. $\dfrac{13}{9}$ 8. $\dfrac{23}{3}$ 9. $\dfrac{21}{5}$

Change into improper fractions:

10. $2\dfrac{1}{2}$ 11. $2\dfrac{3}{8}$ 12. $3\dfrac{2}{3}$ 13. $1\dfrac{2}{5}$ 14. $3\dfrac{4}{9}$ 15. $1\dfrac{5}{8}$

Batch B: *Change into mixed numbers or whole numbers:*

1. $\dfrac{7}{5}$ 2. $\dfrac{9}{7}$ 3. $\dfrac{11}{10}$ 4. $\dfrac{9}{4}$ 5. $\dfrac{13}{5}$ 6. $\dfrac{21}{4}$ 7. $\dfrac{21}{10}$ 8. $\dfrac{11}{5}$ 9. $\dfrac{13}{7}$

Change into improper fractions:

10. $2\dfrac{7}{9}$ 11. $1\dfrac{5}{9}$ 12. $2\dfrac{7}{8}$ 13. $3\dfrac{1}{10}$ 14. $5\dfrac{1}{2}$ 15. $1\dfrac{2}{7}$

Star Challenge 4
9-10 correct = 1 star

Match up these pairs of mixed numbers and improper fractions:

$\dfrac{5}{4}$	$\dfrac{7}{3}$	$\dfrac{19}{9}$
	$\dfrac{11}{9}$	$\dfrac{9}{4}$	
$\dfrac{8}{3}$		$\dfrac{10}{3}$
	$\dfrac{7}{4}$	$\dfrac{11}{3}$	
	$\dfrac{13}{9}$	

$2^1/_3$ $2^1/_9$ $1^1/_4$

$1^3/_4$ $1^4/_9$ $2^1/_4$

$3^1/_3$ $1^2/_9$

$2^2/_3$ $3^2/_3$

• Your teacher has the answers to these.

Section 3: Equivalent fractions

In this section you will:
- work with equivalent fractions;
- find the simplest form of fractions.

D1: Making equivalent fractions

Equivalent fractions can be made by multiplying the top and bottom of a fraction by the same number.

$\dfrac{1}{3}$ is equivalent to $\dfrac{5}{15}$

$\dfrac{1}{3} \xrightarrow{\ \times 5\ } = \dfrac{5}{15}$

Equivalent fractions are the same size.

1. Copy and complete:

   (a) $\dfrac{2}{5} \xrightarrow{\ \times 3\ } = \dfrac{\ \ }{\ \ }$

   (b) $\dfrac{2}{5} \xrightarrow{\ \times 5\ } = \dfrac{\ \ }{\ \ }$

   (c) $\dfrac{2}{5} \xrightarrow{\ \times 4\ } = \dfrac{\ \ }{\ \ }$

   (d) $\dfrac{2}{5} \xrightarrow{\ \times 2\ } = \dfrac{\ \ }{\ \ }$

2. Copy and complete:

   (a) $\dfrac{3}{4} \xrightarrow{\ \times 2\ } = \dfrac{\ \ }{\ \ }$

   (b) $\dfrac{4}{9} \xrightarrow{\ \times 3\ } = \dfrac{\ \ }{\ \ }$

   (c) $\dfrac{3}{5} \xrightarrow{\ \times 5\ } = \dfrac{\ \ }{\ \ }$

   (d) $\dfrac{5}{8} \xrightarrow{\ \times 4\ } = \dfrac{\ \ }{\ \ }$

3. Find the value of each letter:

   (a) $\dfrac{2}{3} \xrightarrow{\ \times a\ } = \dfrac{6}{9}$

   (b) $\dfrac{3}{5} \xrightarrow{\ \times b\ } = \dfrac{15}{25}$

   (c) $\dfrac{2}{7} \xrightarrow{\ \times c\ } = \dfrac{4}{14}$

   (d) $\dfrac{9}{10} \xrightarrow{\ \times d\ } = \dfrac{45}{50}$

   (e) $\dfrac{1}{3} \xrightarrow{\ \times e\ } = \dfrac{4}{12}$

   (f) $\dfrac{4}{7} \xrightarrow{\ \times f\ } = \dfrac{20}{35}$

   (g) $\dfrac{3}{11} \xrightarrow{\ \times g\ } = \dfrac{9}{33}$

   (h) $\dfrac{4}{9} \xrightarrow{\ \times h\ } = \dfrac{40}{90}$

4. Copy each equation. Replace each ☐ with the correct number:

   (a) $\dfrac{1}{2} \xrightarrow{\ \times \Box\ } = \dfrac{4}{\Box}$

   (b) $\dfrac{2}{3} \xrightarrow{\ \times \Box\ } = \dfrac{8}{\Box}$

   (c) $\dfrac{3}{5} \xrightarrow{\ \times \Box\ } = \dfrac{\Box}{20}$

   (d) $\dfrac{3}{7} \xrightarrow{\ \times \Box\ } = \dfrac{9}{\Box}$

- *Check your answers.*

 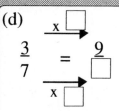

P1: Equivalent fraction practice

Copy and complete each pair of equivalent fractions:

1. $\dfrac{1}{2} = \dfrac{?}{10}$ (×)

2. $\dfrac{1}{3} = \dfrac{?}{12}$ (×)

3. $\dfrac{1}{4} = \dfrac{3}{?}$ (×)

4. $\dfrac{1}{5} = \dfrac{4}{?}$ (×)

5. $\dfrac{1}{6} = \dfrac{?}{24}$ (×)

6. $\dfrac{2}{3} = \dfrac{?}{15}$ (×)

7. $\dfrac{3}{5} = \dfrac{?}{30}$ (×)

8. $\dfrac{5}{7} = \dfrac{20}{?}$ (×)

Copy and complete each pair of equivalent fractions. Use arrows if they help you.

9. $\dfrac{2}{9} = \dfrac{6}{?}$

10. $\dfrac{4}{5} = \dfrac{?}{25}$

11. $\dfrac{7}{8} = \dfrac{?}{16}$

12. $\dfrac{7}{12} = \dfrac{21}{?}$

13. $\dfrac{5}{6} = \dfrac{15}{?}$

14. $\dfrac{5}{8} = \dfrac{?}{24}$

15. $\dfrac{2}{15} = \dfrac{?}{45}$

16. $\dfrac{4}{9} = \dfrac{?}{36}$

• *Check your answers.*

D2: Making equivalent fractions by dividing

> **Equivalent fractions** can also be made by dividing the top and bottom of a fraction by the same number.
>
> $\dfrac{5}{15} = \dfrac{1}{3}$ (÷ 5)

Copy and complete each pair of equivalent fractions:

1. $\dfrac{4}{8} = \dfrac{\;}{\;}$ (÷ 2)

2. $\dfrac{10}{20} = \dfrac{\;}{\;}$ (÷ 5)

3. $\dfrac{6}{9} = \dfrac{\;}{\;}$ (÷ 3)

4. $\dfrac{7}{21} = \dfrac{\;}{\;}$ (÷ 7)

5. $\dfrac{5}{15} = \dfrac{\;}{\;}$ (÷ 5)

6. $\dfrac{3}{6} = \dfrac{1}{\;}$ (÷)

7. $\dfrac{12}{18} = \dfrac{\;}{3}$ (÷)

8. $\dfrac{9}{15} = \dfrac{3}{\;}$ (÷)

Copy and complete each pair of equivalent fractions. They are a mixture of × and ÷

9. $\dfrac{2}{8} = \dfrac{1}{?}$

10. $\dfrac{9}{12} = \dfrac{?}{4}$

11. $\dfrac{2}{3} = \dfrac{12}{?}$

12. $\dfrac{15}{25} = \dfrac{3}{?}$

13. $\dfrac{3}{5} = \dfrac{6}{?}$

14. $\dfrac{12}{16} = \dfrac{?}{4}$

15. $\dfrac{2}{5} = \dfrac{?}{15}$

16. $\dfrac{6}{18} = \dfrac{?}{9}$

• *Check your answers.*

D3: Simplest form

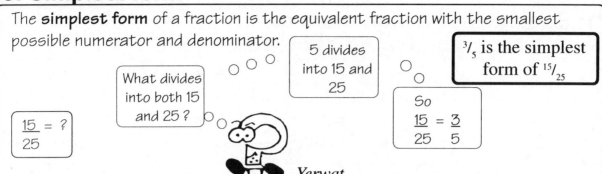

The **simplest form** of a fraction is the equivalent fraction with the smallest possible numerator and denominator.

$\frac{15}{25} = ?$

What divides into both 15 and 25 ?

5 divides into 15 and 25

So $\frac{15}{25} = \frac{3}{5}$

$^3/_5$ is the simplest form of $^{15}/_{25}$

Yerwat

Find the simplest form of each of these fractions:

1. $\frac{16}{20}$ 2. $\frac{6}{18}$ 3. $\frac{20}{25}$ 4. $\frac{14}{21}$ 5. $\frac{12}{20}$ 6. $\frac{10}{15}$ 7. $\frac{9}{24}$ 8. $\frac{15}{35}$

• *Check your answers.*

PRACTICE

P2: Equivalent fraction spiders

The fractions in each spider are equivalent. Copy and complete each spider.

1.
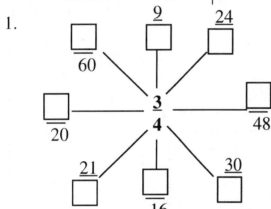

2.
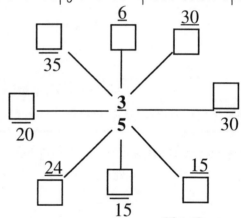

• *Check your answers.*

1. *Copy and complete this equivalent fraction spider.*

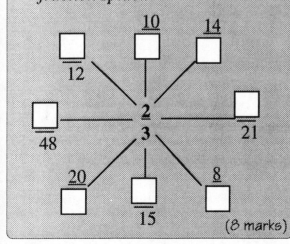

(8 marks)

2. *Copy and complete these equivalent fraction pairs.*

$\frac{3}{7} = \frac{9}{?}$ $\frac{12}{20} = \frac{?}{5}$

$\frac{2}{9} = \frac{?}{36}$ $\frac{12}{15} = \frac{4}{?}$

(4 marks)

3. *Find the simplest form of each of these fractions.*

$\frac{15}{20}$ $\frac{9}{15}$ $\frac{8}{18}$ $\frac{10}{30}$

(8 marks)

• *Your teacher has the answers to these.*

In this section you will:
- change decimals into fractions;
- change decimals into fractions in simplest form.

DEVELOPMENT

D1: Decimals and fractions

The decimal point separates the whole numbers from the bits of numbers.

Thousands T	Hundreds H	Tens T	Units U	.	tenths t	hundredths h	thousandths th	
			0	.	3			$= \frac{3}{10}$
			0	.	0	7		$= \frac{7}{100}$
			0	.	0	0	2	$= \frac{2}{1000}$
			1	.	6			$= 1\frac{6}{10}$
			0	.	5	2		$= \frac{52}{100}$

Copy and complete this table:

Thousands T	Hundreds H	Tens T	Units U	.	tenths t	hundredths h	thousandths th	
			0	.	4			= ......
			0	.	0	3		= ......
			0	.	0	0	7	= ......
			2	.	4			= ......
			0	.	2	9		= ......
			0	.				$= \frac{6}{100}$
			0	.				$= \frac{8}{10}$
			0	.				$= \frac{8}{1000}$
			0	.				$= \frac{57}{100}$
			0	.				$= \frac{31}{1000}$
			...	.				$= 2\frac{1}{10}$
				.				$= 1\frac{17}{100}$
				.				$= 4\frac{31}{1000}$
			0	.	0	3	7	= ......
		1	2	.	5	4	3	= ......

Just keep looking at the labels at the top of the table.

Yerwat

- Check your answers.

D2: Changing decimals to fractions

$$\boxed{\text{T U . t h th}}$$

EXAMPLE:	EXAMPLE:
Q: Write 0.9 as a fraction	Q: Write 0.31 as a fraction

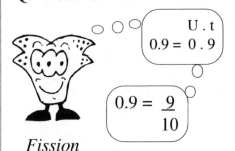

$$\begin{array}{c} \text{U . t} \\ 0.9 = 0 . 9 \end{array}$$

$$0.9 = \frac{9}{10}$$

Fission

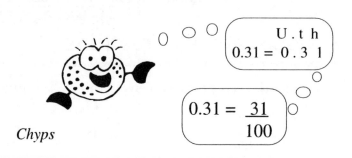

$$\begin{array}{c} \text{U . t h} \\ 0.31 = 0 . 3 1 \end{array}$$

$$0.31 = \frac{31}{100}$$

Chyps

Write these decimals as fractions:

1. **0.7**   2. **0.3**   3. **0.09**   4. **0.01**   5. **0.03**   6. **0.009**

7. **0.11**   8. **0.29**   9. **0.37**   10. **0.05**   11. **0.32**   12. **0.437**

EXAMPLE:

Q: Write 1.7 as a mixed number

A **mixed number** is a whole number and a fraction

$$\begin{array}{c} \text{U . t h} \\ 1.7 = 1 . 7 \end{array}$$

Kooldood

$$1.7 = 1\frac{7}{10}$$

Write these decimals as fractions or mixed numbers:

13. **1.3**   14. **2.6**   15. **4.01**   16. **0.065**   17. **0.08**   18. **0.072**

19. **0.28**   20. **6.5**   21. **0.001**   22. **0.17**   23. **6.8**   24. **3.09**

• *Check your answers*

Star Challenge ★ 6

13-14 correct = 1 star

True (T) or false (F) ?

1. $0.1 = {}^{1}/_{10}$ 2. $0.003 = {}^{3}/_{100}$ 3. $0.005 = {}^{5}/_{1000}$

4. $0.9 = {}^{9}/_{10}$ 5. $2.1 = 2{}^{1}/_{10}$ 6. $3.2 = 3{}^{2}/_{100}$

7. $0.04 = {}^{4}/_{100}$ 8. $3.003 = 3{}^{3}/_{1000}$ 9. $0.15 = {}^{15}/_{10}$

10. $0.16 = {}^{16}/_{100}$ 11. $0.45 = {}^{45}/_{100}$ 12. $0.103 = {}^{103}/_{1000}$

13.   Does $0.73 = {}^{73}/_{100}$ or ${}^{73}/_{10}$?

14. 0.04 does not equal ${}^{4}/_{10}$ Explain why.

• *Your teacher has the answers to these.*

D3: Decimals to fractions in simplest form

Hukka

You know how to:
* change decimals into fractions;
* simplify fractions.

You are now going to apply both of these techniques.

$$0.35 \quad = \quad \underset{\text{fraction}}{\underset{\uparrow}{\frac{35}{100}}} \quad = \quad \underset{\text{simplest form of fraction}}{\underset{\uparrow}{\frac{7}{20}}}$$

$\div 5$ $\div 5$

decimal

Copy and complete:

1. $0.65 = \dfrac{\ldots}{100} = \dfrac{\ldots}{20}$

2. $0.26 = \dfrac{\ldots}{100} = \dfrac{\ldots}{50}$

3. $0.24 = \dfrac{\ldots}{100} = \dfrac{\ldots}{25}$

4. $0.35 = \dfrac{\ldots}{100} = \dfrac{\ldots}{20}$

5. $0.25 = \dfrac{\ldots}{100} = \dfrac{\ldots}{\ldots}$

6. $0.16 = \dfrac{\ldots}{\ldots} = \dfrac{\ldots}{\ldots}$

7. $0.75 = \dfrac{\ldots}{\ldots} = \dfrac{\ldots}{\ldots}$

8. $0.008 = \dfrac{\ldots}{\ldots} = \dfrac{\ldots}{\ldots}$

• *Check your answers.*

PRACTICE

P1: Decimal to fraction practice

Write each decimal as a fraction in its simplest form.
CHECK YOUR ANSWERS AT THE END OF EACH BATCH.

Batch A:
1. **0.4** 2. **0.6** 3. **0.08** 4. **0.22** 5. **0.06** 6. **0.65**

Batch B:
1. **0.2** 2. **0.04** 3. **0.25** 4. **0.44** 5. **0.8** 6. **0.36**

Star Challenge 7

5-6 correct = 1 star

Write each decimal as a fraction in its simplest form.

1. **0.02** 2. **0.24** 3. **0.606** 4. **0.52** 5. **0.64** 6. **0.88**

• *Your teacher has the answers to these.*

Section 5: Decimals, Fractions & Percentages

In this section you will work with simple fraction-decimal-percentage equivalents.

D1: Halves, quarters and three-quarters

$$0.5 \ = \ \tfrac{1}{2} \qquad 4.5 = \ 4\tfrac{1}{2} \qquad 8.5 \ = \ 8\tfrac{1}{2}$$

Copy and complete:

1. $3.5 = \ldots$
2. $5.5 \ = \ldots$
3. $7.5 = \ldots$
4. $2.5 \ = \ldots$
5. $\ldots = 9\tfrac{1}{2}$
6. $10.5 = \ldots$
7. $\ldots = 6\tfrac{1}{2}$
8. $\ldots = 15\tfrac{1}{2}$

$$0.25 = \ \tfrac{1}{4} \qquad 6.25 = \ 6\tfrac{1}{4} \qquad 4.25 \ = \ 4\tfrac{1}{4}$$

Copy and complete:

9. $2.25 \ = \ldots$
10. $3.25 = \ldots$
11. $7.25 = \ldots$
12. $9.25 \ = \ldots$
13. $\ldots = 1\tfrac{1}{4}$
14. $5.25 = \ldots$
15. $\ldots = 8\tfrac{1}{4}$
16. $\ldots = 14\tfrac{1}{4}$

$$0.75 = \ \tfrac{3}{4} \qquad 9.75 = \ 9\tfrac{3}{4} \qquad 5.75 \ = \ 5\tfrac{3}{4}$$

Copy and complete:

17. $4.75 \ = \ldots$
18. $2.75 = \ldots$
19. $1.75 = \ldots$
20. $3.75 \ = \ldots$
21. $\ldots = 6\tfrac{3}{4}$
22. $8.75 = \ldots$
23. $\ldots = 7\tfrac{3}{4}$
24. $\ldots = 10\tfrac{3}{4}$
25. $6.5 = \ldots$
26. $1.25 = \ldots$
27. $\ldots = 3\tfrac{1}{2}$
28. $7.75 \ = \ldots$
29. $\ldots = 6\tfrac{1}{4}$
30. $2.5 \ = \ldots$
31. $\ldots = 2\tfrac{3}{4}$
32. $\ldots = 25\tfrac{1}{2}$

• *Check answers.*

D2: Tenths, hundredths and thousandths revisited

$$0.7 = \tfrac{7}{10} \qquad 0.05 \ = \ \tfrac{5}{100} \qquad 0.001 = \ \tfrac{1}{1000}$$
$$5.3 = \ 5\tfrac{3}{10} \qquad 2.07 \ = \ 2\tfrac{7}{100} \qquad 6.032 = \ 6\tfrac{32}{1000}$$
$$6.2 = \ 6\tfrac{2}{10} \qquad 3.45 \ = \ 3\tfrac{45}{100} \qquad 1.729 = \ 1\tfrac{729}{1000}$$

Copy and complete:

1. $3.7 \ = \ldots$
2. $5.09 = \ldots$
3. $8.21 \ = \ldots$
4. $4.67 \ = \ldots$
5. $1.03 = \ldots$
6. $2.33 = \ldots$
7. $6.003 = \ldots$
8. $9.031 = \ldots$
9. $\ldots = 5\tfrac{9}{10}$
10. $\ldots = 7\tfrac{7}{100}$
11. $\ldots = 1\tfrac{53}{100}$
12. $\ldots = 6\tfrac{37}{1000}$

• *Check answers.*

D3: Decimals and percentages

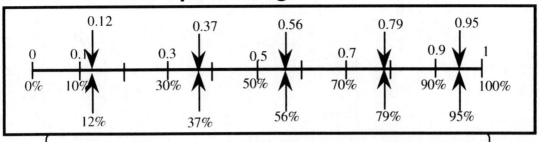

$$0.12 = 12\% \qquad 0.7 = 70\% \qquad 0.07 = 7\%$$

Copy and fill in this table of equivalent decimals and percentages:

Decimal	0.3	0.8	0.73				0.45	0.03
Percentage				51%	23%	35%		
Decimal			0.96	0.33		0.025		
Percentage	64%	40%			5%		$12\tfrac{1}{2}\%$	$37\tfrac{1}{2}\%$

• *Check your answers.*

D4: Fraction–percentage equivalents you should know

LEARN THESE:

$$50\% = \tfrac{1}{2} \qquad 25\% = \tfrac{1}{4} \qquad 10\% = \tfrac{1}{10} \qquad 33\tfrac{1}{3}\% = \tfrac{1}{3} \qquad 12\tfrac{1}{2}\% = \tfrac{1}{8}$$

These basic fraction–percentage pairs can be used to calculate many others.

EXAMPLE

Q: What fraction is 30% ?

A:

$30\% = 3 \times 10\%$

$30\% = 3 \times \tfrac{1}{10} = \tfrac{3}{10}$

Fission

EXAMPLE

Q: What percentage is $\tfrac{3}{8}$?

A:

$\tfrac{3}{8} = 3 \times \tfrac{1}{8}$

$\tfrac{3}{8} = 3 \times 12\tfrac{1}{2}\% = 37\tfrac{1}{2}\%$

Chyps

Work out the percentage equivalent to each of these fractions.
Use the percentage-fraction equivalents in the box.

1. $\dfrac{3}{4}$
2. $\dfrac{9}{10}$
3. $\dfrac{2}{3}$
4. $\dfrac{7}{10}$
5. $\dfrac{7}{8}$
6. $\dfrac{1}{16}$
7. $\dfrac{5}{8}$

Work out the fraction equivalent to each of these percentages:

8. 20% 9. 70% 10. 75% 11. 10% 12. 5% 13. 2.5% 14. 7.5%

Star Challenge 8

All correct = 1 star

VAT is added onto many bills. VAT is charged at $17\tfrac{1}{2}\%$ of the basic price.

$$17\tfrac{1}{2}\% = 10\% + 5\% + 2\tfrac{1}{2}\%$$

The basic price of my TV was £160. 10% of £160 = £16

VAT = value added tax

Work out the VAT that was added on to the £160.

Fill in each box:

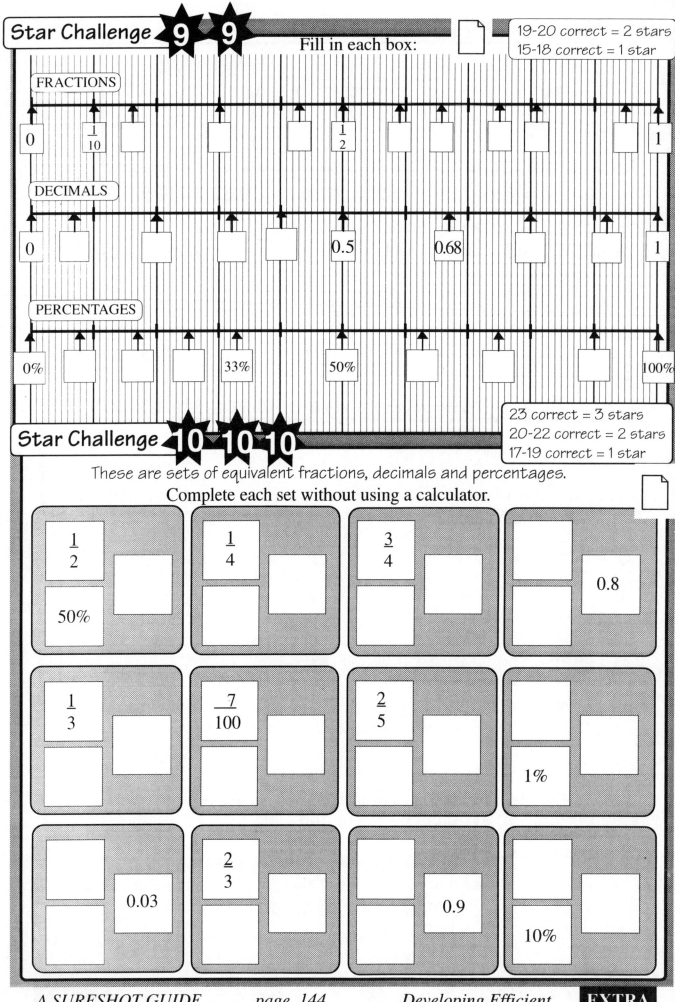

FRACTIONS

0 $\frac{1}{10}$ ☐   ☐   ☐ $\frac{1}{2}$ ☐   ☐   ☐   ☐ 1

DECIMALS

0 ☐   ☐   ☐   ☐ 0.5 0.68 ☐ 1

PERCENTAGES

0% ☐   ☐   ☐ 33% 50% ☐   ☐   ☐ 100%

Star Challenge 10 10 10

These are sets of equivalent fractions, decimals and percentages.
Complete each set without using a calculator.

$\frac{1}{2}$ ☐ / 50%	$\frac{1}{4}$ ☐ / ☐	$\frac{3}{4}$ ☐ / ☐	☐ / 0.8 ☐
$\frac{1}{3}$ ☐ / ☐	$\frac{7}{100}$ ☐ / ☐	$\frac{2}{5}$ ☐ / ☐	☐ / 1% ☐
☐ / 0.03 ☐	$\frac{2}{3}$ ☐ / ☐	☐ / 0.9 ☐	☐ / 10% ☐

Section 6: Working with percentages

In this section you will do calculations involving percentages.

D1: Percentage reasoning

EXAMPLE:

Q: The new intake of trainee Pan–Galactic Explorers have just arrived at the Academy. 12% of them are from the Solar System. The rest are from other Galaxies.

What percentage come from other Galaxies ?

$100\% - 12\% = 88\%$

Sludge

A: 88%

1. 15% of the trainees are humanoid. **What percentage are not humanoid ?**

2. 30% of the trainees speak at least three languages.
    What percentage speak less than three languages ?

3. 35% of the trainees breathe an oxygen–nitrogen mix as found on Earth.
    20% of the trainees need a higher level of oxygen than is found on Earth.
    The rest cannot breathe any form of oxygen.
    What percentage of the trainees cannot breathe oxygen ?

4. In year 2254, 78% of the trainees passed their final exams.
    What percentage failed.

5. 90% of those who failed their exams in 2254 took them again in 2255.
    What percentage didn't retake their exams ?

6. 85% of those who retook their exams passed. **What percentage failed ?**

• *Check your answers.*

D2: Percentages of amounts

LEARN THESE:

$50\% = \frac{1}{2}$ $25\% = \frac{1}{4}$ $10\% = \frac{1}{10}$ $33\frac{1}{3}\% = \frac{1}{3}$ $12\frac{1}{2}\% = \frac{1}{8}$

EXAMPLE   Q: Work out $12\frac{1}{2}\%$ of £80

A:
$$12\frac{1}{2}\% \text{ of } £80$$
$$= \frac{1}{8} \text{ of } £80$$
$$= £10$$

Do-med

Change the percentage to a fraction.
Work out the fraction of the amount.

Work out:

1. 50% of 20 m
2. 75% of 8 cm
3. 10% of £200
4. $33\frac{1}{3}\%$ of 15 cm

5. 25% of 40 kg
6. $33\frac{1}{3}\%$ of 60p
7. 10% of 30 m
8. 50% of 10 m

9. $33\frac{1}{3}\%$ of £9
10. 25% of 8*l*
11. 75% of 4 kg
12. $33\frac{1}{3}\%$ of £18

• *Check your answers.*

P1: Practice in finding percentages of amounts

EXAMPLE: Q: Work out 30% of £50
A: 10% of £50 = $^1/_{10}$ of £50 = £5
So,   30% = £15

20%   = 2 x 10%
$33^1/_3$ = $^1/_3$
So, $66^2/_3$% = $^2/_3$

Batch A: *Work out:*
1.   25% of 16 kg
2.   20% of £30
3. $66^2/_3$% of £300
4.   12.5% of £16
5.   40% of 20*l*
6.   80% of 50p
7.   12.5 % of 80 m
8.   75% of 12 m
9.   30% of 40p
10. 12.5 % of £40
11. 20% of 40 kg
12. $33^1/_3$% of 6 cm

• *Check your answers.*

Batch B: *Work out:*
1. $12^1/_2$% of 16p
2.   30% of 20 cm
3.   20% of £10
4.   40% of 20*l*
5.   25% of 44 mm
6.   75% of 44 mm
7.   20% of 55p
8. $66^2/_3$% of 15 m
9. $33^1/_3$% of £60
10. 10% of £1.20
11. 20% of £2.50
12. $33^1/_3$% of £30

• *Check your answers.*

Star Challenge

15 correct = 2 stars
12-14 correct = 1 star

1.   *Work out the sale price of each of these:*
     (a) TV   – usual price £ 400
     (b) Video recorder – usual price £ 300
     (c) Computer – usual price £ 800

**SALE
25% slashed
off all prices**

2. | Erroll is paid a commission on all his sales. He earns 10% of the amount he sells. |

     Work out how much commission he earns if he sells:
     (a)   £400 worth of goods
     (b)   £2 000 worth of goods
     (c)   £250 worth of goods
     (d)   £1500 worth of goods

3. | Noriko puts $12^1/_2$% service charge onto the bills in her restaurant. |

     Work out how much the service charge is on each of these bills:
     (a)   £80
     (b) £ 24
     (c) £40
     (d) £ 72.80

4.   *Work out the sale price of each of these:*

     **CLOSING
     DOWN SALE
     30%
     off all prices**

     (a)   blankets   £15
     (b)   towels   £4.50
     (c)   duvet covers   £21.30
     (d)   pillows   £9.60

• *Your teacher has the answers to these.*

Section 7: x and ÷ by 10, 100

In this section you will multiply and divide decimals by 10, 100 …

D1: x and ÷ by 10, 100

When you **MULTIPLY** a number by 10 the decimal point moves **1 place to the RIGHT**
When you **MULTIPLY** a number by 100 the decimal point moves **2 places to the RIGHT**

Copy each equation. Replace each ☐ *with the correct number.*

1. **4.31 x 10** = ☐
2. **345 x 100** = ☐
3. **43.95 x 10** = ☐

4. **4.1 x 100** = ☐
5. **3.5 x 10** = ☐
6. **0.1234 x 100** = ☐

When you **DIVIDE** a number by 10 the decimal point moves **1 place to the LEFT**
When you **DIVIDE** a number by 100 the decimal point moves **2 places to the LEFT**

Copy each equation. Replace each ☐ *with the correct number.*

7. **2.73 ÷ 10** = ☐
8. **458 ÷ 100** = ☐
9. **25.65 ÷ 10** = ☐

10. **72.1 ÷ 100** = ☐
11. **2.5 ÷ 10** = ☐
12. **123.4 ÷ 100** = ☐

• *Check your answers.*

P1: x and ÷ by 10, 100 mixed practice

Copy each equation. Replace each ☐ *with the correct number.*
CHECK YOUR ANSWERS at the end of each batch.

Batch A:

1. **5.97 x 10** = ☐
2. **278 x 100** = ☐
3. **31.82 ÷ 10** = ☐
4. **0.0036 x 10** = ☐
5. **0.049 ÷ 100** = ☐

6. **8.3 x 100** = ☐
7. **7.5 ÷ 100** = ☐
8. **0.1234 x 100** = ☐
9. **35.41 ÷ 10** = ☐
10. **14 ÷ 10** = ☐

Batch B:

1. **14.3 x 10** = ☐
2. **3.579 ÷ 10** = ☐
3. **143 ÷ 100** = ☐
4. **0.367 x 100** = ☐
5. **15 ÷ 100** = ☐

6. **270 ÷ 10** = ☐
7. **3500 ÷ 100** = ☐
8. **2435 ÷ 100** = ☐
9. **1.691 x 100** = ☐
10. **0.0004 x 100** = ☐

Batch C:

1. **0.3 x 10** = ☐
2. **4.35 ÷ 100** = ☐
3. **2.51 ÷ 10** = ☐
4. **0.23 x 100** = ☐
5. **2.5 x 100** = ☐
6. **350 x 10** = ☐
7. **4210 ÷ 100** = ☐
8. **125 ÷ 100** = ☐
9. **2.967 x 100** = ☐
10. **0.003 x 100** = ☐

P2: ? = what ?

Copy these equations. Replace each ? with the correct number.

1. **3.57 x ? = 357**
2. **13.82 x ? = 138.2**
3. **59.5 ÷ ? = 5.95**
4. **817.2 ÷ ? = 8.172**
5. **0.742 x ? = 74.2**
6. **0.035 x ? = 3.5**
7. **1500 ÷ ? = 15**
8. **23 x ? = 2300**

• Check your answers.

Star Challenge 12

9-10 correct = 1 star

Copy each equation. Replace each ☐ with the correct number or sign.

1. **43 x 10** = ☐
2. **7.961 x 100** = ☐
3. **15.66 ÷ 10** = ☐
4. **45 x ☐** = **4500**
5. **84.31 x ☐** = **843.1**
6. **2.7 x 100** = ☐
7. **9.98 ÷ 100** = ☐
8. **0.336 x 100** = ☐
9. **4.5 x ☐** = **4500**
10. **7.5 ÷ ☐** = **0.75**

• Your teacher has the answers to these.

Star Challenge 13 13 13

27 correct = 3 stars
24-26 correct = 2 stars
20-23 correct = 1 star

On the next page is a series of boxes.
Each box has a mathematical expression in it.
Match each of the boxes with an equivalent expression
from those outside the boxes.

There is at least one matching expression for each box.
Write the equivalent expression inside the box.

Icee

You will need a pencil and rubber.

Idea

• Your teacher has the answers to these.

Match each of the boxes with an equivalent expression
from those outside the boxes.

37	**3.47 x 10**	**43.7**	**437 ÷ 10**	4.37 x 10
43.7	**7 ÷ 10**	**43 x 10**	**0.3x100+7**	740
34.70				7.43
0.70	**$4 + \dfrac{3}{10} + \dfrac{7}{100}$**	**$3 + \dfrac{7}{10} + \dfrac{4}{100}$**	**$7 + \dfrac{43}{100}$**	10
430				34.7
3.47	**74.3 ÷ 100**	**34.7 ÷ 10**	**0.347 x 100**	
7.43				37.4 ÷10
347 ÷100	**$\dfrac{10}{10}$**	**$\dfrac{100}{10}$**	**$\dfrac{10}{100}$**	4.37
4.37	**3.470**	**43.7 x 100**	**374**	7.43
3470				743
740	**7.43 x 100**	**7.4 + 0.03**	**7 + 0.43**	0.1
37.4 x10	**74 x 10**	**43.7**	**7.4 x 100**	7.34
1				0.743
4.37 x 100	**34.7 x 100**	**73.4 ÷ 10**	**43.7 ÷ 10**	4730

Section 8: Measurement calculations

In this section you will:
- convert from one set of metric units to another using x and ÷ by 10, 100 …;
- work with metric and imperial equivalents.

D1: Working with metric units

1 cm = 10 mm	1 m = 100 cm	1 km = 1000 m

> 1 m = 100 cm
> so, to change m to cm,
> x by 100

Modesto

Copy and complete:

1.	1.35 m = …… cm	6.	34 cm	= …… m	11.	340 mm	= …… cm
2.	3 m = …… cm	7.	256 cm	= …… m	12.	7 mm	= …… cm
3.	2.7 m = …… cm	8.	60 cm	= …… m	13.	2.8 cm	= …… mm
4.	0.72 m = …… cm	9.	4 cm	= …… m	14.	35 cm	= …… mm
5.	0.05 m = …… cm	10.	45 mm	= …… cm	15.	0.08 cm	= …… mm

1000 g = 1 kg
1000 kg = 1 tonne

1000 *ml* = 1 *l*
100 *cl* = 1 *l*

16.	3000 g = …… kg	21.	4 kg	= …… g	26.	80 *cl*	= …… *l*
17.	240 g = …… kg	22.	4.5 kg	= …… g	27.	5 *cl*	= …… *l*
18.	35 g = …… kg	23.	45 kg	= …… g	28.	1 *cl*	= …… *l*
19.	8 g = …… kg	24.	3 tonnes	= …… kg	29.	2000 *ml*	= …… *l*
20.	26.5 g = …… kg	25.	2.5 tonnes	= …… kg	30.	35 *ml*	= …… *l*

- *Check your answers.*

P1: A mixture of metric conversions

Copy and complete:

1.	3.46 m = …… cm	6.	2.3 tonnes	= …… kg	11.	2.3 cm	= …… mm
2.	243 cm = …… m	7.	3.48 cm	= …… mm	12.	9 mm	= …… cm
3.	5.7 kg = …… g	8.	45 mm	= …… cm	13.	43 cm	= …… m
4.	0.72 kg = …… g	9.	75 cm	= …… m	14.	765 m	= …… km
5.	0.03 *l* = …… *ml*	10.	48 *cl*	= …… *l*	15.	3.28 cm	= …… mm

- *Check your answers.*

Star Challenge ★14 14★

> 14-15 correct = 2 stars
> 10-13 correct = 1 star

Copy and complete:

1.	42 cm = …… m	6.	5 tonnes	= …… kg	11.	660 m	= …… km
2.	547 g = …… kg	7.	0.2 km	= …… m	12.	93 g	= …… kg
3.	6.5 m = …… cm	8.	85 m	= …… km	13.	0.6 m	= …… cm
4.	300 *ml* = …… *l*	9.	0.1 kg	= …… g	14.	200 g	= …… kg
5.	0.45 *l* = …… *cl*	10.	3.4 tonnes	= …… kg	15.	0.5 mm	= …… cm

- *Your teacher has the answers to these.*

D2: Using equivalent values to solve problems

1. $\boxed{12'' = 1 \text{ foot} \approx 30 \text{ cm}}$

   Kim wants to buy some shorts when on holiday in Spain.

   In England she looks for waist size 24". **What size should she look for in Spain ?**

2. Caris buys jeans with hip size 90 cm.

   She thinks they are the same size as 36" hips in England. **Is she right ?**

3. $\boxed{1'' \approx 2.5 \text{ cm} = 25 \text{ mm}}$

   Dave is sent by his dad to buy some 2" nails.

   The nails in the D.I.Y. shop are   2 cm   4 cm   5 cm   6 cm

   Which should he buy ?

4. Dave's dad has gone to buy a kitchen cupboard. He wants a cupboard that is 30" wide. The measurements of those in the shop are given in mm.

          500 mm   600 mm   800 mm   900 mm   1000 mm

   Which is the nearest size to the one he wants ?

5. $\boxed{1 \text{ ounce} = 1 \text{ oz} \approx 28 \text{ g}}$

   Peter's grandmother asks him to get her 4 ounces of sweets from the supermarket. The weights of the packets of sweets there are:

          50g   100 g   150 g   200 g   400 g

   Which is the nearest size to the one he wants ?

6. $\boxed{5 \text{ miles} \approx 8 \text{ km}}$

   The distance from Merrivale to Cherree is 15 miles.

   How far is that roughly in km ?

Star Challenge 15

• *Check your answers.*

$\boxed{\text{All correct} = 1 \text{ star}}$

1. $\boxed{1 \text{ kg} \approx 2 \text{ lb} = 2 \text{ pounds}}$

   Sue weighs 120 lb. Her sister, Ellen, gives her weight as 75 kg.

   Which one is heavier ?

2. $\boxed{1 \text{ kg} \approx 2.2 \text{ lb} = 2.2 \text{ pounds}}$

   Mark needs 10lb of sugar to make jam. **How many kilograms should he buy ?**

3. Ethel asks her mother to give her 2 kg of sugar to make jam at school the next day.

   Her mother says "What is that in pounds ?"

   How many pounds of sugar should her mother give her ?

4. $\boxed{1 \text{ litre} \approx 1.75 \text{ pints} \qquad 1 \text{ gallon} = 8 \text{ pints}}$

   The petrol tank on Yossi's car holds 60 litres.

   (a) **Roughly how many pints does it hold ?**

   (b) **What is its capacity in gallons, to the nearest gallon ?**

   • *Your teacher has the answers to these.*

Section 9: Ratios

In this section you will:
- review ratios of enlargements;
- work with equivalent ratios;
- solve problems involving ratios;
- share in ratio.

D1: Reviewing ratios and enlargements

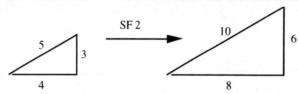

These triangles are similar. Their sides are in the same proportion, or ratio.

The ratio of the longest sides is 5 : 10

The ratio of the shortest sides is 3 : 6

The ratio of the two other sides is 4 : 8

> Read 5 : 10
> as '5 to 10'

The ratio of every pair of corresponding sides is 1 : 2 since every side is doubled in the enlargement.

> 5 : 10   3 : 6   4 : 8   1 : 2
>
> are all **equivalent ratios**
>
> 1 : 2 is the **simplest form** of this ratio.

The shapes in these questions are not drawn to scale.

1.

These two shapes are similar.

(a) What is the ratio of the two longest sides ?

(b) What is the ratio of the two shortest sides ?

(c) What is the ratio of the two other sides ?

(d) What is the simplest form of the ratio of the sides ?

(e) What is the scale factor of the enlargement ?

2.

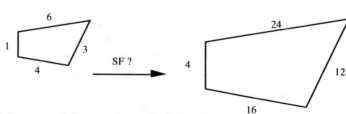

These two shapes are similar.

(a) What are the four ratios of the matching pairs of sides ?

(b) What is the simplest form of this ratio ?

(c) What is the scale factor of the enlargement ?

3. **These two triangles are similar.**

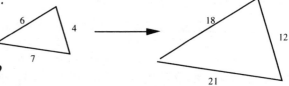

   (a) What are the three ratios of the corresponding pairs of sides ?

   (b) What is the simplest form of the ratio ?

   (c) What is the scale factor of the enlargement ?

4.

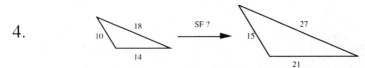

These two triangles are similar.

   (a) What are the three ratios of the corresponding pairs of sides ?

   (b) What is the simplest form of the ratio ?

   (c) What is the scale factor of the enlargement ?

5. These two shapes are similar.

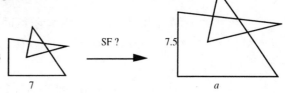

   (a) What is the scale factor of the enlargement ?

   (b) What is the value of a ?

   (c) What is the simplest form of the ratio of the sides ?   • *Check your answers.*

D2: Equivalent ratios

Equivalent ratios		Equivalent fractions
$\div 3 \begin{array}{c} 8 : 24 \\ = 1 : 3 \end{array} \div 3$	are just like	$\dfrac{8}{24} \xrightarrow{\div 3} \dfrac{1}{3} \xleftarrow{\div 3}$
1 : 3 is the simplest form of this ratio		$^1\!/_3$ is the simplest form of this fraction

Find the simplest form of each of these ratios:

  1.   2 : 6   2.   9 : 15   3.   36 : 48   4.   6 : 10   5.   12 : 30

  6.   4 : 6   7.   6 : 18   8.   24 : 12   9.   9 : 6   10.   25 : 30

EXAMPLE   Q   3 : 5 = 6 : a What is a ?
A   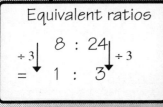 So, <u>a = 10</u>

Find the number that each letter stands for:

  11. 2 : 6 = 8 : b   12. 3 : 4 = c : 16   13. d : 28 = 2 : 7

  14. 3 : 2 = 24 : e   15. 4 : 9 = f : 27   16. g : 6 = 11 : 2

17. In 11MN, the ratio of boys to girls is 2 : 3. There are 10 boys. How many girls are there ?

18. In 11PK, the ratio of boys to girls is also 2 : 3. There are 18 girls. How many boys are there ?

                                                     • *Check your answers*

D3: Mixing in ratio

> Mixing paint colours   a certain shade of green paint is made in this ratio
>   blue : yellow = 3 : 2

1. You use 4 spoonfuls of yellow. How many spoonfuls of blue will you need ?

2. For a large amount of green paint, 12 buckets of blue are used.
    How many buckets of yellow are used ?

> Shortcrust pastry –   flour : fat = 2 : 1

3. (a)   How much flour should you use with 50 g of fat ?
    (b)   How much fat should you use with 50 g of flour ?

> All concrete is made from three ingredients
>   – cement, sand and aggregate (small stones).
> The ratio of cement, sand and aggregate varies according to what the concrete
> is to be used for.
>   For foundations, the mix is 2 : 5 : 7
>   (2 buckets of cement : 5 buckets of sand : 7 buckets of aggregate)

4   Concrete is being mixed for building foundations.
    Henry puts 10 shovels of cement into the mixer.
    How much sand should he put in ?   How much aggregate ?

5. | Foundation mix   2 : 5 : 7 |

Copy and complete this table:

Cement	4	...	1	...	...	...	...
Sand	...	20	...	25	...	15	...
Aggregate	...	...	...	...	70	...	63

6. | General purpose concrete is 1 : 2 : 3 |

    (a) How many spadefuls of sand are needed with 3 spadefuls of cement ?
    (b) How many buckets of aggregate are needed with 4 buckets of sand ?
    (c) Mick uses $1\frac{1}{2}$ barrowloads of aggregate.
        How much cement and sand should he mix with it ?

7. | For concrete paving, the mix is 2 : 3 : 5 |

Copy and complete this table:

Cement	4	...	1	...	...	...	...
Sand	...	21	...	27	...	15	...
Aggregate	...	...	...	...	100	...	40

8. | Fast–set glue   resin : hardener = 4 : 5 |

    (a)   How many drops of hardener should you use with 12 drops of resin ?
    (b)   How many drops of resin should you use with 20 drops of hardener ?

• *Check your answers.*

D4: Sharing in ratio

Example   Q: Emily, Ann and Mary are to share £250 in the ratio 4 : 5 : 1
How much do they each get ?

Big Edd

4 + 5 + 1 = 10
so divide the
money into
10 parts

£250 ÷ 10 = £25

Emily gets 4 parts of
the money − 4 x £25
= £100

Ann gets 5 parts of
the money − 5 x £25
= £125

Mary gets 1 part of
the money − that is,
£25

1.   Share £80 in the ratio 3 : 5   4.   Divide £60 in the ratio 1 : 2 : 7
2.   Share £35 in the ratio 2 : 3   5.   Divide £140 in the ratio 2 : 1 : 4
3.   Share £30 in the ratio 1 : 5   6.   Share £200 in the ratio 2 : 3 : 3

7.   At an election, 4 500 people voted. The ratio of the votes was:
    Labour : Conservative : Liberal Democrat = 4 : 2 : 3
    How many votes did the Liberal Democrats get ?

Star Challenge 16 16

• *Check your answers.*

6 marks = 2 stars
4-5 marks = 1 star

1.   The lengths of two pencils are in the ratio 3 : 5.
     The smaller pencil is 15 cm long.
     How long is the other pencil ?

     Glugl   (1 mark)

2.   A 35 cm piece of string is cut in the ratio 2 : 5.
     What is the length of the shorter piece ?   (1 mark)

3.   Every year the Pan-Galactic Academy publishes its final exam results.
     In 2462, number of trainees who passed : number who failed = 4 : 1
     120 trainees passed. **How many failed ?**

      *Mishrak*

4.   In the new intake at the Pan-Galactic Academy in 2463,
     the ratio of humanoids to insectoids was   5 : 3.
     There were 40 humanoids. **How many insectoids were there ?**   (1 mark)

5.   In the Pan-Galactic Federation, in 2463, there are 240 uninhabited
     planets and 180 inhabited planets.   (1 mark)
     Give the ratio   uninhabited planets : habited planets   in its simplest form

6.   Paul, Shirley and Carol started their own business. At the beginning, Paul
     put £500 into the business, Shirley put in £400 and Carol put in £200.

     (a) **What is the simplest form of the ratio of these amounts.**

     (b) At the end of the first year, they had profits of £3,300.   (2 marks)
          They shared the profits in the same ratio as the money they put in.
          How much did Paul get ?   • *Your teacher has the answers to these.*

Section 10: Return to decimals

In this section you will order decimals.

D1: Ordering decimals

EXAMPLE   Q: Arrange these numbers in order of size, with the smallest first:

0.03   0.51   0. 15

A:

U . t h	
0 . 0 3	$= {}^3/_{100}$
0 . 5 1	$= {}^{51}/_{100}$
0 . 1 5	$= {}^{15}/_{100}$

So, $0.03 < 0.15 < 0.51$

The order is 0.03, 0.15, 0.51

Chyps

Arrange the numbers in order of size, with the smallest first.

1. 0.4   0.2   0.5
2. 0.1   0.01   0.001
3. 0.35   0.17   0.21
4. 0.53   0.35   0. 33
5. 0.23   0.023   0.0023
6. 0.6   0.2   0.9

I want to put 0.34, 0.03, 0.303 in order of size, with the smallest first.
I know an easy way !

0.34 =   0.340
0.03 =   0.030
0.303=   0.303

Fission

I know that 030 < 303 < 340 so the order is 0.03   0.303   0.34

Arrange the numbers in order of size, with the smallest first.

7. 0.23   0.203   0.32
8. 0.05   0.04   0.45
9. 0.7   0.67   0.677
10. 0.1   0.09   0.9
11. 0.007   0.07   0.69
12. 0.15   0.51   0.015

• *Check your answers.*

Arrange the numbers in order of size, with the smallest first.

13. 0.709   0.71   0.7
14. 0.1   0.01   0.11
15. 0.04   0.14   0.014
16. 0.001   0.03   0.2
17. 0.0 , 0.12   0.2   0.133
18. 1.4   0.14   1.14   0.41
19. 2.3   2.03   2.13   2.003
20. 3.05   3.5   3   3.056
21. 1.75   1.57   5.71   5.17

• *Check your answers.*

Star Challenge ⭐17⭐17

14-16 correct = 2 stars
10-13 correct = 1 star

Say whether each of these is TRUE (T) or false (F):

1. $0.6 = 0.60$
2. $0.6 = 0.06$
3. $0.4 = .4$
4. $0.63 > 0.36$
5. $0.51 < 0.15$
6. $5.03 > 5.30$
7. $7 = 7.0$
8. $0.79 \leq 0.8$
9. $0.9 > 0.85$
10. $0.7 < 0.07$
11. $0.214 < 0.215$
12. $0.35 < 0.36$
13. $6 = 0.6$
14. $0.3 = 0.03$
15. $8.1 < 8.11$
16. $5.2 < 5.02$

$<$ is 'less than' $>$ is 'more than'

• *Your teacher has the answers to these.*

THE NATIONAL CURRICULUM ...
... AND BEYOND ...

Sureshot

Understanding
Geometry

EXTRA

Part 2

Understanding Geometry EXTRA *Part 2*
Section 1: Defining area

In this section you will work out areas by counting squares.

DEVELOPMENT

D1: What is area ?

The **area** of a shape is how much surface it has.

The most common unit of area is 1 cm²

1 cm / 1 cm

The area of this shape is 3 cm²

Work out the area of each of these shapes:

A

B

C

D

• *Check your answers.*

Section 2: Areas of rectangles

In this section you will:
- work out areas of rectangles by counting squares;
- work out areas of rectangles using a formula;
- work out areas of rectangles when too much information has been given.

D1: Areas of rectangles by counting squares

Work out the area of each rectangle:

1.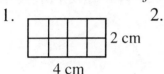
4 cm, 2 cm

2.
3 cm, 3 cm

3.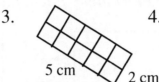
5 cm, 2 cm

4.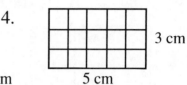
5 cm, 3 cm

5.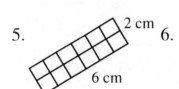
6 cm, 2 cm

6.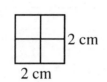
2 cm, 2 cm

7.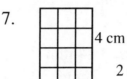
3 cm, 4 cm

8.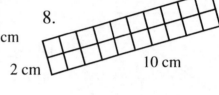
10 cm, 2 cm

- *Check your answers.*

D2: Areas of rectangles using a formula

Area of ☐ = *length* x *width*   ☐ *width*
                                          length $A = l \times w$

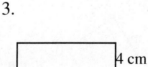
6 cm   Area = 60 cm²
10 cm

Work out the area of each rectangle:

1. 6 cm, 3 cm

2. 5 cm, 5 cm

3. 6 cm, 4 cm

4. 10 cm, 5 cm

5. 6 cm, 9 cm

6.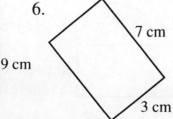
7 cm, 3 cm

7. length = 5 cm
   width = 2 cm

8. length = 20 cm
   width = 4 cm

- *Check your answers.*

P1: Units of area

$A = l \times w$

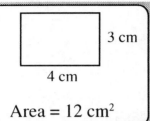

Area = 12 cm²

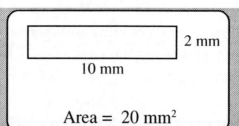

Area = 20 mm²

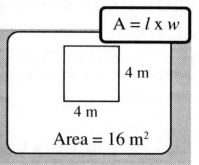

Area = 16 m²

Work out the area of each rectangle. Each answer must have the correct unit of area.

1. 5 cm, 3 cm

2. 2 mm, 4 mm

3. 3 m, 6 m

4. 10 mm, 3 mm

5. 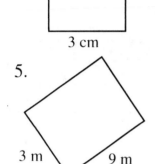 3 m, 9 m

6. length = 14 mm
   width = 2 mm

7. length = 7 m
   width = 5 m

8. length = 3 km
   width = 2 km

9. length = 5 cm
   width = 4 cm

10. length = 3 mm
    width = 4 mm

11. length = 12 m
    width = 3 m

• *Check your answers.*

D3: Choosing your information

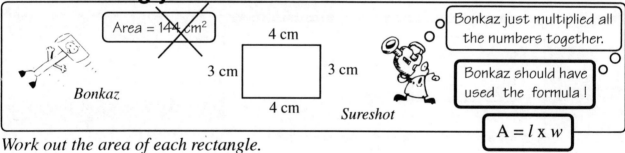

Area = 144 cm²

4 cm

3 cm   3 cm

4 cm

Bonkaz   *Sureshot*

Bonkaz just multiplied all
the numbers together.

Bonkaz should have
used the formula !

$A = l \times w$

Work out the area of each rectangle.
Choose the information you need.   Use the formula.

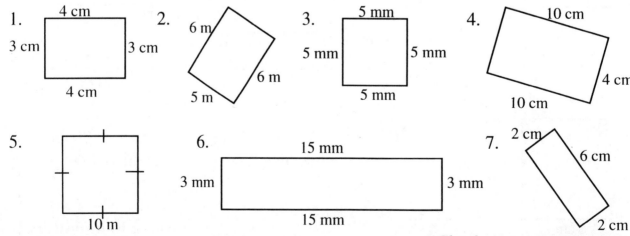

1. 4 cm, 3 cm, 3 cm, 4 cm

2. 6 m, 6 m, 5 m

3. 5 mm, 5 mm, 5 mm, 5 mm

4. 10 cm, 4 cm, 10 cm

5. 10 m

6. 15 mm, 3 mm, 3 mm, 15 mm

7. 2 cm, 6 cm, 2 cm

• *Check your answers.*

Section 3: Compound shapes

In this section you will:
- make compound shapes from rectangles with given areas;
- break down compound shapes into rectangles to work out the area.

D1: Creating L

$A = l \times w$ ⟹ **P** ✂ 📄

Task 1: Measure each rectangle.
Write the length and width INSIDE the rectangle.
Work out the area. Write the area inside the rectangle.

One has been done for you.

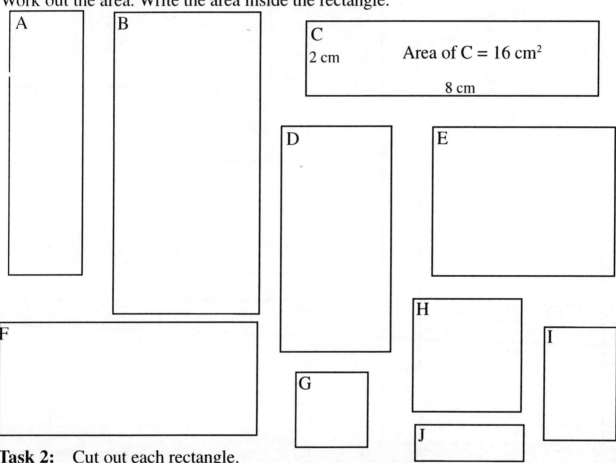

A

B

C
2 cm   Area of C = 16 cm²
                    8 cm

D   E

F   H   I

G   J

Task 2: Cut out each rectangle.

Put two rectangles together to make an L with an area of 50 cm²
Put two rectangles together to make an L with an area of 27 cm²
Put two rectangles together to make an L with an area of 17 cm²
Put two rectangles together to make an L with an area of 25 cm²
Put two rectangles together to make an L with an area of 24 cm²

• *Check answers.*

Star Challenge ⭐1

Task 3: Stick each L into your book.

Beside each L, draw an exact copy of the L, but do not split it into rectangles.

On your copy, write in the dimensions.

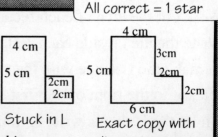

4 cm
5 cm
2cm
2cm
Stuck in L

4 cm
5 cm
3cm
2cm
2cm
6 cm
Exact copy with dimensions on it.

• *Your teacher will need to mark this.*

D2: Reverse Ls

Task 1: Cut round <u>one copy</u> of each L shape.

Stick the L shapes down the left hand side of your page.

Measure the dimensions of each shape and write them on the shape.

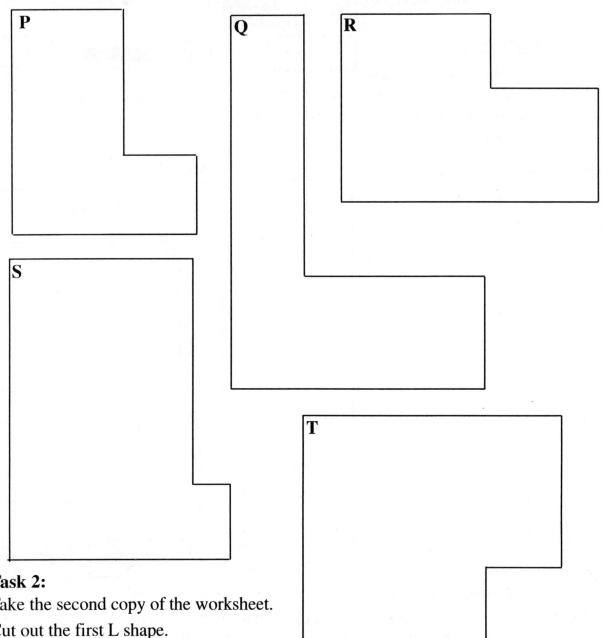

Task 2:

Take the second copy of the worksheet.

Cut out the first L shape.

Cut the L shape into two rectangles.

Measure the length and width of each rectangle.

Write the measurements inside each rectangle. $A = l \times w$

Work out the area of each rectangle.

Write the area inside each rectangle.

Remake the L shape with the two rectangles.

Stick it to the right of the first copy.

Under the L shape, write its total area.

• *Check your answers.*

D3: Compound areas without measuring

For each shape:
- *sketch the shape in your book*
- *write the area of each rectangle inside the rectangle*
- *work out the area of the whole shape.*

$$A = l \times w$$

W 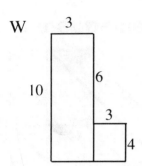 X 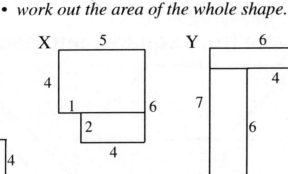 Y 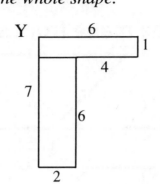 Z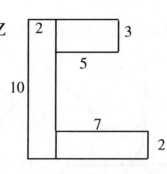

- *Check your answers.*

D4: Now you split them into rectangles

For each shape:
- *make a sketch of the shape in your book*
- *divide the shape up into rectangles*
- *write the area inside each rectangle*
- *work out the area of the whole shape.*

A 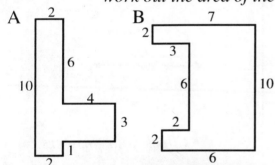 C 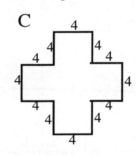 D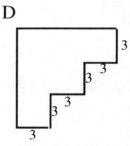

- *Check your answers.*

Star Challenge ⭐2 ⭐2 ⭐2

1 star for each correct shape and its area

For each shape:
- *draw a sketch of the shape in your book;*
- *replace the letters with the correct lengths;*
- *divide the shape up into rectangles;*
- *work out the area of the shape.*

P 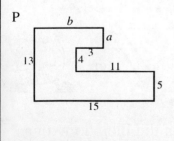 Q 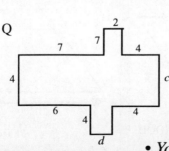 R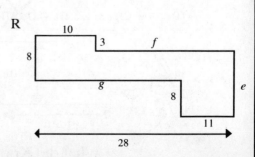

- *Your teacher has the answers to these.*

A SURESHOT GUIDE   page 163   Understanding Geometry Part 2   **EXTRA**

Section 4: Areas of parallelograms

In this section you will work out areas of parallelograms:
 • by counting squares;
 • using a formula.

D1: Parallelograms made from squares and half squares

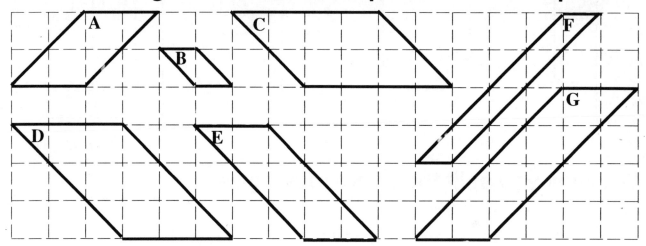

Copy and complete this table:

	length of base	height	area
A			
B			
C			
D			
E			
F			
G			

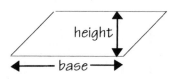

• *Check your answers.*

D2: Using the formula and getting it wrong

Area of a parallelogram = base x height

$A = b \times h$

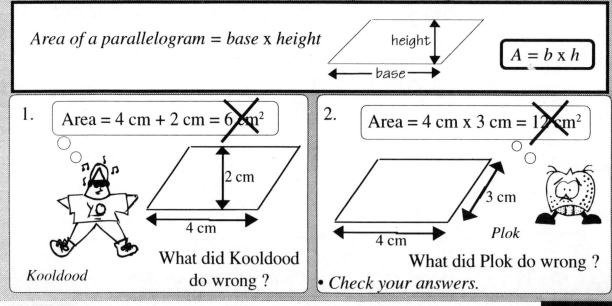

1. Area = 4 cm + 2 cm = 6 cm²

   2 cm
   4 cm

   Kooldood

   What did Kooldood do wrong ?

2. Area = 4 cm x 3 cm = 12 cm²

   3 cm
   4 cm
   Plok

   What did Plok do wrong ?

• *Check your answers.*

D3: Areas of parallelograms using the formula

Area of a parallelogram = base x height $A = b \times h$

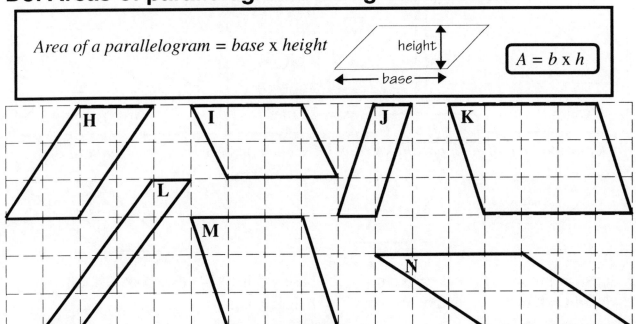

1. Copy and complete this table. Use the formula to work out each area.

	length of base	height	area
H			
I			
J			
K			
L			
M			
N			

2. Measure each of these parallelograms.
   Make a table showing the length of base, the height and the area of each.

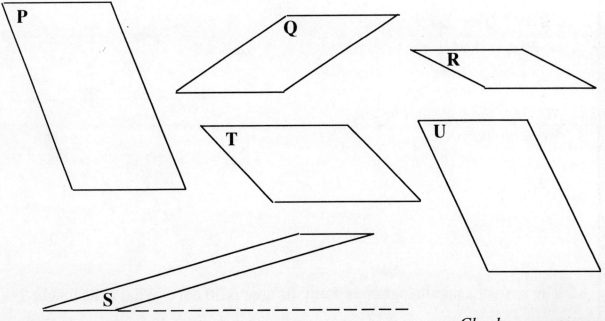

• Check your answers.

D4: Use the correct units and choose the information

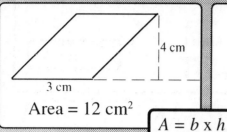

4 cm

3 cm

Area = 12 cm²

$A = b \times h$

5 mm

4 mm

Area = 20 mm²

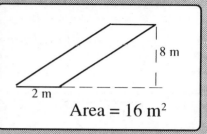

8 m

2 m

Area = 16 m²

Work out the area of each parallelogram. Give each answer the correct unit of area.

1.

3 mm

5 mm

2.
7 cm

2 cm

3.
6 m

3 m

4.
6 cm

10 cm

5. base = 5 mm
   height = 2 mm

6. base = 6 cm
   height = 4 cm

7. base = 5 m
   height = 4 m

8. base = 4 km
   height = 2 km

Work out the area of each parallelogram.
Choose the information you need. Use the formula. $A = b \times h$

9.
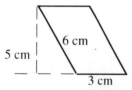
6 cm

5 cm

3 cm

10.
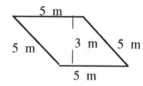
5 m

5 m   3 m   5 m

5 m

• *Check your answers.*

Star Challenge ⭐3⭐3

8 correct = 2 stars
6-7 correct = 1 star

Work out the area of the parallelograms described below.
Each answer must have the correct unit of area.

1. base = 3 cm   height = 6 cm

2. base = 10 mm   height = 5 mm

3. base = 4 m   height = 2 m

4. base = 8 cm   height = 3 cm

5.
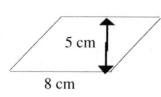
5 cm

8 cm

6.
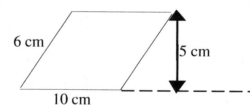
6 cm

5 cm

10 cm

7. *Measure the base and height.*
   Work out the area.

8. The base of a parallelogram is 5 cm. Its area is 30 cm². What is its height ?

• *Your teacher has the answers to these.*

Section 5: Areas of triangles

In this section you will :
- find the connection between the areas of parallelograms and triangles;
- work out the area of any triangle.

DEVELOPMENT

D1: Parallelograms and triangles

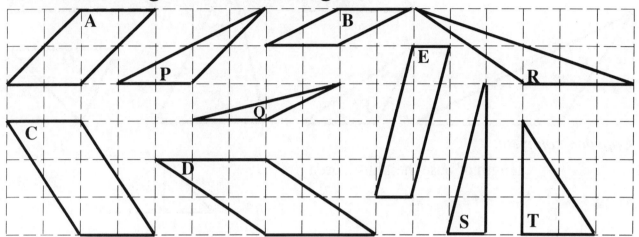

Each triangle is half the area of one of the parallelograms.

Δ P is half the area of parallelogram A

Match up each parallelogram and the triangle which is half its area.

• *Check your answers.*

D2: Rule for the area of a triangle

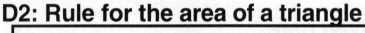

= half of

height

base

Area of Δ = ¹/₂ (base x height)

$A = \frac{1}{2}(b \times h)$

EXAMPLE

3 cm

8 cm

Area = ¹/₂ (3 x 8)
    = ¹/₂ x 24 = 12

Work out the area of each triangle:

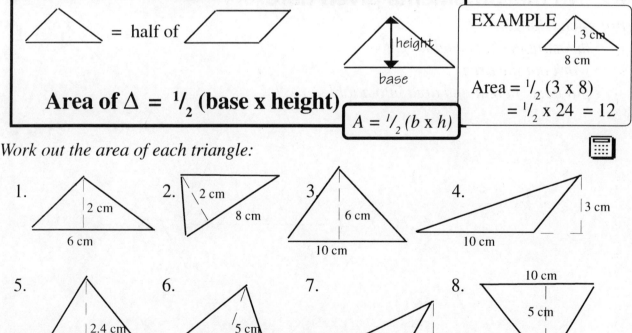

1.
2 cm
6 cm

2.
2 cm
8 cm

3.
6 cm
10 cm

4.
3 cm
10 cm

5.
2.4 cm
10 cm

6.
5 cm
8.2 cm

7.
4.4 cm
8 cm

8.
10 cm
5 cm

• *Check your answers.*

P1: Areas of triangles

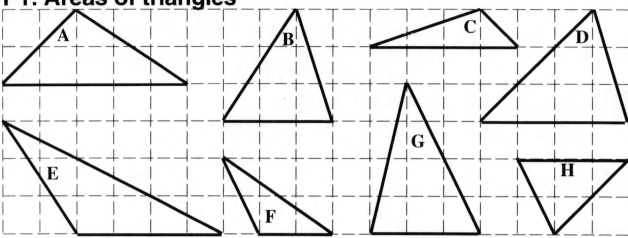

Copyand complete:

	length of base	height	area
A			
B			
C			
D			
E			
F			
G			
H			

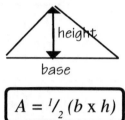

$$A = {}^1/_2 (b \times h)$$

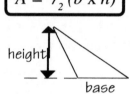

• *Check your answers.*

P2: No measurements given here

For each triangle:
- • *measure the base and height*
- • *work out the area*
- • *put base, height and area into a table.*

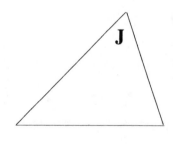

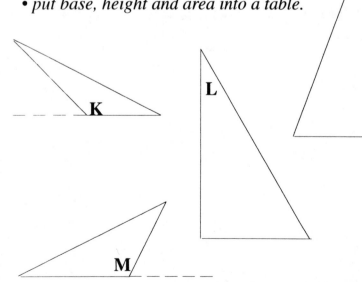

• *Check your answers.*

P1: Altogether now

Rectangle	Parallelogram	Triangle
width, length	height, base	height, base
Area = length x width	Area = base x height	Area = $\frac{1}{2}$(base x height)
$A = l \times w$	$A = b \times h$	$A = \frac{1}{2}(b \times h)$

Work out the area of each shape. Choose the correct information and formula.

Batch A:

1. 3 cm, 5 cm
2. 2 m, 6 m
3. 3 mm, 8 mm
4. 5 cm, 4 cm
5. 3 m, 8 m, 8 m, 3 m
6. 13 cm, 12 cm, 5 cm
7. 4 m, 5 m, 5 m
8. 10 cm, 20 cm

• *Check your answers.*

Batch B:

1. 3 m, 6 m
2. 10 cm, 10 cm, 5 cm
3. 4 cm, 4 cm, 5 cm
4. 5 cm
5. 6 mm, 3 mm
6. 2 m, 10 m
7. 2 cm, 2 cm, 5 cm
8. 5 cm, 4 cm, 6 cm

• *Check your answers.*

Star Challenge ★4★4★4

36 marks = 3 stars
30-35 marks = 2 stars
24-29 marks = 1 star

Work out the area of each shape. Choose the correct information and formula.

1. 4 m, 7 m
2. 10 mm, 12 mm
3. 4 cm, 10 cm
4. 6 cm, 6 cm, 6 cm, 6 cm
5. 4 cm, 3 cm, 6 cm
6. 3 cm, 4 cm, 4 cm
7. 5 mm, 8 mm
8. 5 m, 3 m, 5 m
9. 10 cm, 8 cm, 6 cm
10. 5 cm, 4 cm
11. 6 mm, 3 mm
12. 10 cm, 4 cm, 5 cm

2 marks for each correct area
1 mark for each correct unit

• *Check your answers.*

Section 7: Perimeter

In this section you will work with the perimeters of a variety of shapes.

DEVELOPMENT

D1: Perimeters

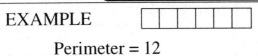 Perimeter = distance round the edge of a shape

 Sureshot

EXAMPLE

Perimeter = 12

Work out the perimeter of each shape:

1.   2.   3. 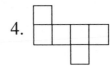   4.   5.

6.   7.   8.   9.   10.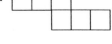

• *Check answers.*

D2: Perimeters using measurements

Work out the perimeter of each shape:

1.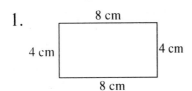
8 cm, 4 cm, 4 cm, 8 cm

2.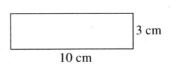
3 cm, 10 cm

3.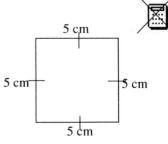
5 cm, 5 cm, 5 cm, 5 cm

4.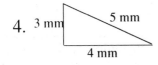
3 mm, 5 mm, 4 mm

5.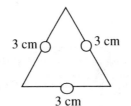
3 cm, 3 cm, 3 cm

6.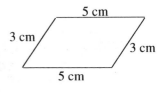
5 cm, 3 cm, 3 cm, 5 cm

7.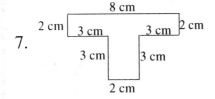
8 cm, 2 cm, 3 cm, 3 cm, 2 cm, 3 cm, 3 cm, 2 cm

8.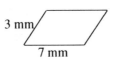
3 mm, 7 mm

9.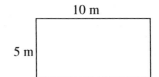
10 m, 5 m

10.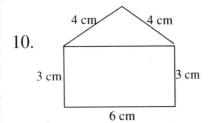
4 cm, 4 cm, 3 cm, 3 cm, 6 cm

11.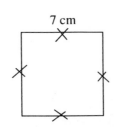
7 cm

12.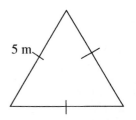
5 m

A SURESHOT GUIDE   page 170   Understanding Geometry Part 2 **EXTRA**

P1: Measure and work out perimeter

Measure each length.
Write the measurements on each diagram.
Work out each perimeter.

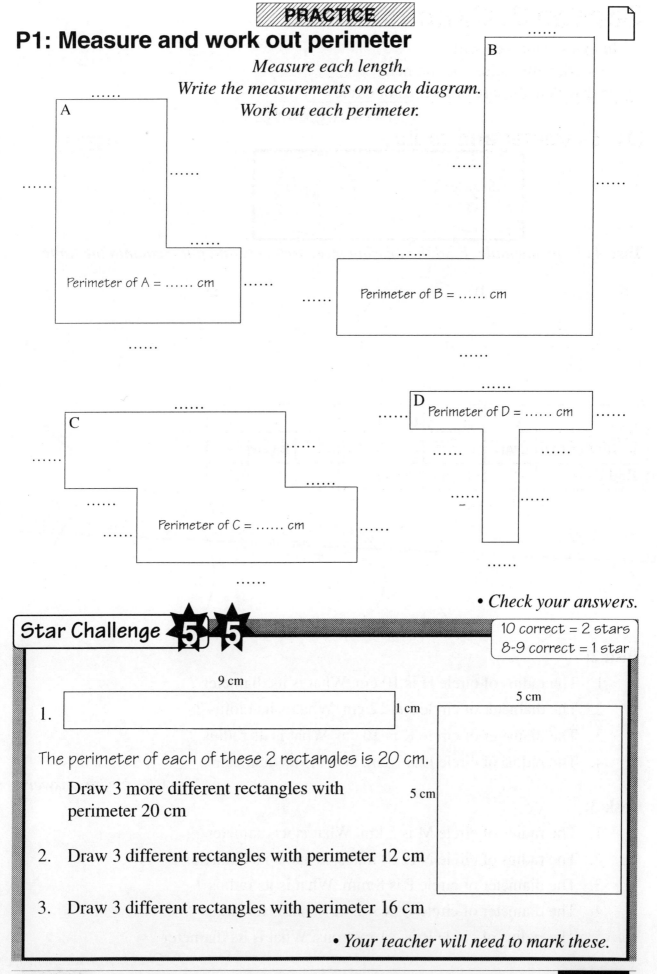

A

......

......

......

......

Perimeter of A = ... cm

......

......

B

......

......

......

......

Perimeter of B = ... cm

......

......

C

......

......

......

......

......

......

Perimeter of C = ... cm

......

......

......

D

......

Perimeter of D = ... cm

......

......

......

......

......

......

......

• *Check your answers.*

Star Challenge 5 5

10 correct = 2 stars
8-9 correct = 1 star

1.
9 cm

1 cm

5 cm

5 cm

The perimeter of each of these 2 rectangles is 20 cm.

Draw 3 more different rectangles with perimeter 20 cm

2. Draw 3 different rectangles with perimeter 12 cm

3. Draw 3 different rectangles with perimeter 16 cm

• *Your teacher will need to mark these.*

Section 8: Circumference

In this section you will:
- work with radius and diameter;
- calculate the circumference of circles.

DEVELOPMENT

D1: Diameter and radius

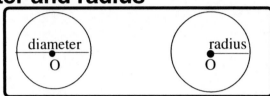

Task 1: *Copy the table. Find the missing measurements and put them into the table.*

A ⃝   B ⃝   C ⃝   D ⃝

Circle	A	B	C	D	E	F	G
Diameter (*d*)	2cm					2.8 cm	
Radius (*r*)		1½cm	½cm				2.2 cm

E ⃝   F ⃝   G ⃝

Task 2:

1. The radius of circle H is 10 cm. What is its diameter ?
2. The diameter of circle J is 12 cm. What is its radius ?
3. The diameter of circle K is 16 cm. What is its radius ?
4. The radius of circle L is 7 cm. What is its diameter ?

• *Check your answers.*

Task 3:

1. The radius of circle M is 5 km. What is its diameter ?
2. The radius of circle N is 10 miles. What is its diameter ?
3. The diameter of circle P is 8 mm. What is its radius ?
4. The diameter of circle Q is 4.2 m What is its radius ?
5. The radius of circle R is 11 metrons. What is its diameter ?

• *Check your answers.*

D2: The circumference of a circle

> The perimeter of a circle has a special name.
> The perimeter of a circle is called **the circumference.**
> The circumference is approximately 3.1 x diameter.
>
> $$C = 3.1 \times d$$

Work out the circumference of a circle …

1. … with diameter 10 cm
2. … with diameter 3 cm
3. … with diameter 4.5 cm
4. … with diameter 6 m
5. … with radius 4 cm
6. … with radius 10 m
7. … with radius 2.1 cm
8. … with radius 15 m
9. … with diameter 7 cm
10. … with radius 7 cm

• *Check your answers.*

Calculating with π *(read this Greek letter as pi)*

We have just used the rule that
" the circumference is approximately 3.1 x diameter"

> It has been known for at least 4000 years that
>
> circumference = a constant value x the diameter
> $$C = \pi d$$
>
> where π = the constant value.   π is read as pi

Task 1: 4000 years ago, the date was 2000BC. In Babylon, they used the formula
$$C = 3 d$$ to work out the circumference of a circle

Use this formula to work out the circumference of the circle …

1. … with diameter 4 cm
2. … with diameter 10 cm
3. … with diameter 2 m
4. … with radius 6 cm
5. … with radius 20 cm

> Work out the diameter first !

Big Edd

• CHECK YOUR ANSWERS BEFORE GOING ON !

Task 2: In Egypt, around 1650 BC, the value 3.16 was used. They used the formula
$$C = 3.16 d$$ to work out the circumference of a circle

Use this formula to work out the circumference of the circle …

6. … with diameter 5 cm
7. … with diameter 8 cm
8. … with diameter 3 m
9. … with radius 7 cm
10. … with radius 10 cm

Task 3: In India, around 500 AD, the value 3.1416 was used. They used the formula
$$C = 3.1416 d$$ to work out the circumference of a circle

Use this formula to work out the circumference of the circle …

11. … with diameter 6 cm
12. … with diameter 90 cm
13. … with diameter 20 cm
14. … with radius 5 cm
15. … with radius 15 cm

• *Check your answers.*

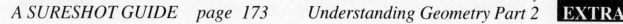

D4: Working out the circumference nowadays

$$C = \pi d$$

Nowadays, we usually
use π = 3.14
or π = 3.142

EXAMPLE   Work out the circumference of the circle with diameter 15 cm.
Use 3.14 as the value of π

| 3. 14 | x | 15 | = | 47.1 | C = 47.1 cm

For these problems, take the value of π as 3.14

Work out the circumference of a circle whose diameter is…

1. …10 cm   2. …3.5 cm   3. …2.05 m   4. …4 mm   5. …56 cm

EXAMPLE   Work out the circumference of the circle with radius 16 cm
Use 3.14 as the value of π

radius = 16 cm tells us that the diameter is 32 cm

| 3. 14 | x | 32 | = | 100.48 | C = 100.48 cm

Yerwat

6. (a) A circle has radius 5 cm. What is the length of its diameter ?
   (b) Work out the circumference of this circle.   [Take π as 3.14]

Work out the circumference of a circle whose radius is …

7. …4 cm   8. …2.1 cm   9. …4½ m   10. …3 mm   11. …20 cm

Work out the circumference of each of these circles. **Take the value of π as 3.142**

12.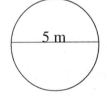
5 m

13.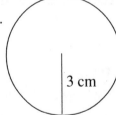
3 cm

14.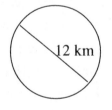
12 km

15.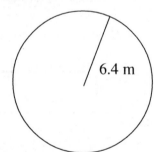
6.4 m

• *Check your answers.*

Star Challenge 6 6 $C = \pi d$ 8-9 correct = 2 stars
                                                          6-7 correct = 1 star

Work out the circumference of each of these circles.
Take the value of π as 3.14

1. circle with diameter 6 cm
2. circle with diameter 8.2 m
3. circle with radius 5 mm
4. circle with radius 2½ cm
5. circle with diameter 2.4 m
6. circle with radius 2.4 m

7.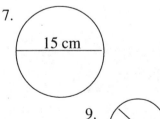
15 cm

8.
12 km

9.
1.6 cm

• *Your teacher will
need to mark these.*

Section 9: Area of a circle

In this section you will calculate the area of a circle.

D1: Using π to work out the area

$$A = \pi r^2$$

r = radius   **Take π as 3.14**

$r^2 = r \times r$

EXAMPLE   Work out the area of the circle with radius 8 cm.
Use 3.14 as the value of π

$\boxed{3.14}$ $\boxed{\times}$ $\boxed{8}$ $\boxed{\times}$ $\boxed{8}$ $\boxed{=}$ $\boxed{200.96}$

A = 200.96 cm²

For these problems, take the value of π as 3.14

Work out the area of a circle whose radius is...

1. ...5 cm   2. ...12 cm   3. ...3.1 m   4. ...3 mm   5. ...25 cm

EXAMPLE   Work out the area of the circle with diameter 14.4 cm
Use 3.14 as the value of π

 diameter = 14.4 cm tells us that the radius is 7.2 cm

$\boxed{3.14}$ $\boxed{\times}$ $\boxed{7.2}$ $\boxed{\times}$ $\boxed{7.2}$ $\boxed{=}$ $\boxed{162.7776}$

Hukka

A = 162.7776 cm²

6. (a) A circle has diameter 20 cm. What is the length of its radius ?
   (b) Work out the area of this circle.   Take π as 3.14

Work out the area of a circle whose diameter is ...

7. ...6 cm   8. ...10 cm   9. ...4.8 m   10. ...4 mm   11. ...24 cm

Work out the area of a circle whose ...

12. ...radius is 10 m   13. ...diameter is 16 cm   14....radius is 7 cm
15. ...diameter is 4.8 m   16. ...radius is 13 cm   17....radius is 100 m

Star Challenge 7 7 • *Check your answers.*

8-9 correct = 2 stars
6-7 correct = 1 star

Work out the area of each of these circles:
Take the value of π as 3.14

1. circle with radius 11 cm
2. circle with diameter 6.2 m
3. circle with radius 4 mm
4. circle with diameter 18 cm
5. circle with diameter 3.6 cm
6. circle with radius 3.6 cm

7.
5.5 cm

8.
6.6 m

9.
2.2 mm

• *Your teacher will need to mark these.*

Section 10: Circumference and area

In this section you will work with circumferences and areas of circles.

PRACTICE

P1: Circle calculations

$\pi = 3.14$ $C = \pi d$ $A = \pi r^2$

Use the value of π on your calculator or π = 3.14. Give answers to 3 s.f.
For each circle work out (a) the circumference (b) the area

Batch A:
1. radius = 6 cm
2. diameter = 4.6 m
3. diameter = 8.6 mm
4. radius = 3.1 m
5. radius = 20 feet
6. diameter = 6.4 km
7. diameter = 16 inches
8. radius = 0.5 cm
9. diameter = 0.4 m

CHECK YOUR ANSWERS. Do you need more practice ?

Batch B:
1. radius = 5.8 cm
2. diameter = 2.8 cm
3. diameter = 12.2 mm
4. radius = 8.5 cm
5. radius = 50 m
6. diameter = 8.4 cm
7. diameter = 14 km
8. radius = 2.1 cm
9. diameter = 0.6 m

• *Check your answers.*

P2: Circle problems

1. A netball goal is a circular ring.
   Its diameter is 39 cm.
   Work out its circumference to the nearest cm.

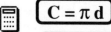 $C = \pi d$
 $A = \pi r^2$
$\pi = 3.14$

2.  A tree stump is approximately circular.
   Its diameter is 84 cm.
   Work out its circumference to the nearest cm.

3. A circular swimming pool has radius 12m.
   Work out the perimeter of the pool and the surface area of the water.

4. A picnic plate has diameter 23 cm.
   Work out the circumference of the plate and the area of its top surface.

5. A circle has radius 11.5 cm. Work out the length of the side of the square
   with the same area as the circle, to the nearest cm

6. A circular pond has diameter 10 m.
   It is surrounded by a path 1 m wide.
   Work out the area of the path.

7.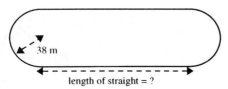

   length of straight = ?

   A running track has two semicircular ends of radius 38 m.
   The total length of the inside lane is 400 m. What is the length of each straight ?

• *Check your answers.*

E1: Rolling problems

$\pi = 3.14$ $C = \pi d$

When a circle rolls through one revolution, the distance it travels forward is its circumference.

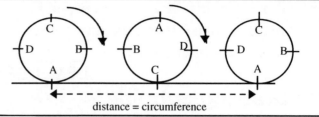

distance = circumference

1. A 10p coin has diameter 2.4 cm. How far does it travel when it rolls
   (a) one revolution   (b)   five revolutions ?

2. A cycle wheel has diameter 0.62 m.
   (a) How far has the wheel travelled after 1 revolution ?
   (b) How far has the wheel travelled after 100 revolutions ?

3. Sue's car wheel has diameter 0.72 m.
   How far has the wheel travelled after 1 revolution ?

4. A golf ball has a diameter 4.27 cm.
   (a) How far does it travel when it makes 1 revolution ?
   (b) It rolls 50 cm in a straight line. How many complete turns does it make ?

   • *Check your answers.*

Star Challenge 8 8

13-16 correct = 2 stars
10-12 correct = 1 star

For each of these circles, calculate:
   (a) the circumference   (b) the area

$\pi = 3.14$ $C = \pi d$ $A = \pi r^2$

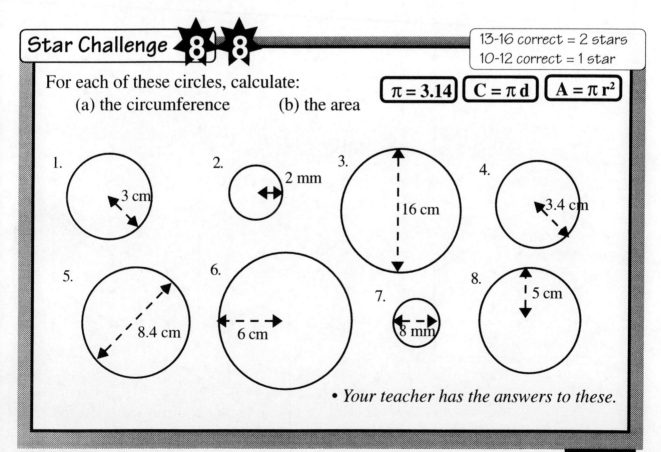

1. 3 cm
2. 2 mm
3. 16 cm
4. 3.4 cm
5. 8.4 cm
6. 6 cm
7. 8 mm
8. 5 cm

• *Your teacher has the answers to these.*

Section 11: Cuboids

In this section you will :
- draw cuboids on isometric paper;
- read and make isometric drawings;
- make nets of cuboids.

DEVELOPMENT

D1: Drawing cuboids

Complete each of these drawings of cuboids:

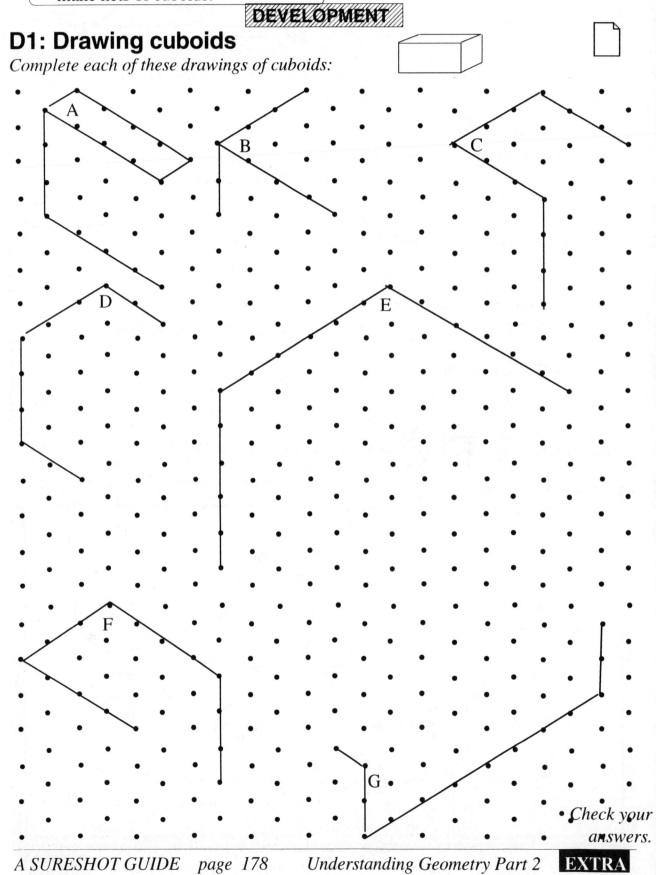

D2: Making isometric drawings

cubes isometric paper

When making isometric drawings, you draw a line whenever you can see an edge.
An edge is where two faces meet.
If the object you are drawing is made from cubes,
you do NOT draw lines to show the individual cubes.

1. Copy and complete each drawing:

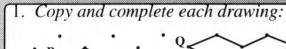

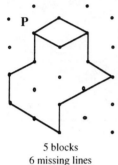

5 blocks
6 missing lines

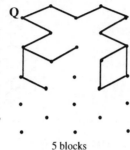

5 blocks
7 missing lines

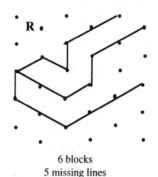

6 blocks
5 missing lines

Star Challenge 9

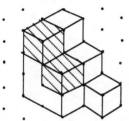

2. Make this shape.
   Remove the shaded cubes.
   Draw the new shape.

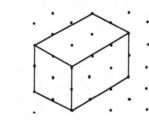

3. A larger version is
   made of this shape
   with every edge twice
   as long. Draw it.

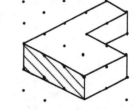

4. Make this shape.
   Tilt it so it stands up
   on the shaded face.
   Draw it. All correct = 1 star

• Check your answers.

D3: Nets of cuboids

Task 1: Draw each of
these accurately.
Cut them out.

If a shape like this will fold
up to make a box, we say
it is a net for a box.

Only one of these is a net
for a box.
Which one is it ?

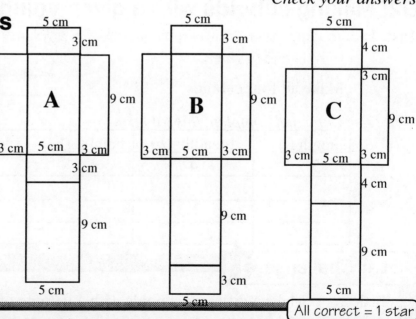

Star Challenge 10

Task 2: Draw the net accurately in your book.
Draw in flaps so that you could glue the box together.

• Show the net
to your teacher.

All correct = 1 star

Section 12: Volume

In this section you will :
- work out volumes by counting cubes;
- calculate volumes of cuboids.

DEVELOPMENT

D1: What is volume ?

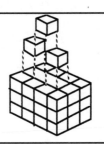

The **volume** of a shape is the number of cubes needed to make the shape.

Make each of these shapes.
Write down the volume of each shape.
Write your answers in the form   Volume of A = ... cubes

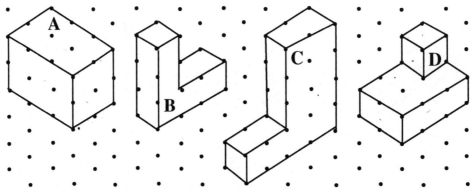

• *Check your answers.*

D2: Making cuboids with a given volume

Task 1:   You can make 4 different cuboids with a volume of 20 cubes.
Here is one of them.

Make all four cuboids.

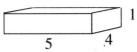

Copy and complete this table:

length (*l*)	breadth (*b*)	height (*h*)	volume (*V*)
5	4	1	20
			20
			20
			20

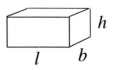

• *Check your answers.*

Star Challenge ⭐ 1 | All correct = 1 star |

Task 2:   Make 4 different cuboids with a volume of 18 cubes.
Make a table like that in Task 1. Complete the table.

• *Your teacher will need to mark this.*

D3: Volumes of cuboids

Volume of cuboid = length x breadth x height

$$V = l \times b \times h$$

EXAMPLE	Work out the volume of this cuboid.

$V = l \times b \times h$ => $V = 8 \times 5 \times 3$

= 120 cm³

If the sides are in cm, then the volume is in cm³

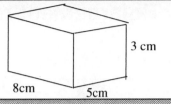

Work out the volume of each cuboid. Each answer must have the correct unit.

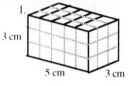
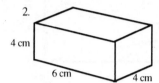

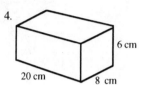

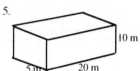
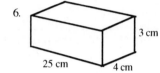
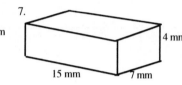
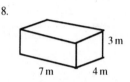

• *Check your answers.*

P1: Picking the right information

Each of these measurements are in cm.

<u>BUT – in many of the diagrams, too much information has been given.</u>

Find the volume of each cuboid, in cm³.

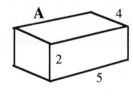
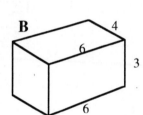
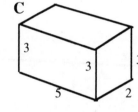

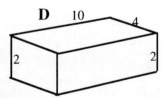
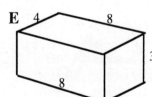
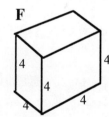

Star Challenge 12

All correct = 1 star

The volume of each of these cuboids is 60 cm³.
Each of the measurements is in cm.
Find the measurement that each letter stands for.

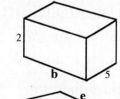
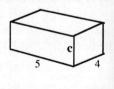
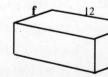

• *Your teacher has the answers.*

Section 13: Enlargements

In this section you will enlarge shapes using positive scale factors.

D1: Enlargement review

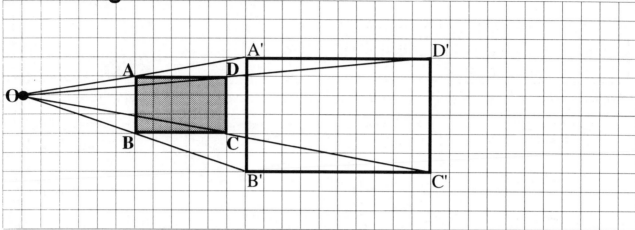

The rectangle ABCD has been enlarged with a scale factor 2 from O (the centre of enlargement).
To do this:

- OA is drawn and extended. A' is twice as far away from O as A.
- OB is drawn and extended. B' is twice as far away from O as B.
- OC is drawn and extended. C' is twice as far away from O as C.
- OD is drawn and extended. D' is twice as far away from O as D..

Task 1: Use the diagram above. Enlarge rectangle ABCD with a scale factor 3 from O.
Label the new rectangle A"B"C"D".

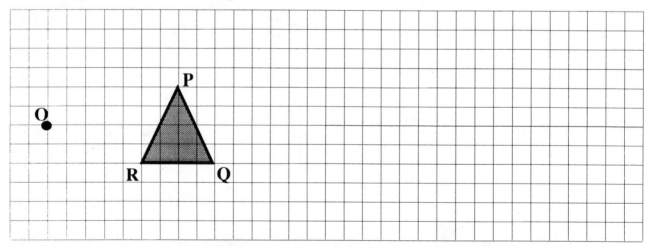

Task 2: Use the second diagram. Enlarge ΔPQR with a scale factor 2 from O.
Label the new triangle P'Q'R'.

Task 3: Use the second diagram. Enlarge ΔPQR with a scale factor 3 from O.
Label the new triangle P"Q"R".

Task 4: Use the third diagram.
Enlarge ΔRST with scale
factor 2 from O.
Label the new triangle R'S'T'

- *Check your answers.*

P1: Using an edge

1. Draw a triangle something like this.
   Use A as the centre of enlargement.
   Enlarge with scale factors 2, 3, 4.

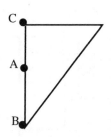

2. Repeat, on a fresh diagram,
   with B as the centre of enlargement.

3. Repeat with C as the centre of enlargement.

• *Check your answers.*

Star Challenge ◄13►

All correct = 1 star

Find the centre

Kite 1 has vertices (corners) (8,4), (9,6) (8,7) (7,6)
Kite 1 has vertices (2,0), (4,4) (2,6) (0,4)
Kite 2 is an enlargement of Kite 1.

Work out :

  (a) the scale factor of the enlargement
  (b) the coordinates of the centre of enlargement.

• *Your teacher will need to mark this.*

Star Challenge ◄14-14►

6 correct = 2 stars
4-5 correct = 1 star

Enlarge to fit ?

1. A photograph is 15.2 cm long by 9.8 cm wide.
   It is enlarged to fit a frame that is 38 cm long.

   (a) What is the scale factor of the enlargement ?

   (b) What is the width of the enlarged photograph ?

2. This is a logo for a firm
   making equipment for
   children's playgrounds.

   The larger version goes on their packaging.
   It is an enlargement of the smaller version.

   The smaller version goes on their letterhead.

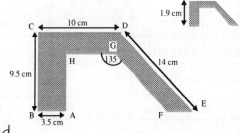

   (a) What is the scale factor of the enlargement <u>up to</u> the packaging size ?

On the letterhead logo, what is:

   (b) the length corresponding to CD ?

   (c) the length corresponding to DE ?

   (d) the obtuse angle corresponding to the angle FGH ?

• *Your teacher will need to mark this.*

All correct = 3 stars
1-2 errors = 2 stars
3-5 errors = 1 star

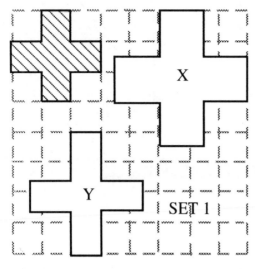

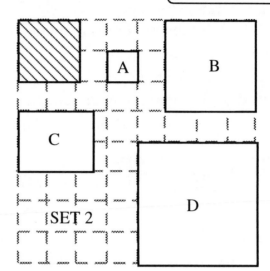

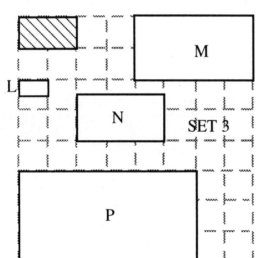

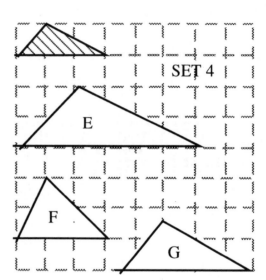

Copy and complete this table:

	SET 1	SET 2	SET 3	SET 4
shape	X Y	A B C D	L M N P	E F G
enlargement?				
scale factor ?				

enlargement ?
Is the shape an enlargement of the shaded shape – answer Y or N

scale factor ?
Give a the scale factor of the enlargement FROM the shaded shape

•*Your teacher will need to mark this.*

Developing Efficient Calculator Techniques EXTRA
ANSWERS

Section 1: Divisibility p6

D1: Which answers are whole numbers

A: Yes B: No C: Yes D: Yes E: No F: No G: Yes H: No I: Yes J: No

D2: What does 'divisible by' mean ?

1. No   2. Yes   3. No   4. No   5. Yes   6. Yes   7. Yes   8. No   9. Yes
10. No   11. No   12. Yes   13. | 35 | 63 | 49 | 56 | 21 | 84 | 14. | 40 | 16 | 24 | 92 | 12 | 108 | 52 |

D3: Numbers that are divisible by 2, 5 or 10

1. | 60 | 30 | 70 | 100 | 40 | 300 | 240 | 450 | 2. A number that is divisible by 10 ends in 0
3. | 55 | 70 | 80 | 20 | 85 | 900 | 225 | 15 | 4. A number that is divisible by 5 ends in 0 or 5
5. | 24 | 40 | 16 | 68 | 28 | 678 | 120 | 2472 | 6. A number that is divisible by 10 ends in 0, 2, 6, or 8

D3: Using divisiblity rules

Task 1: | 90 | 120 | 250 | 430 | 3570 |

Task 2: | 65 | 90 | 75 | 105 | 120 | 250 | 250 | 205 | 255 | 430 | 3570 |

Task 3: | 24 | 90 | 34 | 12 | 412 | 666 | 5432 | 102 | 120 | 250 | 946 | 430 | 3570 | 432 |

D4: "Divisible by' and ''multiples of''

1. 20, 30, 40, 50   2. 12, 15, 18   3. 20, 25, 30, 35, 40, 55   4. 21, 28
5. 45 30 75 60

Section 2: Quotients and Remainders   p10

D1: Introducing quotients and remainders

1. 4 with 1 left over   2. 2 with 2 left over   3. 1 with 1 left over
4. 1 with 3 left over   5. 2 with 1 left over   6. 1 with 2 left over
7. 2 with 1 left over   8. 2 with 1 left over   9. 5 with 2 left over
10. 2 with 2 left over

11.

	13 ÷ 2	10 ÷ 3	5 ÷ 4	7 ÷ 5	10 ÷ 4	11 ÷ 5	11 ÷ 3
quotient	6	3	1	1	2	2	3
remainder	1	1	1	2	2	1	2

D2: Using a calculator to find quotients and remainders

1. 4   2. 10   3. 15   4. 8   5. 6   6. 10   7. 9   8. 6   9. 18   10. 50
11. 1   12. 1   13. 1   14. 2   15. 2
16. q 2. r 3   17. q 12. r 1   18. q 18. r 1   19. q 98. r 2   20. q 6. r 7

Section 3: Factors and prime numbers   p12

D1: What are factors ?

1. Numbers in boxes are | 1 | 2 | 4 | 8 | 16 | 2. Numbers in boxes are | 1 | 2 | 3 | 6 |
3. Numbers in boxes are | 1 | 2 | 3 | 4 | 6 | 12 | 4. True   5. True   6. | 1 | 2 | 4 | 8 |
7. | 1 | 2 | 5 | 10 | 8. | 1 | 3 | 9 |
9. Numbers in boxes are | 1 | 2 | 4 | 5 | 10 | 20 | 10. Numbers in boxes are | 1 | 2 | 3 | 4 | 6 | 8 | 12 | 24 |

D2: Factor pairs

1. 6 ÷ 2 = 3   6 is divisible by 2 | 2 | is a factor of 6
   6 ÷ 3 = 2   6 is divisible by | 3 | | 3 | is a factor of 6
2. 6 ÷ 1 = | 6 | 6 is divisible by | 6 | | 1 | is a factor of 6
   6 ÷ 6 = | 1 | 6 is divisible by | 6 | | 6 | is a factor of 6

3. 1 & 10   2 & 5   4. 1 & 18   2 & 9   3 & 6   5. 1 & 20   2 & 10   4 & 5

D3: A systematic way of getting all the factors of a number

1. 1, 15, 3, 5   2. 1, 24, 2, 12, 3, 8, 4, 6   3. 1, 30, 2, 15, 3, 10, 5, 6
4. 1 25, 5   5. 1, 36, 2, 18, 3, 12, 4, 9, 6   6. 1, 40, 2, 20, 4, 10
7. 1, 49, 7   8. 1, 48, 2, 24, 3, 16, 4, 12, 6, 8

D4: From factors to prime numbers

1.
1	1		6	1, 2, 3, 6		11	1, 11		16	1,2,4,8,16	5
2	1, 2		7	1, 7		12	1,2,3,4,6,12		17	1, 17	2
3	1, 3		8	1, 2, 4, 8		13	1, 13		18	1,2,3,6,9,18	6
4	1, 2, 4		9	1, 3, 9		14	1, 2, 7, 14		19	1, 19	2
5	1, 5		10	1, 2, 5, 10		15	1, 3, 5, 15		20	1,2,4,5,10,20	6

2. 2, 3, 5, 7, 11, 13, 17, 19

D5: Prime factors

1. The first eight prime numbers are : 2, 3, 5, 7, 11, 13, 17, 19
2. The factors of 15 are 1, 3, 5, 15   The prime factors of 15 are 3, 5
3. The factors of 20 are 1, 2, 4, 5, 10, 20   The prime factors of 20 are 2, 5
4. 2,3   5. 3, 7   6. 2, 3   7. 2   8. 2, 5   9. 2, 7   10. 2, 3

E1: Prime factors of large numbers – using factor trees

1.   2.   3.

Prime factors are 3 & 5   Prime factors are 2, 3 & 5   Prime factors are 2 & 5

5. 3, 5   6. 2, 3   7. 2, 3, 5   8. 3, 5, 7
9. 3, 5   10. 3, 5, 11   11. 7, 13

Section 4: Squares, cube and roots   p16

D1: Squares and cubes

1. 5 x 5 x 5   2. 169   3. 216   4. 225   5. 441
6. 12.25   7. 1   8. 1331   9. 64   10. 20.25
11. 15129   12. 33076161   13. 343

14.
2	10	7	3	5	8	6	12	21
4	100	49	9	25	64	36	144	441

15.
6	4	11	10	8	15	2	7	14
216	64	1331	1000	512	153375	8	343	2744

ANSWERS : page 185

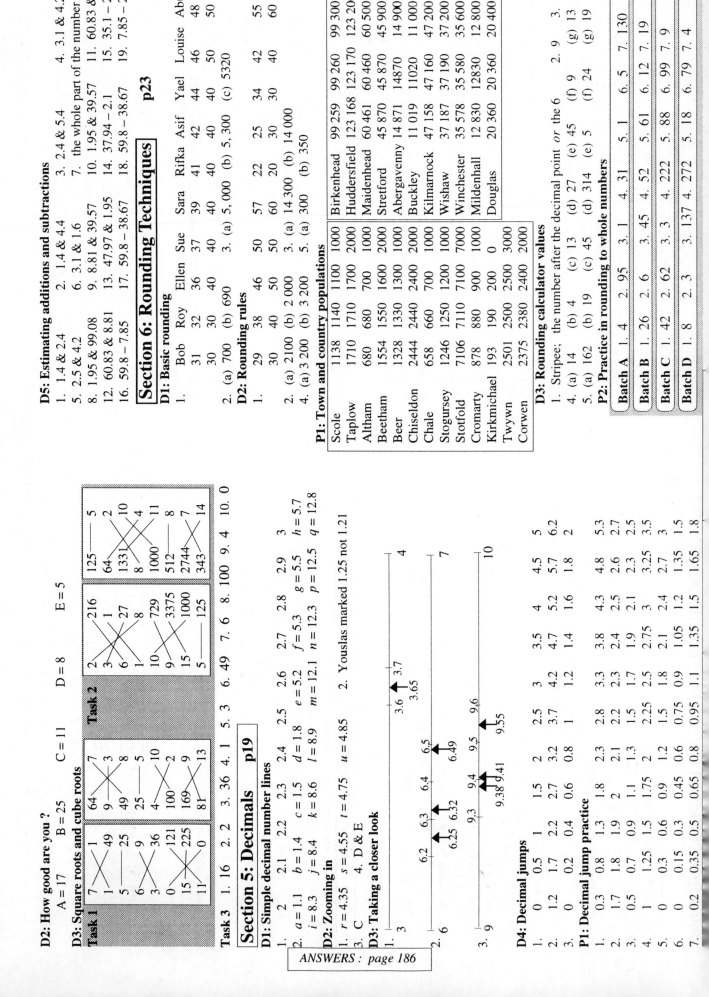

D2: How good are you?

A = 17   B = 25   C = 11   D = 8   E = 5

D3: Square roots and cube roots

Task 1

7 — 1		64 — 7
1 — 49		9 — 3
5 — 25		49 — 8
6 — 9		25 — 5
3 — 36		4 — 10
0 — 121		100 — 2
15 — 225		169 — 9
11 — 0		81 — 13

Task 2

2 — 216		125 — 5
3 — 1		64 — 2
6 — 27		1331 — 10
1 — 8		8 — 4
10 — 729		1000 — 11
9 — 3375		512 — 8
15 — 1000		2744 — 7
5 — 125		343 — 14

Task 3   1. 16   2. 2   3. 36   4. 1   5. 3   6. 49   7. 6   8. 100   9. 4   10. 0

Section 5: Decimals   p19

D1: Simple decimal number lines

1. 2   2.1   2.2   2.3   2.4   2.5   2.6   2.7   2.8   2.9   3

2. $a=1.1$ $b=1.4$ $c=1.5$ $d=1.8$ $e=5.2$ $f=5.3$ $g=5.5$ $h=5.7$
   $i=8.3$ $j=8.4$ $k=8.6$ $l=8.9$ $m=12.1$ $n=12.3$ $p=12.5$ $q=12.8$

D2: Zooming in

1. $r=4.35$ $s=4.55$ $t=4.75$ $u=4.85$

2. Youslas marked 1.25 not 1.21

3. C   4. D & E

D3: Taking a closer look

1.
   6.2   6.3   6.4   6.5   3.6 ⟵ 3.7   9.3   9.4 ⟵ 9.6
   6.25 6.32 6.49   3.65   9.38 9.41 9.5 9.55

D4: Decimal jumps

1.	0	0.5	1	1.5	2	2.5	3	3.5	4	4.5	5
2.	1.2	1.7	2.2	2.7	3.2	3.7	4.2	4.7	5.2	5.7	6.2
3.	0	0.2	0.4	0.6	0.8	1	1.2	1.4	1.6	1.8	2

P1: Decimal jump practice

1.	0.3	0.8	1.3	1.8	2.3	2.8	3.3	3.8	4.3	4.8	5.3
2.	1.7	1.8	1.9	2	2.1	2.2	2.3	2.4	2.5	2.6	2.7
3.	0.5	0.7	0.9	1.1	1.3	1.5	1.7	1.9	2.1	2.3	2.5
4.	1	1.25	1.5	1.75	2	2.25	2.5	2.75	3	3.25	3.5
5.	0	0.3	0.6	0.9	1.2	1.5	1.8	2.1	2.4	2.7	3
6.	0	0.15	0.3	0.45	0.6	0.75	0.9	1.05	1.2	1.35	1.5
7.	0.2	0.35	0.5	0.65	0.8	0.95	1.1	1.35	1.5	1.65	1.8

ANSWERS : page 186

D5: Estimating additions and subtractions

1. 1.4 & 2.4   2. 1.4 & 4.4   3. 2.4 & 5.4   4. 3.1 & 4.2
5. 2.5 & 4.2   6. 3.1 & 1.6   7. the whole part of the number
8. 1.95 & 99.08   9. 8.81 & 39.57   10. 1.95 & 39.57   11. 60.83 & 99.08
12. 60.83 & 8.81   13. 47.97 & 1.95   14. 37.94 − 2.1   15. 35.1 − 2.1
16. 59.8 − 7.85   17. 59.8 − 38.67   18. 59.8 − 38.67   19. 7.85 − 2.1

Section 6: Rounding Techniques   p23

D1: Basic rounding

1.

	Bob	Roy	Ellen	Sue	Sara	Rifka	Asif	Yael	Louise	Abu
	31	32	36	37	39	41	42	44	46	48
	30	30	40	40	40	40	40	40	50	50
	50	55							42	34
	50	60							40	30

2. (a) 700   (b) 690   3. (a) 5,000   (b) 5,300   (c) 5320

D2: Rounding rules

1.

29	38	46	57	22	25	34	42	55
30	40	50	60	20	30	30	40	60

2. (a) 2100   (b) 2 000   3. (a) 14 300   (b) 14 000
4. (a) 3 200   (b) 3 200   5. (a) 300   (b) 350

P1: Town and country populations

Scole	1138	1140	1100	1000
Taplow	1710	1710	1700	2000
Altham	680	680	700	1000
Beetham	1554	1550	1600	2000
Beer	1328	1330	1300	1000
Chiseldon	2444	2440	2400	2000
Chale	658	660	700	1000
Stogursey	1246	1250	1200	1000
Stotfold	7106	7110	7100	7000
Cromarty	878	880	900	1000
Kirkmichael	193	190	200	0
Twywn	2501	2500	2500	3000
Corwen	2375	2380	2400	2000
Birkenhead	99 259	99 260	99 300	99 000
Huddersfield	123 168	123 170	123 200	123 000
Maidenhead	60 461	60 460	60 500	60 000
Stretford	45 870	45 870	45 900	46 000
Abergavenny	14 871	14870	14 900	15 000
Buckley	11 019	11020	11 000	11 000
Kilmarnock	47 158	47 160	47 200	47 000
Wishaw	37 187	37 190	37 200	37 000
Winchester	35 578	35 580	35 600	36 000
Mildenhall	12 830	12830	12 800	13 000
Douglas	20 360	20 360	20 400	20 000

D3: Rounding calculator values

1. Stripee; the number after the decimal point *or* the 6   2. 9   3. 13
4. (a) 14   (b) 4   (c) 13   (d) 27   (e) 45   (f) 9   (g) 13   (h) 137
5. (a) 162   (b) 19   (c) 45   (d) 314   (e) 5   (f) 24   (g) 19   (h) 95

P2: Practice in rounding to whole numbers

Batch A	1. 4	2. 95	3. 1	4. 31	5. 1	6. 5	7. 130	8. 7
Batch B	1. 26	2. 6	3. 45	4. 52	5. 61	6. 12	7. 19	8. 7
Batch C	1. 42	2. 62	3. 3	4. 222	5. 88	6. 99	7. 9	8. 5
Batch D	1. 8	2. 3	3. 137	4. 272	5. 18	6. 79	7. 4	8. 677

Section 7: Decimal places   p28

D1: Rounding to 1 decimal place
1. 6.1 2. 10.8 3. 8.3 4. 27.9 5. 9.1
6. 15.8 7. 15.3 8. 76 9. 3.6 10. 22.4

P1: Rounding square roots to 1 d.p.

	1.	2.	3.	4.	5.	6.
Batch A	4.8	21.2	6.2	31.1	15.7	18.1
Batch B	8.2	21.4	19.5	5.9	56.3	6.9
Batch C	22.2	8.5	15.6	24.1	6.1	3.7

P2: Rounding answers to 1 d.p.
1. 5.3 2. 98.7 3. 1.6 4. 13.7 5. 1.8
6. 34.9 7. 4.1 8. 1.6

D2: Rounding to 2 d.p.
1. 4.36 2. 17.75 3. 21.73 4. 4.58 5. 8.94 6. 8.46
7. 24.49 8. 20.52 9. 3.69 10. 7.68 11. 15.78 12. 18.35

D1: Rounding to 1 decimal place
1. 24.595 2. 9.466 3. 1.7775 4. 25.314 5. 21.794
6. 145.587 7. 28.178 8. 50.595 9. 30.51 10. 40.04
11. 8.87 12. 603.17 13. 8.10 14. 391.25 15. 31.702
16. 2.277 17. 10.339 18. 131.257 19. 13.491 20. 5.0133

Section 8: Significant figures   p30

D1: How close can you get ?
Task 1   Round 3 : 30 – not close enough   Round 5 : 300 – 2 digits used
Round 7 : 600 – not close enough   Round 8 : 200 – not close enough & 2 digits used
Round 10 : 400 – not close enough & 2 digits used

Task 2   4   70   50   90   90   100   100   300   2000   40000
0.2   0.4   0.06   0.008

Task 3   9   38   620   840   470   120   4700   0.23   0.033   380   1600

D2: Significant figures
1. 43 2. 5.2 3. 6.5 4. 25 5. 33 6. 8.5
7. 26.7 8. 95.9 9. 3.69 10. 521 11. 45.8 12. 1.36
13. 4000 14. 70 15. 600 16. 400 17. 90 18. 100
19. 6200 20. 880 21. 900 22. 1600 23. 3400 24. 4400
25. 0.02 26. 0.005 27. 0.6 28. 0.05 29. 0.6 30. 0.0005

P1: Mixed practice
Batch A 1. 50 2. 40 3. 3 4. 32
5. 12 6. 230 7. 359 8. 107 9. 0.229
Batch B 1. 5 2. 10 3. 3 4. 3.9
5. 38 6. 29 7. 167 8. 9.14 9. 176

Section 9: Changing fractions into decimals   p32

D1: Fractions into decimals
1. 0.5 2. 0.25 3. 0.75 4. 0.1 5. 0.7
6. 0.3 7. 0.4 8. 0.025 9. 0.375 10. 0.35
11. 0.2 12. 0.9 13. 0.16 14. 0.625 15. 0.22

P1: Using decimals to search for equivalent fractions
Task 1 $^{46}/_{89}$ Task 2   Set A: $^{20}/_{56}$ Set B : $^{450}/_{608}$ Set C : $^{30}/_{128}$

Section 10: Fractions into decimals again   p34

D1: Changing fractions into decimals to 2 d.p.
1. 0.33 2. 0.21 3. 0.71 4. 0.11 5. 0.15 6. 0.13
7. 0.41 8. 0.16 9. 0.47 10. 0.39 11. 0.29 12. 0.28

P1: Practice in changing fractions into decimals

	1.	2.	3.	4.		5.	6.	7.	8.	9.
Batch A	0.125	0.375	0.429	0.385		0.412	0.615	0.739	0.4	0.571
Batch B	0.12	0.667	0.067	0.625		0.389	0.722	0.821	0.938	0.897
Batch C	0.7	0.613	0.4	0.438		0.44	0.552	0.579	0.719	3.074

D2: Recurring decimals
1. 0.5555... 2. 0.6363... 3. 0.56363... 4. 0.563563... 5. 0.2563563...
6. $0.\dot{4}5\dot{6}$ 7. 0.456 8. 0.12345
9. $0.\dot{2}$ 10. $0.\dot{3}$ 11. $0.\dot{6}$ 12. $0.8\dot{3}$ 13. $0.\dot{4}\dot{5}$
14. 0.17 15. 0.018 16. 0.15 17. 0.387 18. $0.230\dot{4}$
19. $0.88\dot{9}$ 20. 0.3108

Section 11: Fractions, Decimals and Percentages   p36

D1: Decimals and percentages

0.1	0.6	0.62	0.73	0.24	0.15	0.25	0.05
10%	60%	62%	73%	24%	15%	25%	5%

0.56	0.4	0.86	0.35	0.41	0.025	0.105	0.375
56%	40%	86%	35%	41%	2.5%	10.5%	37.5%

D2: Changing fractions to percentages
Task 1: Bio Farming 74%   Space Navigation 95%   Maths 96%
Weapon Repairs 80%   Communications 85%   Astronomy 80%
Survival skills 75%   Galacto-Speak 92%   Electronics 80%

Task 2: Maths   Task 3: Bio Farming   Task 4: 84.1% Yes

Understanding Geometry EXTRA *Part 1* ANSWERS

Section 1: Mirror symmetry p46

D1: Finding Lines of symmetry   D2: Creating mirror symmetry

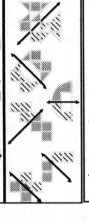

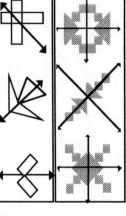

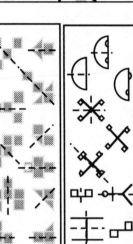

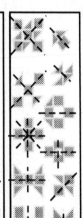

P1:How many lines of symmetry ?

A 4 B 1 C 2 D 4 E 2 F 3
G 3 H 2 I 1 J 1 K 6 L 3
M 1 N 1

Section 2: Rotational symmetry p49

D1: Circle Patterns

Circle Pattern	A	B	C
Order of rotational symmetry	2	3	1

D2:Rotational symmetry

Task 1:

R	S	P	C	E	O	T
2	4	2	4	3	8	1

Task 2:

	A	B	C	D	E	F	G	H	I	J	K	L
order	1	1	2	2	2	1	4	2	2	1	4	1
lines	1	1	2	0	1	0	2	0	1	4	0

Section 3: Angle review p52

D1: Classifying angles

Task 1: 90°; smaller than 90°, between 180° and 360°, between 90° and 180°

Task 2: A : right B: reflex   C: acute   D: right   E: reflex   F: acute
G: reflex   H: reflex   I: reflex   J: obtuse   K: obtuse

D3: Percentage test marks
1. 85%   2. 85%   3. 68%   4. 45%
5. 46%   6. 43%   7. 47%   8. 62%

P1: Practice in changing fractions into percentages

Batch A	1. 85%	2. 72%	3. 81%	4. 60%	5. 80%
	6. 60%	7. 47%	8. 34%	9. 84%	10. 71%

Batch B	1. 75%	2. 63%	3. 79%	4. 96%	5. 75%
	6. 97%	7. 42%	8. 88%	9. 57%	10. 76%

Batch C	1. 65%	2. 41%	3. 44%	4. 78%	5. 65%
	6. 85%	7. 77%	8. 36%	9. 51%	10. 33%

Section 12: Working with fractions, decimals & % p38

D1: Percentage reasoning
1. 59%   2. 35%   3. 25%   4. 11%   5. 7%

D2: Percentages of amounts
1. £4   2. 60p   3. 75p   4. £2.40   5. £44.80   6. £1.70
7. £27.20   8. £4.80   9. £5.74   10. 96p   11. 99p   12. £16.50

D3: Fractions of amounts
1. £60   2. £12.80   3. £10   4. £12   5. £7.50   6. 4.80
7. £11.25   8. £26.25   9. 10p   10. 12p   11. 24p   12. £24

P1: Practice in finding percentages and fractions of amounts

Batch A:	1. £5.50	2. £10	3. £1.05	4. £27	5. 42p	6. £1.33
	7. £9.20	8. £6.30	9. £9.75	10. £14	11. £5.16	12. £6.25

Batch B:	1. 51p	2. £27	3. £27	4. £36	5. £16.20	6. £1.12
	7. £9	8. £3.90	9. £28	10. £10.20	11. £1.32	12. £8.30

Batch C:	1. 60p	2. £30	3. £1.38	4. £2.50	5. £57.60	6. £100
	7. £57	8. £1.94	9. £13.80	10. £16.50	11. £3.91	12. £25

D4: Additions and reductions
1. £162.80   2. £427.50   3. £39.05   4. £255   5. £17.38   6. £13 482   7. £161

D5: Expressing one quantity as a percentage of another

Task 1: Pow 30%   Hoblin 90%   Modesto 96%

Task 2: Chyps 86%   Driller 88%   Frizzbang 45%

Task 3: (a) 20p   (b) 20/320   (c) 6.25%

Task 4: (a) £75   (b) 25%

E1: Do the words mean 'up' or 'down' ?
1. £20   2. £10   3. loss   4. £10   5. No   6. Yes
7. £5 000   8. 1990 & 1991   9. £420   10. loss   11. increased   12. £320   13. £9

ANSWERS : page 188

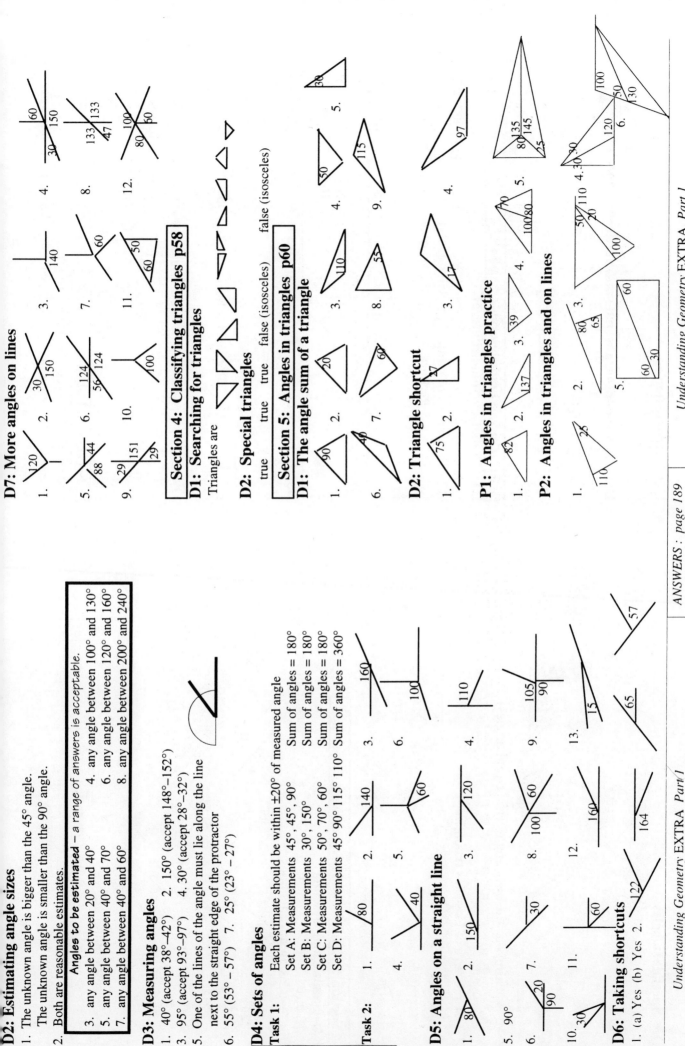

D2: Estimating angle sizes

1. The unknown angle is bigger than the 45° angle.
   The unknown angle is smaller than the 90° angle.
2. Both are reasonable estimates.

   Angles to be estimated – a range of answers is acceptable.
   3. any angle between 20° and 40°   4. any angle between 100° and 130°
   5. any angle between 40° and 70°   6. any angle between 120° and 160°
   7. any angle between 40° and 60°   8. any angle between 200° and 240°

D3: Measuring angles

1. 40° (accept 38°–42°)   2. 150° (accept 148°–152°)
3. 95° (accept 93°–97°)   4. 30° (accept 28°–32°)
5. One of the lines of the angle must lie along the line
   next to the straight edge of the protractor
6. 55° (53° – 57°)   7. 25° (23° – 27°)

D4: Sets of angles

Task 1:   Each estimate should be within ±20° of measured angle

Set A: Measurements 45°, 45°, 90°   Sum of angles = 180°
Set B: Measurements 30°, 150°   Sum of angles = 180°
Set C: Measurements 50°, 70°, 60°   Sum of angles = 180°
Set D: Measurements 45° 90° 115° 110°   Sum of angles = 360°

Task 2:

D5: Angles on a straight line

D6: Taking shortcuts

1. (a) Yes   (b) Yes   2.

Understanding Geometry EXTRA Part 1

D2: More angles on lines

Section 4: Classifying triangles   p58

D1: Searching for triangles

Triangles are   true   true   true   false (isosceles)   false (isosceles)

D2: Special triangles

Section 5: Angles in triangles   p60

D1: The angle sum of a triangle

D2: Triangle shortcut

P1: Angles in triangles practice

P2: Angles in triangles and on lines

Understanding Geometry: EXTRA Part 1

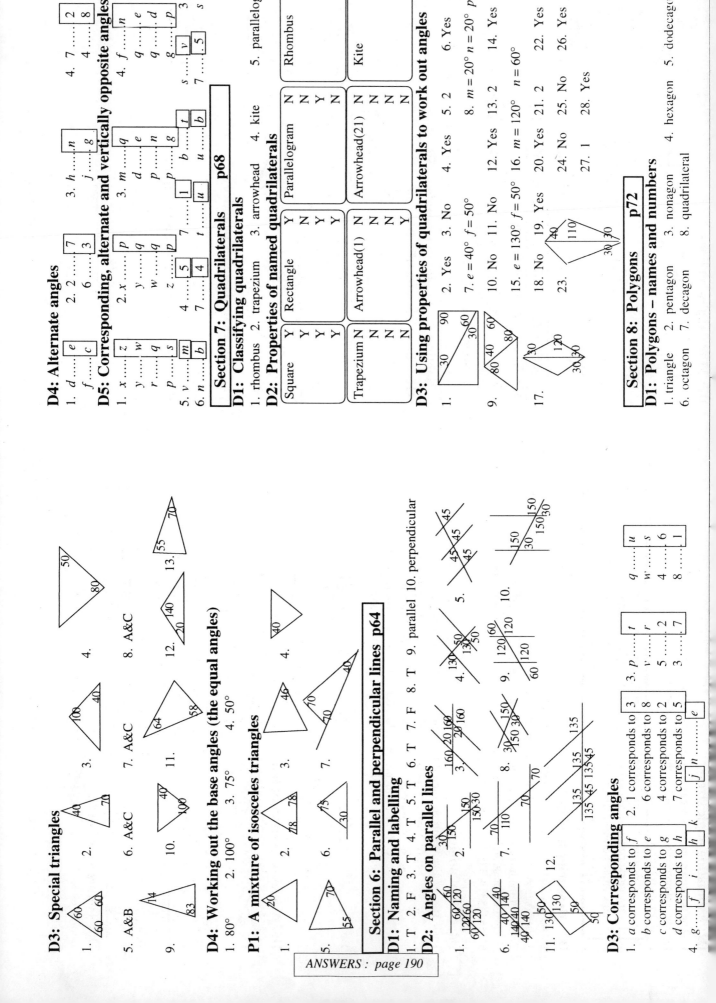

D4: Alternate angles

1. d ..... e 2. 2 7   3. h ..... n 4. 7 2
    f ..... c 6 ..... 3 j ..... g 4 8

D5: Corresponding, alternate and vertically opposite angles

1. x ..... z 2. x ..... p 3. m ..... q 4. f ..... n
    y ..... w y ..... q d ..... e q ..... e
    r ..... q w ..... q p ..... n q ..... d
    p ..... s z ..... p p ..... g g ..... p

5. v ..... m 7 5   1 b ..... t s 3   6
6. n ..... b 4 u u ..... b 7 ..... 5 m

Section 7: Quadrilaterals   p68

D1: Classifying quadrilaterals

1. rhombus   2. trapezium   3. arrowhead   4. kite   5. parallelogram

D2: Properties of named quadrilaterals

	Square	Rectangle	Parallelogram	Rhombus
	Y	Y	N	N
	Y	N	N	Y
	Y	Y	Y	Y
	Y	Y	N	Y

	Trapezium	Arrowhead(1)	Arrowhead(21)	Kite
	N	N	N	N
	N	N	N	Y
	N	Y	N	N
	N	Y	N	Y

D3: Using properties of quadrilaterals to work out angles

1.   2. Yes   3. No   4. Yes   5. 2   6. Yes
7. $e = 40°$ $f = 50°$ 8. $m = 20°$ $n = 20°$ $p = 70°$
9.   10. No   11. No   12. Yes   13. 2   14. Yes
15. $e = 130°$ $f = 50°$ 16. $m = 120°$ $n = 60°$
17.   18. No   19. Yes   20. Yes   21. 2   22. Yes
23.   24. No   25. No   26. Yes   27. 1   28. Yes

Section 8: Polygons   p72

D1: Polygons – names and numbers

1. triangle   2. pentagon   3. nonagon   4. hexagon   5. dodecagon
6. octagon   7. decagon   8. quadrilateral

D3: Special triangles

1.   2.   3.   4.
5. A&B   6. A&C   7. A&C   8. A&C
9.   10.   11.   12.   13.

D4: Working out the base angles (the equal angles)

1. 80°   2. 100°   3. 75°   4. 50°

P1: A mixture of isosceles triangles

1.   2.   3.   4.
5.   6.   7.

Section 6: Parallel and perpendicular lines   p64

D1: Naming and labelling

1. T   2. T   3. F   4. T   5. T   6. T   7. F   8. T   9. parallel   10. perpendicular

D2: Angles on parallel lines

1.   2.   3.   4.   5.
6.   7.   8.   9.   10.
11.   12.

D3: Corresponding angles

1. a corresponds to f 2. 1 corresponds to 3   3. p ..... t q ..... u
    b corresponds to e 6 corresponds to 8 v ..... r w ..... s
    c corresponds to g 4 corresponds to 2   5 2   4 6
    d corresponds to h 7 corresponds to 5   3 7   8 1

4. g ..... f i ..... h k ..... j n ..... e

5. LEFT 45 FORWARD 30 RIGHT 90 FORWARD 90 RIGHT 90
FORWARD 30 RIGHT 90 FORWARD 30

6. FORWARD 40 RIGHT 90 FORWARD 40 RIGHT 90 FORWARD 40
RIGHT 90 FORWARD 40 RIGHT 90 FORWARD 20 RIGHT 45
FORWARD 28 RIGHT 90 FORWARD 28 RIGHT 90 FORWARD 28
RIGHT 90 FORWARD 28

7. FORWARD 30 RIGHT 90 FORWARD 50 RIGHT 90 FORWARD 30
RIGHT 90 FORWARD 50 RIGHT 90 FORWARD 10 RIGHT 90 PEN UP
FORWARD 10 PEN DOWN FORWARD 30 LEFT 90 FORWARD 10
LEFT 90 FORWARD 30 LEFT 90 FORWARD 10   (If you have an alternative
set of instructions as you move inwards, ask your teacher to check it)

D2: Drawing different angles

1. FORWARD 30 RIGHT 120 FORWARD 30 RIGHT 120 FORWARD 30

2. RIGHT 30 FORWARD 40 RIGHT 120 FORWARD 40 RIGHT 120
FORWARD 40

3. RIGHT 90 FORWARD 40 LEFT 60 FORWARD 40 LEFT 60 FORWARD 40
FORWARD 40

4. FORWARD 40 RIGHT 45 FORWARD 30 RIGHT 135 FORWARD 40
RIGHT 45 FORWARD 30

5. (a) LEFT 45 FORWARD 30 RIGHT 45 FORWARD 30 RIGHT 45
FORWARD 30 RIGHT 45 FORWARD 30 RIGHT 45 FORWARD 30
RIGHT 45 FORWARD 30 RIGHT 45 FORWARD 30 RIGHT 45
FORWARD 30 (8 lots of forward 30)

(b) RIGHT 90 FORWARD 30 LEFT 45 FORWARD 30 LEFT 45 FORWARD 30
LEFT 45 FORWARD 30 LEFT 45 FORWARD 30 LEFT 45
FORWARD 30 (8 lots of forward 30)

(c) RIGHT 90 FORWARD 30 RIGHT 60 FORWARD 30 RIGHT 60
FORWARD 30 RIGHT 60 FORWARD 30 RIGHT 60 FORWARD 30
RIGHT 60 FORWARD 30 (6 lots of forward 30)

D2: Properties of some polygons

1. A B D G H I 2. P Q V 3. square 4. rhombus 5. equilateral

D3: Constructing regular polygons

1. (a) isosceles (b) 360 ÷ 5 = 72   3. (a) 60°
4. centre angle is 40°   5. centre angle is 36°
6. (a) centre angle is 45° (d) 4 rectangles and 1 square   (e) right-angled
7. Icosagon (20 sides)

Section 9: Angles in polygons   p76

D1: Exterior angles in a polygon

Task 1: 1. $x = 90°$ $y = 130°$ 2. $p = 120°$ $q = 100°$ 3. $n = 50°$
4. $m = 30°$ 5. $s = 60°$ $t = 65°$ 6. $u = 70°$

Task 2: When walking round the sides of a concave polygon you turn through more than 360°. For any indent, you turn "in" and then "out" through the same angle.

D2: The sum of the interior angles of a polygon

Task 1: Sum of interior angles of quadrilateral = sum of interior angles of the two Δs

Task 2:

4	2	360°
5	3	540°
6	4	720°
7	5	900°
8	6	1080°
20	18	3240°
50	48	8640°
n	$n-2$	$(n-2) \times 180°$

Task 3: $S = (n-2) \times 180°$

Task 4: $a = 35°$ $b = 105°$ $x = 60°$

Task 5: A concave polygon does not split into Δs in the same way.

D3: Angles in regular polygons

1. (a) 72° (b) 108° $(180-72)$ 2. (a) 540° (b) $540 ÷ 5 = 108$
3. 120° 4. 135° 5. 144°

Section 10: Drawing shapes with a computer   p79

D1: Right-angled shapes

1. FORWARD 50 RIGHT 90 FORWARD 50 RIGHT 90 FORWARD 50
RIGHT 90 FORWARD 50

2. RIGHT 90 FORWARD 40 LEFT 90 FORWARD 40 LEFT 90
FORWARD 40 LEFT 90 FORWARD 40

3. RIGHT 90 FORWARD 60 LEFT 90 FORWARD 30 LEFT 90
FORWARD 60 LEFT 90 FORWARD 30

4. FORWARD 40 RIGHT 90 FORWARD 40 RIGHT 90 FORWARD 40
RIGHT 90 FORWARD 40 RIGHT 135 FORWARD 28 RIGHT 90 FORWARD 28
or RIGHT 45 FORWARD 28 RIGHT 90 FORWARD 28 RIGHT 135
FORWARD 40 RIGHT 90 FORWARD 40 RIGHT 90 FORWARD 40
RIGHT 90 FORWARD 40

Developing Efficient Non-Calculator Techniques

EXTRA *Part 1* ANSWERS

Section 1: Multiples and divisibility p82

D1: From multiples to primes

Task 1: Task 3: Task 5: Task 7:

Task 2: straight lines down the page

Task 4: diagonal lines down the page

Task 6: 2 straight lines down the page

Task 8: dots in diagonal lines

Task 9: Numbers that should be circled are
2 3 5 7 11 13 17 19 23 29 31 37 41 43 47 53 59 61 67 71 73 79 83 89 97

Check these carefully – you will need to use these primes in Sections 2 & 3

D2: Multiples and divisibility
1. Yes 2. Yes 3. No 4. No 5. 37 is not shaded in the multiples of 7 table
6. 22 24 26 28 30 7. 27 30 33 36 39 8. 40 45 50 55 60 65 70
9. 14 21 28 35 42 49 10. 24 30 36 42 48 11. 38 56 12. 87
13. 85 95 14. 56

D3: Simple rules for divisibility
1. 340 890 2. 340 890 125 65 3. 340 890 64 92 28 566 7248 356

D4: Digit sums
1. 439 has digit sum 7   357 has digit sum 6   5112 has digit sum 9
3289 has digit sum 11   31569 has digit sum 6
2. 357, 5112, 31569 3. 1473 21444 7935 4. All final digit sums are 9
5. If the final digit sum is 9, then the number is divisible by 9

Section 2: Multiples, factors and primes p85

D1: Using a table square
1. 36 2. 70 3. 63 4. 52 5. 182 6. 72 7. 84 8. 64
9. 143 10. 84 11. 8 12. 9 13. 12 14. 13 15. 7 16. 6
17. 4 18. 12 19. 8 20. 9 21. 8 22. 6 23. 9 24. 14 25. 14

D2: What are factors ?
1. T 2. T 3. F 4. T 5. T 6. F 7. T 8. T
9. F 10. T 11. T 12. T 13. T 14. T 15. 1 2 4 8
16. 1 2 7 14 17. 1 5 25 18. 1 2 4 8 16 19. 1 2 3 4 6 12

D3: Factor pairs
1. 1 & 6, 2 & 3 2. 1 & 10. 2 & 5 3. 1 & 18. 2 & 9. 3 & 6
4. 1 & 20. 2 & 10, 4 & 5 5. 1 & 28. 2 & 14. 4 & 7 6. 1 & 12. 2 & 6. 3 & 4
7. 1 & 15. 3 & 5 8. 1 & 21. 3 & 7 9. Expected three are 4 & 15, 5 & 12. 6 & 10
(but there are also 1 & 60. 2 & 30. 3 & 20) 10. 1 & 50. 2 & 25. 5 & 10

ANSWERS : page 192

D4: Factor diagrams
1. Numbers in boxes should be 1, 2, 3, 6   2. Numbers in boxes should be 4, 8
3. Numbers in boxes should be 1, 2, 3, 4, 6, 12
4. Numbers in boxes should be 1, 2, 3, 4, 6, 9, 12, 18, 36
5. Numbers in boxes should be 1, 2, 4, 5, 10, 20
6. Numbers in boxes should be 1, 2, 3, 4, 6, 8, 12, 24

Section 3: Square and cube numbers   p89

D1: Square and cube review
1. 25 2. 100 3. 36 4. 144 5. 169 6. 81 7. 64 8. 49
9. 121 10. 169 11. 196 12. 225 13. 16 14. 81 15. 169 = 13 x 13
16. 25 36 144 81 9 121
17. The first ten square numbers are 1 4 9 16 25 36 49 64 81 100
18. $1^3 = 1 \times 1 \times 1 = 1$ $3^3 = 3 \times 3 \times 3 = 27$ 19. 64   20. 125

E1: Digit cube chains
Task 1: $12 \longrightarrow 9 \longrightarrow 729 \longrightarrow 1080 \longrightarrow 513 \longrightarrow 153$
Task 2: $13 \longrightarrow 28 \longrightarrow 520 \longrightarrow 133 \longrightarrow 55 \longrightarrow 250$

$14 \longrightarrow 65 \longrightarrow 341 \longrightarrow 92 \longrightarrow 737 \longrightarrow 713 \longrightarrow 371$
$15 \longrightarrow 126 \longrightarrow 225 \longrightarrow 141 \longrightarrow 66 \longrightarrow 432 \longrightarrow 99 \longrightarrow 1458 \longrightarrow 702 \longrightarrow 351$
$16 \longrightarrow 217 \longrightarrow 352 \longrightarrow 160 \longrightarrow 217$

$17 \longrightarrow 344 \longrightarrow 155 \longrightarrow 251 \longrightarrow 134 \longrightarrow 92 \longrightarrow 737 \longrightarrow 713 \longrightarrow 371$
$18 \longrightarrow 513 \longrightarrow 153$

Section 4: Index notation   p93

D1: Review of powers
1. 16 2. 125 3. 49 4. 1000 5. 32 6. 27 7. 64 8. 16
9. 64 10. 36 11. 2^4 12. 3^4 13. 7^2 14. 9^2 15. 2^6 16. 48
17. 108 18. 200 19. 9 20. 343 21. 55 22. 13 23. 64

Section 5: Techniques for addition & multiplication   p94

D1: Addition review
1. 189 2. 439 3. 291 4. 732 5. 587 6. 1048 7. 1002 8. 37
9. 110 10. 79 11. 171 12. 508 13. 304 14. 441 15. 851 16. 1046

D2: Multiplication review
1. 42 2. 75 3. 74 4. 215 5. 444 6. 644 7. 642 8. 1848
9. 3122 10. 3522

P1: Multiplication practice
Batch A
1. 84 2. 192 3. 260 4. 252 5. 984 6. 456 7. 3708
8. 2106 9. 567 10. 4576

Section 6: Techniques for division   p99

D1: Sharing with counters

1. 3   2. 2   3. 4   4. 2   5. 2   6. 3   7. (a) 3 (b) 1
8. (a) 3 (b) 1   9. (a) 4 (b) 1   10. (a) 2 (b) 2   11. (a) 2 (b) 1   12. (a) 3 (b) 2
13. 5   14. 3   15. 4   16. 2   17. 6   18. 4   19. 3   20. 7

D2: Division using the table square

1. 8   2. 3   3. 3   4. 3   5. 7   6. 8   7. 4   8. 6
9. 8   10. 6   11. 6   12. 5   13. 11   14. 9   15. 7   16. 8
17. 5   18. 9   19. 13   20. 14

D3: Setting out division sums

1. 5   2. 6   3. 8   4. 4   5. 6   6. 9   7. 7   8. 8
9. 9   10. 4

D4: More difficult division sums

1. 19   2. 24   3. 51   4. 74   5. 88   6. 105   7. 45   8. 136
9. 92   10. 46   11. 135   12. 81   13. 51   14. 23   15. 14

P1: Division practice

Batch A	1. 237	2. 123	3. 95	4. 13	5. 24
	6. 150	7. 29	8. 46	9. 19	10. 107
Batch B	1. 48	2. 119	3. 82	4. 53	5. 127
	6. 62	7. 74	8. 314	9. 135	10. 74
Batch C	1. 157	2. 52	3. 127	4. 318	5. 53
	6. 64	7. 17	8. 55	9. 78	10. 78

P2: Division puzzles

1. 342 & 432   2. 233, 323, 332   3. 189, 192, 219, 225, 252, 255

D5: Dividing 3-dogot number by 2-digit numbers

1. 17   2. 23   3. 29   4. 42   5. 56   6. 43   7. 27   8. 21
9. 87   10. 36   11. 32   12. 13   13. 61   14. 37   15. 51

P3: Large number division practice

Batch A	1. 11	2. 46	3. 22	4. 12	5. 45
	6. 29	7. 43	8. 26	9. 17	10. 12
Batch B	1. 51	2. 26	3. 43	4. 71	5. 29
	6. 14	7. 13	8. 72	9. 18	10. 23

Section 7: Checking calculations   p103

D1: Using approximations to check multiplications

1. 3000: sum ≈ 300 x 10   2. 2800: sum ≈ 140 x 20   3. 1 400: ≈ 70 x 20
4. (a) Zuk and Pow   (b) It is no easier to work out than the original sum

D2: Using approximations to check divisions

1. Didi: sum ≈ $^{1600}/_{50}$ = 32   2. 5.8; ≈ $^{360}/_{60}$ = 6

Batch B

1. 96   2. 308   3. 294   4. 639   5. 1530   6. 180   7. 4944   8. 5733
9. 1356   10. 875

Batch C

1. 111   2. 260   3. 588   4. 245   5. 780   6. 203   7. 1902   8. 6399
9. 3192   10. 1295

P2: Different totals

1. 35 x 4 = [140]   53 x 4 = [212]   45 x 3 = [135]   54 x 3 = [162]
2. 34 x 7 = [238]   43 x 7 = [301]   37 x 4 = [148]   73 x 4 = [292]
   47 x 3 = [141]   74 x 3 = [222]   6 different totals
3. 54 x 4 = [216]   45 x 4 = [180]   44 x 5 = [220]   3 different totals

D3: Multiplication by 10, 100, 1000

1. 50   2. 130   3. 500   4. 1700   5. 9000   6. 150   7. 2700   8. 620
9. 34000   10. 110   11. 6800   12. 7000   13. 85000   14. 4600   15. 570   16. 1400

D4: Multiplication by 20, 30 ... 200, 300 ...

1. 80   2. 150   3. 600   4. 2700   5. 12000   6. 320   7. 2000   8. 420
9. 2400   10. 450   11. 3500   12. 5500   13. 600   14. 1500   15. 900   16. 21000
17. 2400   18. 350019. 4000   20. 1600   21. 12000   22. 3600   23. 18000   24. 2000

D5: Another method of multiplication

1. 52   2. 135   3. 108   4. 460   5. 204   6. 296   7. 385   8. 738

D6: Multiplying larger numbers

1. 312   2. 900   3. 1404   4. 378   5. 1836   6. 2795   7. 1846   8. 7728
9. 1008   10. 795   11. 1092   12. 256   13. 693   14. 1530   15. 3145   16. 3627

D7: Multiplying a 3-digit number by a 2-digit number

1. 9204   2. 3537   3. 5175   4. 14878   5. 46332

P3: Multiplication practice

Batch A	1. 3000	2. 10148	3. 10044	4. 34980	5. 10045
	6. 11025	7. 37164	8. 16606	9. 46592	10. 25489
Batch B	1. 12342	2. 10741	3. 21556	4. 38740	5. 13644
	6. 17404	7. 17208	8. 46646	9. 28282	10. 43617
Batch C	1. 16892	2. 25155	3. 27360	4. 17464	5. 16560
	6. 41616	7. 30422	8. 22932	9. 45472	10. 4386
Batch D	1. 19875	2. 47120	3. 38718	4. 39372	5. 26010
	6. 49245	7. 62216	8. 70266	9. 18528	10. 20768

How Likely Is It ? EXTRA   ANSWERS

Section 3: Probability lines   p109

D1: The probability line

Task 1: [fruit drop] [chocolate] [toffee] [toffee or chocolate]

Task 2: [wine gum] [toffee] [toffee or choc] [toffee, fruit drop or choc]
[fruit drop] [toffee or choc]

P1: Counter probability

1. Blue — [R] [R or W]
2. Yellow — [W] [R] [R or W]
3. Blue — [W] [R] [R or G]
4. [W] [G or W] [B or G]
5. [R] [G] [R or B] [R or G]
6. Orange — [Y] [R] [P] [R/G/B] [R/G/B]
7. Red — [O] [W] [G] [P] [P/W/G] [P or W]

P2: Estimating probabilities

1. Event P is B   Event Q is A   Event R is C   Event S is D
2. [W] [R or G] [R, G or W]
   [R]

Section 4: Experimental probabilities   p113

EXP 2: Two coins

Task 3:

Table 3 bar chart: four bars approximately the same height

Table 4 bar chart: 2H and 2T approx the same height. one of each is twice the height.

Task 4: 1. Table 3   2. All four results are approx the same, so prob of each is $\frac{1}{4}$
3. $\frac{1}{4}$ 4. $\frac{1}{2}$ 5. about 1000   6. about 1000   7. about 2000
8. The more trials you do, the more accurate are the experimental probabilities.

E1: Experimental cheats

Exp 1: Group C   Results should be approximately the same. These are well out.

Exp 2: Group Q   These are OK for predicted values – but experimental values are not so exact.

Section 5: Equally likely outcomes   p 116

D1: Equally likely or not

1. Y   2. N   3. Y   4. N   5. Y   6. N   7. Y   8. Y   9. N   10. N
11. Y   12. N   13. N   14. Y   15. N   16. N   17. N   18. N   19. N   20. N

Section 6: Working out probabilities   p 117

D1: Simple probabilities

1. chance is 1 out of 5   prob(white) = $\frac{1}{5}$
   chance is 4 out of 5   prob(black) = $\frac{4}{5}$
2. chance is 2 out of 7   prob(white) = $\frac{2}{7}$
   chance is 5 out of 7   prob(black) = $\frac{5}{7}$
3. chance is 4 out of 5   prob(white) = $\frac{4}{5}$
   chance is 1 out of 5   prob(black) = $\frac{1}{5}$
4. prob(white) = $\frac{3}{7}$ prob(black) = $\frac{4}{7}$
5. prob(white) = 0   prob(black) = 1
6. prob(white) = $\frac{3}{8}$ prob(black) = $\frac{5}{8}$

D2: More difficult probabilities

1. $\frac{1}{5}$, $\frac{2}{5}$, $\frac{2}{5}$
2. $\frac{1}{7}$, $\frac{3}{7}$, $\frac{3}{7}$
3. $\frac{2}{7}$, $\frac{3}{7}$, $\frac{2}{7}$
4. $\frac{2}{8}$, $\frac{4}{8}$, $\frac{2}{8}$
5. 1 out of 6 : $\frac{1}{6}$ $\frac{1}{6}$ $\frac{2}{6}$
6. 1 out of 8 : $\frac{1}{8}$ $\frac{2}{8}$ $\frac{2}{8}$ $\frac{3}{8}$
7. $\frac{1}{10}$ $\frac{2}{10}$ $\frac{3}{10}$ $\frac{3}{10}$

P1: One dice probabilities

1. $\frac{1}{6}$ 2. $\frac{1}{6}$ 3. $\frac{1}{2}$ or $\frac{3}{6}$
4. $\frac{2}{6}$ 5. $\frac{2}{6}$ 6. $\frac{1}{2}$ or $\frac{3}{6}$
7. 0   8. $\frac{1}{2}$ or $\frac{3}{6}$ 9. $\frac{2}{6}$

P2: Two dice probabilities

1.

7	8	9	10	11	12
6	7	8	9	10	11
5	6	7	8	9	10
4	5	6	7	8	9
3	4	5	6	7	8
2	3	4	5	6	7

2. 36
3. $\frac{2}{36}$ 4. $\frac{1}{36}$ 5. $\frac{5}{36}$
6. $\frac{6}{36}$ 7. $\frac{5}{36}$ 8. $\frac{9}{36}$
9. $\frac{10}{36}$ 10. $\frac{15}{36}$ 11. $\frac{7}{36}$
6. 4   7. 12   8. 6

P3: Probabilities with a pack of cards

1. 52   2. 13   3. 13   4. 26   5. 4

Batch A: 1. $\frac{26}{52}$ or $\frac{1}{2}$ 2. $\frac{13}{52}$ or $\frac{1}{4}$
6. $\frac{4}{52}$ 7. $\frac{8}{52}$

Batch B: 1. $\frac{4}{52}$ 2. $\frac{1}{52}$ 3. $\frac{2}{52}$ 4. $\frac{16}{52}$ 5. $\frac{4}{52}$
6. $\frac{2}{52}$ 7. $\frac{2}{52}$ 8. $\frac{1}{52}$ 9. $\frac{2}{52}$ 10. $\frac{2}{52}$

P4: Mixed practice

1. $\frac{2}{6}$ or $\frac{1}{3}$ 2. $\frac{2}{5}$ 3. (a) $\frac{1}{4}$ (b) $\frac{1}{2}$ (c) 0   4. 1   5. $\frac{1}{4}$ 6. 0
7. 0   8. $\frac{1}{80}$ 9. $\frac{5}{80}$ 10. $\frac{3}{5}$ 11. (a) $\frac{1}{4}$ (b) $\frac{2}{6}$ (c) $\frac{4}{6}$ 12. $\frac{2}{9}$

D4: Common mistakes

1. (a) outcomes are not equally likely (b) $\frac{1}{4}$ (c) $\frac{3}{4}$
2. (a) Total number of outcomes is 3 (b) $\frac{1}{3}$ (c) $\frac{2}{3}$
3. Modesto
4. red $\frac{3}{8}$ blue $\frac{1}{4}$ yellow $\frac{3}{8}$

D4: Sums of probabilities

1. (a) $\frac{2}{5}$ (b) $\frac{3}{5}$ 2. It is certain that you will get either a black or white counter.
3. $\frac{3}{4}$ 4. $\frac{1}{3}$ 5. 0.4   6. 0.3   7. 0.6

Section 7: Methods of estimating probabilities   p 124

D1: Choose the right method

1. S   2. O   3. D   4. D   5. S   6. S   7. S or D   8. D
9. O   10. D   11. D   12. S   13. E   14. D

Developing Efficient Non-Calculator Techniques
EXTRA *Part 2* ANSWERS

Section 1: Fractions are easy   p130

D1: What fraction is … ?

1. A $\frac{1}{3}$ B $\frac{3}{4}$ C $\frac{2}{5}$ D $\frac{3}{8}$ E $\frac{4}{9}$ F $\frac{5}{12}$ G $\frac{3}{10}$ H $\frac{7}{8}$
2. A $\frac{2}{3}$ B $\frac{1}{4}$ C $\frac{3}{5}$ D $\frac{5}{8}$ E $\frac{5}{9}$ F $\frac{7}{12}$ G $\frac{7}{10}$ H $\frac{1}{8}$
3. $\frac{5}{7}$ 4. $\frac{7}{11}$
5. P $\frac{3}{7}$ Q $\frac{3}{8}$ R $\frac{3}{6}$ S $\frac{4}{9}$ T $\frac{4}{10}$ U $\frac{5}{10}$
6. P $\frac{3}{7}$ Q $\frac{2}{8}$ R $\frac{1}{6}$ S $\frac{3}{9}$ T $\frac{3}{10}$ U $\frac{1}{10}$
7. P $\frac{1}{7}$ Q $\frac{3}{8}$ R $\frac{2}{6}$ S $\frac{2}{9}$ T $\frac{3}{10}$ U $\frac{4}{10}$
8. $\frac{4}{5}$ 9. $\frac{1}{3}$ 10. $\frac{1}{4}$ 11. $\frac{1}{5}$ 12. $\frac{3}{28}$

D2: Fractions of amounts

1. 2 2. 3 3. 3 4. 3 5. 5 6. 2 7. 2 8. 2

P1: Fractions of amounts practice

1. 3p 2. 3 lorries 3. £5 4. 2 cm 5. 4p 6. 3 boys
7. 5 sweets 8. 2 lemons 9. 3 apples 10. £3 11. 2 horses 12. 7 m

D3: More complex fractions of amounts

1. (a) 2 (b) 4 (c) 6 (d) 8 2. (a) 3 (b) 6 3. (a) 3 (b) 9

P2: More complex fraction practice

Batch A:
1. (a) £2 (b) £4 2. (a) £5 (b) £15 3. (a) £3 (b) £6 (c) £12 (d) £15
4. (a) £4 (b) £16 (c) £12 5. 4 toffees 6. £6 7. 6 boys
8. 10 girls 9. 12 white mice 10. 6 sticky buns 11. £12 12. 20 matches 13. £20

Batch B:
1. £10 2. £9 3. 12 boys 4. 6 girls 5. 15 cm 6. £80
7. 15 sweets 8. 10 cars 9. £35 10. 8 cm 11. 14 kittens 12. 4 flowers

Section 2: Words and fractions   p134

D1: Getting the words right

1. (a) 9 (b) 7 (c) proper fraction 2. (a) 8 (b) 5 (c) top heavy fraction
3. (a) 3 & 2 (b) $3\frac{3}{5}$ $1\frac{1}{3}$ $4\frac{6}{7}$ (c) $\frac{3}{4}$ $2\frac{1}{9}$ $2\frac{1}{7}$ $\frac{19}{23}$ $\frac{13}{15}$ (d) $4\frac{1}{3}$ $12\frac{1}{5}$ $\frac{15}{9}$ $\frac{40}{33}$ $12\frac{1}{7}$
(e) $\frac{3}{4}$ $2\frac{1}{9}$ $3\frac{3}{5}$ $1\frac{1}{3}$ (f) $\frac{40}{33}$ $\frac{19}{23}$ 4. $\frac{4}{3} = 1\frac{1}{3}$

D2: Changing improper fractions into mixed numbers

1. $1\frac{1}{2}$ 2. $1\frac{1}{3}$ 3. $2\frac{1}{3}$ 4. $2\frac{1}{3}$ 5. $1\frac{1}{5}$ 6. 2 7. $1\frac{1}{9}$ 8. $6\frac{2}{3}$ 9. $5\frac{1}{4}$

D3: Changing mixed numbers into improper fractions

1. $\frac{5}{2}$ 2. $\frac{13}{8}$ 3. $\frac{7}{3}$ 4. $\frac{11}{3}$ 5. $\frac{9}{5}$ 6. $\frac{33}{10}$ 7. $\frac{44}{9}$ 8. $\frac{23}{6}$

P1: Mixed number practice

Batch A: 1. $4\frac{1}{2}$ 2. $1\frac{2}{3}$ 3. $4\frac{1}{4}$ 4. $1\frac{3}{4}$ 5. $1\frac{3}{5}$ 6. 3 7. $1\frac{4}{9}$ 8. $7\frac{2}{3}$
9. $4\frac{1}{5}$ 10. $\frac{5}{2}$ 11. $\frac{19}{4}$ 12. $\frac{11}{7}$ 13. $7\frac{1}{5}$ 14. $\frac{31}{9}$ 15. $\frac{13}{8}$

Developing Efficient Non-Calculator Techniques EXTRA Part 2

Section 8: Listing equally likely outcomes   p125

D1: Lu–Lu

1. 1, 2, 3, 4, 5, 6, 7, 8, 9, 10
2.

Score	Outcomes	
0	0000	
1	1000	
2	2000	
3	1200	3000
4	1300	4000
5	1400	2300
6	2400	1230
7	1240	3400
8	1340	
9	2340	
10	1234	

3. 16
4. $\frac{1}{16}$
5.

Score	0	1	2	3	4
Prob	$\frac{1}{16}$	$\frac{1}{16}$	$\frac{2}{16}$	$\frac{2}{16}$	$\frac{2}{16}$

Score	5	6	7	8	9	10
Prob	$\frac{2}{16}$	$\frac{2}{16}$	$\frac{2}{16}$	$\frac{1}{16}$	$\frac{1}{16}$	$\frac{1}{16}$

6. (a) $\frac{2}{16}$ (b) $\frac{3}{16}$ (c) $\frac{5}{16}$ (d) $\frac{5}{16}$

D2: Dominoes

1.

Total Score	Outcomes			
12	66			
11	65			
10	64	55		
9	63	54		
8	62	53	44	
7	61	52	43	
6	60	51	42	33
5	—	50	41	32
4	—	40	31	22
3	—	—	30	21
2	—	—	20	11
1	—	—	—	10
0	—	—	—	00

D2: Dominoes (contd)

2. (a) 2 (b) 3 (c) 4 (d) 1
3. (a) $\frac{2}{10}$ (b) $\frac{3}{28}$ (c) $\frac{1}{28}$ (d) $\frac{4}{28}$ (e) $\frac{2}{28}$
   (f) $\frac{1}{28}$ (g) $\frac{5}{28}$ (h) $\frac{12}{28}$ (i) $\frac{6}{28}$ (j) $\frac{16}{28}$

P1: Systematic methods of getting …

1. (HHH) (HHT) (HTH) (THH) (TTH)
   (THT) (HTT) (TTT)
2. (white, red) (white, green) (white blue)
   (black, red) (black, green) (black, blue)
3. (black, black) (black, silver) (black, purple)
   (blue, black) (blue, silver) (blue, purple)
   (grey, black) (grey, silver) (grey, purple)
4. *The table should contain these 12 combinations:*
   (Cola, Dead Rat)   (Cola, Squashed Fly)   (Cola, Dried Toad)
   (Orange, Dead Rat)   (Orange, Squashed Fly)   (Orange, Dried Toad)
   (Lemon, Dead Rat)   (Lemon, Squashed Fly)   (Lemon, Dried Toad)
   (Raspberry, Dead Rat)   (Raspberry, Squashed Fly)   (Raspberry, Dried Toad)
5. rows are (1,7) (1,8) (1,9) (2,7) (2,8) (2,9)
   (3,7) (3,8) (3,9) (4,7) (4,8) (4,9)

E1: Beat the teacher

Task 1: The game is not fair because the teacher wins most times.

Task 3:

Score	2	3	4	5	6	7	8	9	10	11	12
Prob	$\frac{1}{36}$	$\frac{2}{36}$	$\frac{3}{36}$	$\frac{4}{36}$	$\frac{5}{36}$	$\frac{6}{36}$	$\frac{5}{36}$	$\frac{4}{36}$	$\frac{3}{36}$	$\frac{2}{36}$	$\frac{1}{36}$

Task 4: Teacher wins on 5, 6, 7, 8 or 9.
Prob teacher wins is $\frac{4}{36} + \frac{5}{36} + \frac{6}{36} + \frac{5}{36} + \frac{4}{36} = \frac{24}{36}$ or $\frac{2}{3}$

How Likely Is It ? EXTRA

ANSWERS : page 195

ANSWERS : page 195

D1: Decimals and fractions

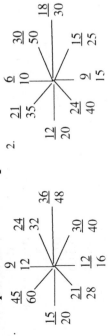

0.4	=	$\frac{4}{10}$
0.03	=	$\frac{3}{100}$
0.007	=	$\frac{7}{1000}$
2.4	=	$2\frac{4}{10}$
0.29	=	$\frac{29}{100}$
0.06	=	$\frac{6}{100}$
0.8	=	$\frac{8}{10}$
0.008	=	$\frac{8}{1000}$
0.57	=	$\frac{57}{100}$
0.031	=	$\frac{31}{1000}$
2.1	=	$2\frac{1}{10}$
1.17	=	$1\frac{17}{100}$
4.031	=	$4\frac{31}{1000}$
0.037	=	$\frac{37}{1000}$
12.543	=	$12\frac{543}{1000}$

D2: Changing decimals to fractions

1. $\frac{7}{10}$ 2. $\frac{3}{10}$ 3. $\frac{9}{100}$ 4. $\frac{1}{100}$
5. $\frac{3}{100}$ 6. $\frac{9}{1000}$ 7. $\frac{11}{100}$ 8. $\frac{29}{100}$
9. $\frac{37}{100}$ 10. $\frac{5}{100}$ 11. $\frac{32}{100}$ 12. $\frac{437}{1000}$
13. $1\frac{3}{10}$ 14. $2\frac{6}{10}$ 15. $4\frac{1}{100}$ 16. $\frac{65}{1000}$
17. $\frac{8}{100}$ 18. $\frac{72}{1000}$ 19. $\frac{28}{100}$ 20. $6\frac{5}{10}$
21. $\frac{1}{1000}$ 22. $\frac{17}{100}$ 23. $6\frac{8}{10}$ 24. $3\frac{9}{100}$

D3: Changing decimals to fractions in simplest form

1. $\frac{65}{100} = \frac{13}{20}$ 2. $\frac{26}{100} = \frac{13}{50}$
3. $\frac{24}{100} = \frac{6}{25}$ 4. $\frac{35}{100} = \frac{7}{20}$
5. $\frac{25}{100} = \frac{1}{4}$ 6. $\frac{16}{100} = \frac{4}{25}$
7. $\frac{75}{100} = \frac{3}{4}$ 8. $\frac{8}{1000} = \frac{1}{125}$

P1: Decimal to fraction practice

Batch A: 1. $\frac{2}{5}$ 2. $\frac{3}{5}$ 3. $\frac{2}{25}$
4. $\frac{11}{50}$ 5. $\frac{3}{50}$ 6. $\frac{13}{20}$

Batch B: 1. $\frac{1}{5}$ 2. $\frac{1}{25}$ 3. $\frac{1}{4}$
4. $\frac{11}{25}$ 5. $\frac{4}{5}$ 6. $\frac{9}{25}$

D1: Halves, quarters and three-quarters

1. $3.5 = 3\frac{1}{2}$ 2. $5.5 = 5\frac{1}{2}$ 3. $7.5 = 7\frac{1}{2}$ 4. $2.5 = 2\frac{1}{2}$
5. $9.5 = 9\frac{1}{2}$ 6. $10.5 = 10\frac{1}{2}$ 7. $6.5 = 6\frac{1}{2}$ 8. $15.5 = 15\frac{1}{2}$
9. $2.25 = 2\frac{1}{4}$ 10. $3.25 = 3\frac{1}{4}$ 11. $7.25 = 7\frac{1}{4}$ 12. $9.25 = 9\frac{1}{4}$
13. $1.25 = 1\frac{1}{4}$ 14. $5.25 = 5\frac{1}{4}$ 15. $8.25 = 8\frac{1}{4}$ 16. $14.25 = 14\frac{1}{4}$
17. $4.75 = 4\frac{3}{4}$ 18. $2.75 = 2\frac{3}{4}$ 19. $1.75 = 1\frac{3}{4}$ 20. $3.75 = 3\frac{3}{4}$
21. $6.75 = 6\frac{3}{4}$ 22. $8.75 = 8\frac{3}{4}$ 23. $7.75 = 7\frac{3}{4}$ 24. $10.75 = 10\frac{3}{4}$
25. $6.5 = 6\frac{1}{2}$ 26. $1.25 = 1\frac{1}{4}$ 27. $3.5 = 3\frac{1}{2}$ 28. $7.75 = 7\frac{3}{4}$
29. $6.25 = 6\frac{1}{4}$ 30. $2.5 = 2\frac{1}{2}$ 31. $2.75 = 2\frac{3}{4}$ 32. $25.5 = 25\frac{1}{2}$

D2: Tenths, hundredths and thousandths revisited

1. $3.7 = 3\frac{7}{10}$ 2. $5.09 = 5\frac{9}{100}$ 3. $8.21 = 8\frac{21}{100}$ 4. $4.67 = 4\frac{67}{100}$
5. $1.03 = 1\frac{3}{100}$ 6. $2.33 = 2\frac{33}{100}$ 7. $6.003 = 6\frac{3}{1000}$ 8. $9.031 = 9\frac{31}{1000}$
9. $5.9 = 5\frac{9}{10}$ 10. $7.07 = 7\frac{7}{100}$ 11. $1.53 = 1\frac{53}{100}$ 12. $6.037 = 6\frac{37}{1000}$

D3: Decimals and percentages

Decimal	0.3	0.8	0.73	0.51	0.23	0.35	0.45	0.03
Percentage	30%	80%	73%	51%	23%	35%	45%	3%

Batch B: 1. $1\frac{2}{5}$ 2. $1\frac{2}{7}$ 3. $1\frac{1}{10}$ 4. $2\frac{1}{4}$ 5. $2\frac{3}{5}$ 6. $5\frac{1}{4}$ 7. $2\frac{1}{10}$ 8. $2\frac{1}{5}$
9. $1\frac{6}{7}$ 10. $\frac{25}{9}$ 11. $\frac{14}{9}$ 12. $\frac{23}{8}$ 13. $\frac{31}{10}$ 14. $\frac{11}{2}$ 15. $\frac{9}{7}$

D1: Making equivalent fractions

1. (a) $\frac{6}{15}$ (b) $\frac{10}{25}$ (c) $\frac{8}{20}$ (d) $\frac{4}{10}$
2. (a) $\frac{6}{8}$ (b) $\frac{12}{27}$ (c) $\frac{15}{25}$ (d) $\frac{20}{32}$
3. $a = 3$ $b = 5$ $c = 2$ $d = 5$ $e = 4$ $f = 5$ $g = 3$ $h = 10$
4. (a) $\frac{1}{2} = \frac{4}{8}$ (×4)   (b) $\frac{2}{3} = \frac{8}{12}$ (×4)   (c) $\frac{3}{5} = \frac{12}{20}$ (×4)   (d) $\frac{3}{7} = \frac{9}{21}$ (×3)

P1: Equivalent fraction practice

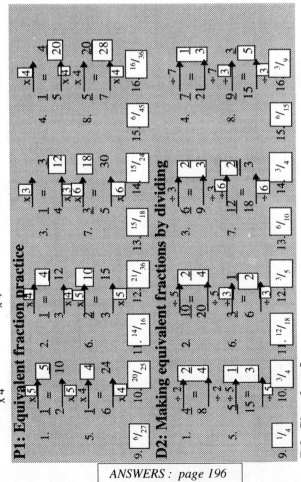

D2: Making equivalent fractions by dividing

D3: Simplest form

1. $\frac{4}{5}$ 2. $\frac{1}{3}$ 3. $\frac{4}{5}$ 4. $\frac{2}{3}$ 5. $\frac{3}{5}$ 6. $\frac{2}{3}$ 7. $\frac{3}{8}$ 8. $\frac{3}{7}$

P2: Equivalent fraction spiders

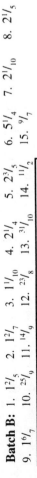

1. $\frac{45}{60}$ $\frac{9}{12}$ $\frac{24}{32}$ $\frac{36}{48}$ $\frac{15}{20}$ $\frac{21}{28}$ $\frac{12}{16}$ $\frac{30}{40}$

2. $\frac{21}{35}$ $\frac{6}{10}$ $\frac{30}{50}$ $\frac{18}{30}$ $\frac{24}{40}$ $\frac{9}{15}$ $\frac{15}{25}$ $\frac{12}{20}$

ANSWERS : page 196

P1: A mixture of metric conversions

1. 346 cm 2. 2.43 m 3. 5700 g 4. 720 g 5. 30 *ml*
6. 2300 kg 7. 34.8 mm 8. 4.5 cm 9. 0.75 m 10. 0.48 *l*
11. 23 mm 12. 0.9 cm 13. 0.43 m 14. 0.765 km 15. 32.8 mm

6. 24 km

D2: Using equivalent values to solve problems

1. 60 cm 2. Yes 3. 5 cm 4. 800 mm 5. 100g

Section 9: Ratios   p152

D1: Reviewing ratios and enlargements

1. (a) 7 : 21 (b) 3 : 9 (c) 5 : 15 (d) 1 : 3 (e) 3
2. (a) 6 : 24, 1 : 4, 4 : 16, 3 : 12 (b) 1 : 4 (c) 4
3. (a) 6 : 18, 7 : 21, 4 : 12 (b) 1 : 3 (c) 3
4. (a) 10 : 15, 18 : 27, 14 : 21 (b) 2 : 3 (c) 1.5
5. (a) 2.5 (b) 17.5 (c) 2 : 5

D2: Equivalent ratios

1. 1 : 3 2. 3 : 5 3. 3 : 4 4. 3 : 5 5. 2 : 5 6. 2 : 3
7. 1 : 3 8. 2 : 1 9. 3 : 2 10. 5 : 6 11. 24 12. 12
13. 8 14. 16 15. 12 16. 33 17. 15 girls 18. 12 boys

D3: Mixing in ratio

1. 6 2. 8 3. (a) 100 g (b) 25 g 4. 25 shovels of sand,35 shovels of aggregate

5.
4	8	1	10	20	6	18
10	20	2.5	25	50	15	45
14	28	3.5	35	70	21	63

7.
4	14	1
6	21	1.5
10	35	2.5

6. (a) 6 (b) 6 (c) ½ & 1

8. (a) 15 (b) 16
18	40	10	16
27	60	15	24
45	100	25	40

7. 1 500

D4: Sharing in ratio

1. £30 : £50 2. £14 : £21 3. £5 : £25 4. £6 : £12 : £42
5. £40 : £20 : £80 6. £50 : £75 : £75

Section 10: Return to decimals   p156

D1: Ordering decimals

1. 0.2 0.4 0.5 2. 0.001 0.01 0.1 3. 0.17 0.21 0.35
4. 0.33 0.35 0.53 5. 0.0023 0.023 0.23 6. 0.2 0.6 0.9
7. 0.203 0.23 0.32 8. 0.04 0.05 0.45 9. 0.67 0.677 0.7
10. 0.09 0.1 0.9 11. 0.007 0.07 0.69 12. 0.015 0.15 0.51
13. 0.7 0.709 0.79 14. 0.01 0.1 0.11 15. 0.014 0.04 0.14
16. 0.001 0.03 0.2 17. 0.02 0.12 0.133 0.2 18. 0.14 0.41 1.14 1.41
19. 2.003 2.03 2.13 2.3 20. 3 3.05 3.056 3.5 21. 1.57 1.75 5.17 5.71

Decimal	0.64	0.4	0.96	0.33	0.05	0.025	0.125	0.375
Percentage	64%	40%	96%	33%	5%	2½%	12½%	37½%

D4: Fraction-percentage equivalents you ought to know

1. 75% 2. 90% 3. 66⅔% 4. 70% 5. 87½% 6. 6¼% 7. 62½%
8. 20/100 or 1/5 9. 70/100 or 7/10 10. 3/4 11. 1/10 12. 1/20 13. 1/40 14. 3/40

Section 6: Working with percentages   p145

D1: Percentage reasoning

1. 85% 2. 70% 3. 45% 4. 22% 5. 10% 6. 15%

D2: Percentages of amounts

1. 10 m 2. 6 cm 3. £20 4. 5 cm 5. 10 kg 6. 20p
7. 3 m 8. 5 m 9. £3 10. 2l 11. 3 kg 12. £6

P1: Practice in finding percentages of amounts

Batch A: 1. 1.4 kg 2. £6 3. £200 4. £2 5. 8l 6. 40p
7. 10 m 8. 9 m 9. 12p 10. £5 11. 8 kg 12. 2 cm

Batch B: 1. 2p 2. 6 cm 3. £2 4. 8l 5. 11 mm 6. 33 mm
7. 11p 8. 10 m 9. £20 10. 12p 11. 50p 12. £10

Section 7: x and ÷ by 10, 100   p147

D1: x and ÷ by 10, 100

1. 43.1 2. 34500 3. 439.5 4. 410 5. 35 6. 12.34
7. 0.273 8. 4.58 9. 2.565 10. 0.721 11. 0.25 12. 1.234

P1: x and ÷ by 10, 100 mixed practice

Batch A: 1. 59.7 2. 27800 3. 3.182 4. 0.036 5. 0.00049
6. 830 7. 0.075 8. 12.34 9. 3.541 10. 1.4

Batch B: 1. 143 2. 0.3579 3. 1.43 4. 36.7 5. 0.15
6. 27 7. 35 8. 24.35 9. 169.1 10. 0.04

Batch C: 1. 3 2. 0.0435 3. 0.251 4. 23 5. 250
6. 3500 7. 42.1 8. 1.25 9. 296.7 10. 0.3

P2: ? = ?
1. 100 2. 10 3. 10 4. 100 5. 100 6. 100 7. 100 8. 100

Section 8: Measurement calculations   p150

D1: Working with metric units

1. 135 cm 2. 300 cm 3. 270 cm 4. 72 cm 5. 5 cm
6. 0.34 m 7. 2.56 m 8. 0.6 m 9. 0.04 m 10. 4.5 cm
11. 34 cm 12. 0.7 cm 13. 28 mm 14. 350 mm 15. 0.8 mm
16. 3 kg 17. 0.24 kg 18. 0.035 kg 19. 0.008 kg 20. 0.265 kg
21. 4000 g 22. 4500 g 23. 45000 g 24. 3000 kg 25. 2500 kg
26. 0.8 *l* 27. 0.05 *l* 28. 0.01 *l* 29. 2 *l* 30. 0.035 *l*

Understanding Geometry EXTRA *Part 2* ANSWERS

Section 1: Defining area   p158
D1: What is area ?
A = 28 cm²   B = 20 cm²   C = 42 cm²   D = 34 cm²

Section 2: Areas of rectangles   p159
D1: Areas of rectangles by counting squares
1. 8 cm²   2. 9 cm²   3. 10 cm²   4. 15 cm²
5. 12 cm²   6. 4 cm²   7. 12 cm²   8. 20 cm²

D2: Areas of rectangles using a formula
1. 18 cm²   2. 25 cm²   3. 24 cm²   4. 50 cm²
5. 54 cm²   6. 21 cm²   7. 10 cm²   8. 80 cm²

P1: Units of area
1. 15 cm²   2. 8 mm²   3. 18 m²   4. 30 mm²
5. 27 m²   6. 28 mm²   7. 35 m²   8. 6 km²
9. 20 cm²   10. 12 mm²   11. 36 m²

D3: Too much information
1. 12 cm²   2. 30 m²   3. 25 mm²   4. 40 cm²
5. 100 m²   6. 45 mm²   7. 12 cm²

Section 3: Compound shapes   p161
D1: Creating L
Task 1:

	A	B	C	D	E	F	G	H	I	J
length	7	8	8	6	5	7	2	3	3	3
width	2	4	2	3	4	3	2	3	2	1
area	14	32	16	18	20	21	4	9	6	3

Task 2: B & D   F & I   A & J   C & H   E & G

D2: Reverse Ls
Task 2: (There are two sets of answers for each shape, depending on how you cut up the L shape)
P *either* 12 + 10 = 22 *or* 18 + 4 = 22
Q *either* 14 + 21 = 35 *or* 20 + 15 = 35
R *either* 8 + 21 = 29 *or* 20 + 9 = 29
S *either* 12 + 30 = 42 *or* 40 + 2 = 42
T *either* 28 + 10 = 38 *or* 30 + 8 = 38
U *either* 18 + 8 = 26 *or* 20 + 6 = 26

D3: Compound areas without measuring
W: 30 + 12 = 42   X: 20 + 8 = 28   Y: 12 + 6 = 18
Z: 10 + 15 + 14 = 39

ANSWERS : page 198

D4: Now you split them into rectangles
A: 32   B: 50   C: 80   D: 54

Section 4: Areas of parallelograms   p164
D1: Parallelograms made from squares and half squares
A 2 2 4
B 1 1 1
C 4 2 8
D 3 3 9
E 2 3 6
F 1 4 4
G 2 4 8

D2: Using the formula and getting it wrong
1. Kooldood added instead of multiplying.
2. The second measurement should have been the height – it wasn't.

D3: Areas of parallelograms using the formula
1.
H 2 3 6
I 3 2 6
J 1 3 3
K 4 3 12
L 1 4 4
M 3 3 9
N 4 2 8

2.
P 3 5 15
Q 3 2 6
R 3 1 3
S 2 2 4
T 4 2 8
U 3 4 12

D4: Use the correct units and choose the information
1. 15 mm²   2. 14 cm²   3. 18 m²   4. 60 cm²
5. 10 mm²   6. 24 cm²   7. 20 m²   8. 8 km²
9. 15 cm²   10. 15 m²

Section 5: Areas of triangles   p167
D1: Parallelograms and triangles
A & P   B & Q   C & T   D & R   E & S

D2: Rule for the area of a triangle
1. 6 cm²   2. 8 cm²   3. 30 cm²   4. 15 cm²
5. 12 cm²   6. 20.5 cm²   7. 17.6 cm²   8. 25 cm²

P1: Areas of triangles
A 5 2 5   E 4 3 6
B 3 3 4½   F 2 2 2
C 4 1 2   G 3 4 6
D 4 3 6   H 3 2 3

D4: Working out the circumference nowadays

1. 31.4 cm 2. 10.99 cm 3. 6.437 cm 4. 12.56 cm 5. 175.84 cm
6. (a) 10 cm (b) 31.4 cm 7. 25.12 cm 8. 13.188 cm 9. 28.26 cm
10. 18.84 mm 11. 125.6 cm 12. 15.71 m 13. 18.852 cm
14. 37.704 km 15. 40.2176 m

Section 9: Area of a circle p175

D1: Using π to work out the area

1. 78.5 cm² 2. 452.16 cm² 3. 30.1754 m² 4. 28.26 cm²
5. 1962.5 cm² 6. (a) 10 cm (b) 314 cm² 7. 28.26 cm²
8. 78.5 cm² 9. 18.0864 m² 10. 12.56 mm² 11. 452.16 cm²
12. 314 m² 13. 200.96 cm² 14. 153.86 cm² 15. 18.0864 m²
16. 530.66 cm² 17. 31400 m²

Section 10: Circumference and area p176

P1: Circle calculations

Batch A:

	Q1	Q2	Q3	Q4	Q5	Q6	Q7	Q8	Q9
(a)	37.7	14.4	27.0	19.5	126	20.1	50.2	3.14	1.26
(b)	113	16.6	58.1	30.2	1260	32.2	201	0.785	0.126

Batch B:

	Q1	Q2	Q3	Q4	Q5	Q6	Q7	Q8	Q9
(a)	36.4	8.79	38.3	53.6	314	26.4	44.0	13.2	1.88
(b)	106	6.15	117	227	7850	55.4	154	13.8	0.283

P2: Circle problems

1. 122 cm 2. 264 cm 3. 75.36 m & 452.16 m²
4. 72.22 cm & 415.265 cm² 5. 20 cm 6. 34.54 m² 7. 80.68 m

E1: Rolling problems

1. (a) 7.536 cm (b) 37.68 cm 2. (a) 1.9486 m (b) 194.68 m
3. 2.2608m 4. (a) 13.4078 cm (b) 3

P2: No measurements given here

I	4	5	10
J	4	3	6
K	2	2	2
L	3	5	7½
M	3	2	3
N	6	5	15

P3: Altogether now

Batch A 1. 15 cm² 2. 12 m² 3. 12 mm² 4. 10 cm²
5. 24 m² 6. 30 cm² 7. 10 m² 8. 100 cm²

Batch B 1. 9 m² 2. 50 m² 3. 8 cm² 4. 25 cm²
5. 18 mm² 6. 10 m² 7. 10 m² 8. 12 cm²

Section 7: Perimeter p170

D1: Perimeters

1. 10 2. 12 3. 12 4. 14 5. 14
6. 10 7. 12 8. 12 9. 14 10. 14

D2: Perimeters using measurements

1. 24 cm 2. 26 cm 3. 20 cm 4. 12 mm 5. 9 cm 6. 16 cm
7. 26 cm 8. 20 mm 9. 30 m 10. 20 cm 11. 28 cm 12. 15 m

P1: Measure and work out perimeter

A = 22 cm B = 30 cm C = 24 cm D = 18 cm (If you get some
wrong, ask your teacher to check your measurements.)

Section 8: Circumference p172

D1: Diameter and radius

Task 1:

	A	B	C	D	E	F	G
	2 cm	3 cm	1 cm	5 cm	4 cm	2.8 cm	4.4 cm
	1 cm	1½ cm	½ cm	2½ cm	2 cm	1.4 cm	2.2 cm

Task 2: 1. 20 cm 2. 6 cm 3. 8cm 4. 14 cm 5. 22 metrons
Task 3: 1. 10 km 2. 20 miles 3. 4 mm 4. 2.1 m

D2: The circumference of a circle

1. 31 cm 2. 9.3 cm 3. 13.95 cm 4. 18.6 cm 5. 24.8 cm
6. 62 m 7. 13.02 cm 8. 93 cm 9. 21.7 cm 10. 43.4 cm

D3: Calculating with π

1. 12 cm 2. 30 cm 3. 6 m 4. 36 cm 5. 120 cm
6. 15.8 cm 7. 25.28 cm 8. 9.48 m 9. 44.24 cm 10. 63.2 cm
11. 18.8496 cm 12. 282.744 cm 13. 62.832 cm 14. 31.416 cm 15. 94.248 cm

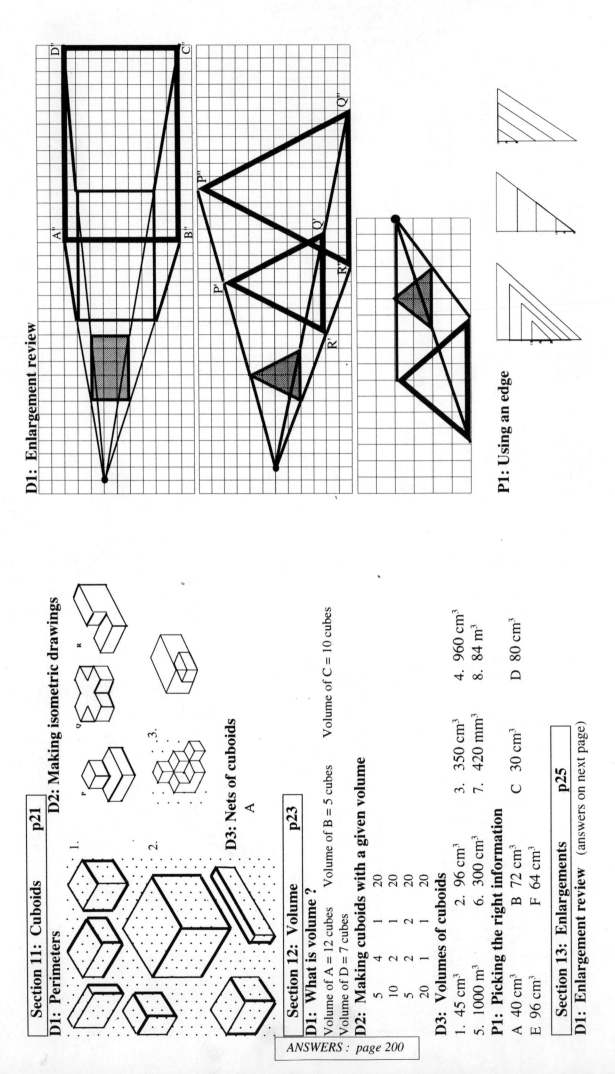

D1: Enlargement review

P1: Using an edge

Section 11: Cuboids   p21

D1: Perimeters

D2: Making isometric drawings

1.   2.   3.

P   Q   R

D3: Nets of cuboids   A

Section 12: Volume   p23

D1: What is volume ?

Volume of A = 12 cubes   Volume of B = 5 cubes   Volume of C = 10 cubes
Volume of D = 7 cubes

D2: Making cuboids with a given volume

5	4	1	20
10	2	1	20
5	2	2	20
20	1	1	20

D3: Volumes of cuboids

1. 45 cm³   2. 96 cm³   3. 350 cm³   4. 960 cm³
5. 1000 m³   6. 300 cm³   7. 420 mm³   8. 84 m³

P1: Picking the right information

A 40 cm³   B 72 cm³   C 30 cm³   D 80 cm³
E 96 cm³   F 64 cm³

Section 13: Enlargements   p25

D1: Enlargement review   (answers on next page)

ANSWERS : page 200